Who's Who in the Ancient Near East

Who's Who in the Ancient Near East

Gwendolyn Leick

London and New York

First published 1999
by Routledge
11 New Fetter Lane, London EC4P 4EE

Simultaneously published in the USA and Canada
by Routledge
29 West 35th Street, New York, NY 10001

Typeset in Sabon by Routledge
Printed and bound in Great Britain by TJ International Ltd,
Padstow, Cornwall

British Library Cataloguing in Publication Data
A catalogue record for this book is available from the British Library

Library of Congress Cataloging in Publication Data
A catalogue record has been requested for this title

ISBN 0–415–13230–4 (hbk)

Contents

List of Maps

Preface

This book was the idea of Richard Stoneman, editor of the Classics List at Routledge. It follows the format of the *Who's Who* series, being a biographical dictionary of people who were important in the history of the ancient Near East and whose memory has survived the long passage of time that separates their world from ours. Many of these societies were to some extent literate and there are documents in the various languages of the region. Although by no means all original sources have as yet been translated and analysed, there is a considerable body of transcribed material, secondary and tertiary literature. For this volume, a reference book that is also meant to provide information for non-specialists, I have not used any unpublished original texts but have relied instead on works that are relatively easy to access, such as the *Cambridge Ancient History* series and similar historical treatises, supplemented by more specialised studies and articles. The sources of my information are listed under each entry. The entries often reflect the opinions and conclusions of the quoted authors rather than my own and should give an idea of the current state of scholarship. Some periods and places have attracted more attention than others. This is generally determined by the availability of sources; new excavations, and particularly the discovery of archives, force a revision of the always provisional conclusions.

In single-author reference works the specialisation of the writer is both a strength and a weakness. As an Assyriologist I have more access to Mesopotamian material and there are proportionally more entries on Babylonia and Assyria in this book. For Iranian and Anatolian history I have relied more on the standard works.

The majority of entries concern kings and local rulers. As explained in my Introduction it was the ruler's prerogative to perpetuate his name. However, like a contemporary *Who's Who*, I have also included intellectuals, writers, businessmen, generals and a few ecclesiasts. I have included as many women as I could find, though merely private individuals are excluded. All these categories can be accessed through the index. Some entries were included to direct the reader's attention to an interesting article or book on a period or subject, and the specific entry serves as representative of an often much larger cast of people. On the whole, the selection aims to be both orthodox in its general range and individualistic, especially with respect to private individuals.

As far as the actual names of persons are concerned, I have not translated them; some, especially the Babylonian and Assyrian ones, have a discernable meaning, others do not. For works specifically concerned with personal names see Ranke 1905, Stamm 1939, Tallqvist 1966, Laroche 1966, Lipiński 1994, Gelb *et al.* 1943, Mayrhofer 1979, Archi 1988, Limet 1968, di Vito 1993.

Chronology

The chronological framework is somewhat wider than in most popular works on the ancient Near East. I have gone beyond the traditional cut-off point, the death of Alexander in 323, to include the Hellenistic period to the second century BC because I believe the reign of Macedonian rulers did not produce a sharp break in the cultural continuity of the Near East and that such an assumption projects an over-estimation of Greek impact. I have therefore included Seleucid, Ptolemaic and Parthian rulers although the various Anatolian principalities and minor states of the second half of the 1st millennium BC are admittedly under-represented.

There is still considerable scholarly disagreement as to all dates up to the middle of the 2nd millennium. I have usually followed the so-called Middle Chronology, as used by the *Cambridge Ancient History* and A. Kuhrt's *The Ancient Near East* (2 vols, 1995), but have occasionally adopted the one preferred by the author of a particular source, as indicated in the bibliographical reference. The 'Outline of the main historical periods' that appears after the Glossary is intended as a very general guide; for more detailed tables see the *Cambridge Ancient History* and Kuhrt.

All dates, unless otherwise indicated, are BC.

Geography

The areas that constitute the ancient Near East is another issue on which opinions are divided and it also depends on what period is under consideration. I have proceeded from the position that places Mesopotamia in the centre of cultural and political developments; direct and historically verifiable connection with this centre serves as the main criterion for inclusion. Hence for the 3rd millennium I have only included Mesopotamian and Elamite persons. In the 2nd millennium many more groups acquired literacy and states began to interact with each other across increasingly large distances, so the geographical frame is much wider, including also Syria-Palestine, Anatolia and Egypt. In the 1st millennium this network grew even wider with the multinational empires of the Assyrians,

Achaemenids and Alexander. For the latter two, I have restricted the choice of entries to those persons who had particular relevance to the Mesopotamian and Syro-Palestinian region.

Notes on the use of *Who's Who in the Ancient Near East*

Glossary

The Glossary contains concise information for the non-specialist and clarifies historical terminology.

Cross-references

Cross-references to entries in the main part of the book are printed in small capitals. Cross-references within the Glossary have an asterisk (*).

Index

The index lists names of people mentioned in the text who do not have a separate entry, as well as professional groups (e.g. scribes) and ethnic affiliation (e.g. Aramaic), text categories (e.g. chronicles, stelae), historical periods, place names, etc.

Abbreviations

CAH *Cambridge Ancient History*
RlA *Reallexikon der Assyriologie*

Introduction

Like any other *Who's Who* this volume contains information on people 'who made a name for themselves': public personages, kings and queens, chieftains and rebels, senior officials and generals. Yet this rather clichéd phrase has a peculiar aptness in the context of the ancient Near East. Its perhaps most enduring legacy was the development of urbanism and state societies. The traditional kinship-based solidarity had been loosened, and status differentials based not only on inherited membership of distinct clans but on personal merit and enterprise became possible. In the Mesopotamian (and the Egyptian) world of the 3rd millennium there was a growing awareness of historical time, made possible through writing. Within this historical framework the individual could leave his mark. Personal achievements could be transmitted to posterity; one did not just make a name for oneself to impress contemporaries but a name to outlast even one's lineage, a name that would last forever. The desire for a personalised perpetuation of memory was to remain characteristic for all literate societies in the ancient Near East at all periods. We need to examine briefly how this was achieved, as several media were available.

Votive inscriptions

The earliest records for people included in this volume are brief inscriptions on objects such as the mace of Mesilim, a king of Kish, from around 2500. The practice of marking things with the engraved signs for the name and title of a person is much older and goes back to the custom of placing seal impressions on containers and parts of buildings, in order to link them with an institution or an official with administrative responsibility. This was already standard procedure in the 4th millennium. The problem for us is that we cannot read the seal legends since the writing system of the period was mainly logographic and its links with any known language remain impenetrable. Otherwise the officials and overseers who worked at the great estates of Uruk and other cities would be known to us by name. Only when the cuneiform system had matured enough to represent a particular idiom by linking logograph and phoneme through the principle of homophony do the records became legible for the modern scholar. It has become clear that because the original purpose of writing was prosaically bureaucratic, the first names to be transmitted were those of administrators and 'civil servants'. But with the growing influence of a warrior class, which in the course of the Early Dynastic period produced individuals who achieved power through force and ambition, we find them making use of writing to inscribe their name 'forever' and to perpetuate their deeds. The lion-mace of Mesilim is a small limestone, carved in high relief with six lions attacking bovines, an iconographic motif well known from cylinder seals. The signs that read 'Mesilim king of Kish' are engraved across the relief. This mace was not a tool or weapon but a votive offering to be deposited in the temple at Tello, where French archaeologists found it in the early twentieth century. The votive gift was forever linked with the donor by means of the inscription. It legitimatised and eternalised the act of offering through the writing of the name. It was also meant to reduce the risk of the offering's theft by identifying the original donor. We also find the individuation of intent which is so characteristic for this age of early state formation. The brief text has multiple levels of meaning. It communicated to the gods that an act of reciprocal exchange had been initiated; a precious artefact was dedicated by a person in return for divine blessing. It proclaimed the status of the donor not just by the value and rarity of the object and the title 'king' but by the inscription itself, since only the elite had access to literacy. Wealthy patrons would curry favour with the powerful by offering him an inscribed object 'for his life'. A significant proportion of the people in this book, especially from the early periods, are there because of votive inscriptions on something durable that was deposited in the relative safety of a temple. Nor did this habit disappear in later times. Wherever literacy was adopted in the various peripheral areas of the first state societies, inscribed stones and vases proliferated, usually magically protected by curses against thieves and despoilers. Assyrian and Babylonian monarchs, familiar with foundation deposits and memorial stelae from previous ages, would specifically address a future prince, recommending their inscribed objects to his care. Even in the late 2nd millennium AD, inscribed plaques were deposited on the moon, inscribed with the names of astronauts and the American president.

Year names and eponyms

The will to perpetuate the memory of particular political achievements within a consciously conceived historical framework is very clearly demonstrated by the practice of year names. The system of organising memory according to outstanding events is often found in non-centralised and non-literate societies where the orally transmitted collective memory focuses on happenings that break the cyclical monotony of living. The rulers of the Akkad Dynasty, the first administratively coherent and centralised state in 3rd-millennium Mesopotamia, introduced a system of dating that was to have general currency for the whole country. Years were named on hindsight after a significant event; the current year was provisionally called 'year after such and such took place'. They recorded successful wars and thus reflected the expansion of the state. They also emphasised the role of the supreme ruler as the instigator of successful conquest and defence. Secondarily, they also recorded the inauguration of high officials, and of public works, such as the building of fortifications, the restoration of temples, the dedication of statues, etc. Lists of such year names were collected and enabled years to be dated consecutively. The practice was in use for centuries and, especially in the absence of other data, furnishes useful historical information. A fair number of rulers whose other inscriptions did not survive are known only from year names.

Year names were a southern Mesopotamian invention; the Assyrians dated differently, by naming the year after a special official or eponym, as well as according to regnal years of kings. In the case of the former the name of the official became synonymous with a certain time. The list of eponyms inscribed on the rows of stelae on public view at Assur was a manifestation of historical time. They were used alongside genealogical lists of kings that reflect the traditional reckoning of biological time as the succession of generations, the main form of dating in the pastoralist societies of the Near East.

Annals

The most highly developed literary efforts to perpetuate a personalised history are the first-millennium Assyrian royal annals. They are always in the form of a personal statement ('I, Sennacherib, king of Assyria...') of their achievements in chronological order, couched as a formal report addressed to the gods of the nation. The purpose of such annals was not the writing of history in the modern sense but to present an idealised official version of actual events that dwelled on victory and passed over defeat in silence. It also placed the king in the centre of historical processes that he could shape according to his will, in so far as he acted with divine guidance and approval. The tone of these annals is never personal. The kings, like their carved images on reliefs and stelae, are representatives of an ideal type: warriors and conquerors, patrons of architectural projects, leading participants in cult rituals.

Private sources

In contrast to the self-conscious efforts to perpetuate the memory of an individual of high status are other more random and indirect prosopographic sources. The bureaucratic machinery of institutions such as temple and palace estates has preserved the names of thousands of people: employees, supervisors, workers, slaves. The 3rd-millennium archive of Ebla is an early example. The judicial court records list plaintiffs and accused parties, witnesses, judges and legal clerks. Business archives have also been recovered that feature the names of numerous persons engaged in trade, investment, transport, etc. Such sources are most voluminous in the cuneiform medium of writing due to the physical durability of the clay, and are virtually absent from those regions and periods that used more perishable media of writing or indeed lacked such institutions in the first place. These unofficial records deserve to be studied, although the biographical details are fragmentary at best. Most often only the name remains in a particular context as the recipient of wages or goods. Although names are interesting in themselves, as far as the framework of a *Who's Who* is concerned, the information is too scant and the likely impact of the personality too opaque. However, I did include some bankers and merchants and officials, if only to direct the reader's attention to the existence of such sources. Like those people we know from letters that have survived in some archives, they represent the more private world that has been opened up by paleography; the rediscovery of their existence, even more a matter of chance, is one of the rewards of engaging in a biographical search.

Colophons

Some important tablet collections, of scholarly rather than economic importance, were identified by colophons at the bottom of each tablet, a bibiographical device to make cataloguing easier. The scribes would cite the title of the composition or series, the number of lines, the provenance of an original version if a copy was being made and, importantly, record the name, professional title, and sometimes the pedigree of the writer. This practice first appeared in the Middle Babylonian period, and is much in evidence in the tablet collections discovered in the Assyrian palace library at Nineveh. Such colophons are a main source of information concerning scholars and intellectuals of the ancient Near East.

Oral tradition

The fact that so much written material has survived must not delude us into thinking that the ancient Near East was a completely literate world. Only a small elite ever had recourse to the written word and very few knew of chronicles and king lists or could actually read the inscribed monuments set up by their rulers of old. The majority of people lived within an oral and aural tradition. This did not preclude some historical awareness, but in order for the past event or personality to be remembered they needed to be made memorable. Bare facts take on a life of their own in the retelling; the deeds of ancestors or bygone kings become interwoven with legend. Tribal memory can preserve such narratives for a long time; some may become paradigmatic myths. If these stories are written down the oral and literate fuse to create a text that is both of a time and part of other times.

The protagonists may well have lived, but since their deeds are 'folklorised', they lack the direct link between person, event and the written record that historians like to have clearly established. The 'unreliable' memory of the oral tradition, because of the vividness of its artifice, tends to serve the resistance hero better than the conqueror. It lodges his name in the imagination of generations while the rather pedantic and pathetic royal proclamations of battles won and the exact number of enemies slain remain of interest only to specialists. The oral tradition and written evidence of a particular time sometimes end up complementing each other, as in the case of the Greek historians' writings, supplemented by annals or letters from the time of the protagonists. The Hellenistic historians who wrote about the exotic 'other', many of whom lived generations ago in distant countries, were not uncritical of their sources, oral or otherwise, and especially for the later periods that this book is concerned with, their accounts are often the only information there is. Like the work of the chroniclers of the Bible, whose attitude to history is no doubt different, but who also shaped an oral tradition into personalised history, the testimony of Greek historians for the closing phases of the ancient Near East is the link with our own world since it has informed western perception of the past for centuries.

This *Who's Who* is not just a compendium of long-dead kings and bureaucrats. Through biblical and classical streams of tradition they belong to later ages too. Through the discoveries of archaeology over the last hundred years and the ongoing process of decipherment, interpretation and publication, they belong to the modern age; they are a newly discovered part of contemporary knowledge. The initial impetus for the stabilisation of memory by writing, which was at first in the service of bureaucracy, has left an enormous legacy, but not least it has made it possible for some 700 or so individuals to be included in a *Who's Who* for the earliest documented historical periods.

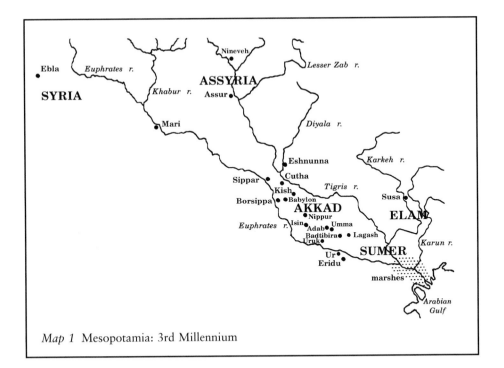

Map 1 Mesopotamia: 3rd Millennium

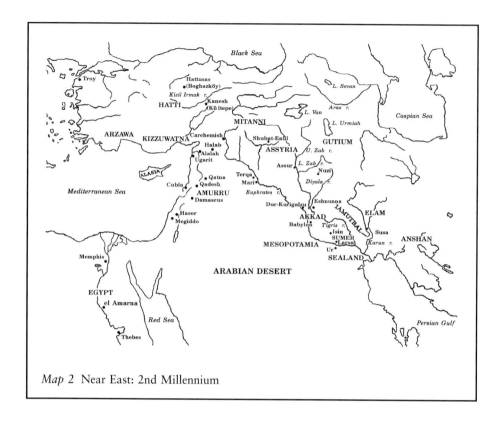

Map 2 Near East: 2nd Millennium

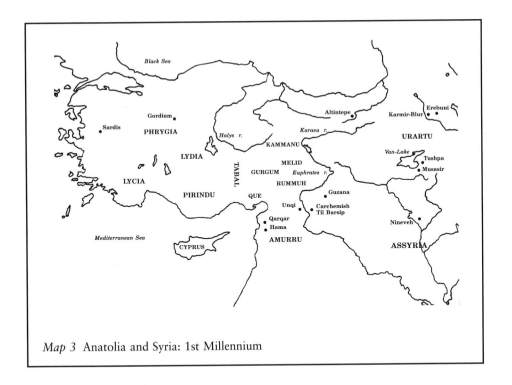

Map 3 Anatolia and Syria: 1st Millennium

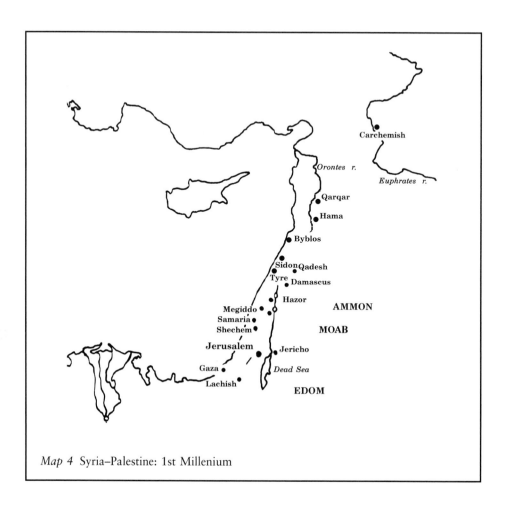

Carchemish

Orontes r.

Euphrates r.

Qarqar

Hama

Byblos

Sidon Qadesh

Tyre Damascus

Hazor

AMMON

Megiddo

Samaria

Shechem

MOAB

Jerusalem

Gaza

Lachish

Jericho

Dead Sea

EDOM

Map 4 Syria–Palestine: 1st Millenium

A

A-anepada
Early Dynastic king of the First Dynasty of Ur (*c*. 2500), son of MESANEPADA. His name appears on votive offerings. He probably built the temple at 'Ubaid.

Sollberger and Kupper 1971: IB5a–c; Gadd 1971, in CAH I/2: 245

Aba-Enlil-dana (Aramean Ahiqar)
High official under SENNACHERIB and ESARHADDON (7th century). Under his Aramean name, Ahiqar, he became famous as the author of a series of wisdom texts written in Aramaic.

Grayson 1991, in CAH III/2: 132

Abalgamash
King of Warakhshi (the region adjoining Elam to the north) (*c*. 24th century). Together with HISHEP-RATEP, king of Elam, he began a revolt against the Akkadian king RIMUSH, who wrote about this campaign. The battle took place between Awan and Susa. Rimush won and took over 4,000 prisoners, plus a great amount of gold and copper, which he dedicated to the god Enlil in Nippur.

Gadd 1971, in CAH III/2: 436–7; Hinz 1972: 73

Abba'el
King of Halab (Aleppo), son of HAMMURAPI I of Yamhad, contemporary with SAMSU-ILUNA of Babylon (18th century). His brother, YARIM-LIM I, became ruler of Alalakh. Abba'el managed to regain lost territories for the kingdom of Yamhad.

Klengel 1992: 60–2

Abdi-Ashirta
Amorite leader, well known from the correspondence found at Amarna (14th century). He was the main adversary of RIB-ADDI.

Youngblood 1980; Moran 1992: *passim*

Abdi-Heba
Ruler of Jerusalem in the Amarna period. He was installed by AMENO-PHIS IV, who maintained an Egyptian occupation force in the city at that

time (14th century). Some of the letters he wrote to the Egyptian sovereign are preserved in the Amarna correspondence.

Moran 1992: 321, 325–7, 331

Abdi-milkutti (= Abdi-milki)

King of Sidon who rebelled against the Assyrian king SENNACHERIB in 677. When Esarhaddon captured the city, Abdi-milki escaped by boat but was later caught 'like a fish' and beheaded.

Grayson 1991, in CAH III/2: 125; Culican, ibid: 469–70

Abiba'al

King of Tyre, possible founder of a new dynasty that was to make Tyre into a major sea-faring and politically important city in the 10th century.

Klengel 1992: 203; Katzenstein 1973: 74ff.

Abi-esuh

King of Babylon in the Old Babylonian period, son and successor of SAMSU-ILUNA (1711–1684). The year names record that he had several successful confrontations with Kassite troops. However, he also lost some territories, especially in the Middle Euphrates area.

Saggs 1995: 114; Frayne 1990: 404–10

Abih-il see Ebih-il

Abijah

King of Judah, son and successor of REHOBOAM (913–911). According to II Chr. 13 he conducted a successful campaign against the northern kingdom, Israel, then still ruled by JEROBOAM I, in which he occupied the cult centre of Bethel.

Mitchell 1982, in CAH III/1: 461–2

Abi-milki

Ruler of Tyre during the reign of AMENOPHIS IV (14th century). His letters to the pharaoh were among those discovered in the Amarna archives. He supplied the pharaoh with intelligence in return for Egypt's support in his own struggles.

Moran 1992: 146–55

Abi-rattash

Early (fourth or fifth) ruler of the Kassite Dynasty in Babylon. According to later sources he was an ancestor of AGUM III KAKRIME. The length of his reign is unknown.

Brinkman 1976: 85–6

Abisare

King of Larsa, successor of GUNGUNUM (1905–1895). According to his year names, he won a victory over Isin in his tenth year and engaged in large-scale canal building projects.

Edzard 1957: 108–9

Abishemu

Ruler of Gubla (classical Byblos) at the time of pharaoh Amenemhet III (late 19th century).

Klengel 1992: 43

Abi-simti

Royal lady at the court of Ur during
the Third Dynasty, probably the wife
and queen (Sumerian *nin*) of AMAR-SIN
and SHU-SIN's mother.

Steinkeller 1981, Agostino 1998

Achaemenes (= Persian Hakhamanish)

Persian king, reputed founder of the
house of the Achaemenids, succeeded
by his son TEISPES. If he is a historical
figure, he may have been the king who
fought with the Elamites under HUM-
BAN-NIMENA against the Assyrians in
691.

Hinz 1972: 150

Adad-apla-iddina

Eighth king of the Second Dynasty of
Isin, successor of MARDUK-SHAPIK-
ZERI (1069–1048). He was apparently
not of royal descent. According to the
New Babylonian Chronicle he was a
usurper, while the Assyrian Synchronistic History states that he was
appointed by the Assyrian king
ASHUR-BEL-KALA as ruler over Babylon
and married his daughter. Whether he
was of Aramean descent or a Babylonian is uncertain, since the genealogy
given in his inscriptions is contradictory. At any rate he continued to
use Babylonian royal titles.

The Babylonian Chronicles mention
the revolt of the Arameans against
him, as well as incursions by the
Suteans. It is also likely that Assyrian
campaigns against Babylonian territories happened during his reign. His
royal inscriptions report the rebuilding of the city walls of Babylon and
Kish, and of temples throughout the
land.

Frame 1995: 50–63; Brinkman 1968: 135–44;
Grayson 1975: 203–4

Adad-idri *see* Ben-Hadad II

Adad-it'i *see* Hadad-yis'i

Adad-nirari I

Assyrian king, son and successor of
ARIK-DEN-ILI (1307–1275). He initiated the practice, later widely
adopted by Assyrian kings, of leaving
detailed reports of his military opera-
tions. In general, there is a large
amount of inscribed material from
his reign, not just building and votive
inscriptions, but chronicles, edicts,
and letters to other sovereigns.

His most decisive victory was over
Mitanni. He advanced to the capital
Washshukanni and took its ruler
SHATTUARA I prisoner. Having deported him to Assyria, Adad-nirari
allowed him to return. The revolt that
followed Shattuara's death forced the
Assyrian king to march against Mitanni again. He destroyed numerous
cities and deported parts of the
population. He moved the Babylonian
frontier further towards the Diyala
region and generally expanded his
territory. His rule seems to have been
accepted, as reports of a successful
march into the Jezireh emphasise, for
he was able to gather large amounts of
tribute without any challenge.

In his long reign he undertook
numerous and ambitious building

projects. He had canals dug, strengthened or built city walls and quays, and restored various temples, mainly at the capital Assur and at Nineveh.

Munn-Rankin 1975, in CAH II/2: 274–61; Grayson 1972: 57–79; Grayson 1975: 204–5; Grayson 1991: 142–62; Kuhrt 1995: 353–4

Adad-nirari II

Assyrian king, son and successor of ASHUR-DAN II (911–891).

He fought his battles in much the same areas as his father, extending and consolidating his successes. He undertook several journeys to collect tribute and to display the might of Assyria as a major power which punished those who withheld their obligations of paying tribute. He probably also undertook the reorganisation of the army to make it able to respond more promptly to any challenge.

The Synchronistic History reports clashes with the Babylonians, and ascribes victory to the Assyrian king over SHAMASH-MUDAMMIQ. In 891 a new peace agreement was drawn up between NABU-SHUMA-UKIN I, king of Babylon, and Adad-nirari, sealed by the exchange of daughters in dynastic marriages. This led to a realignment of the border and friendly relations between the two countries that were to last some eighty years.

Grayson 1976: 81–97; 1982, in CAH III/1: 249–51; Kuhrt 1995: 481–3

Adad-nirari III

Assyrian king, son and successor of SHAMSHI-ADAD V (810–783). Sources for his reign are not abundant. Campaigns in the early part of his reign were conducted by his generals, especially NERGAL-ILIA, and the prominence of senior officials in the royal inscriptions is a typical feature of this period. The royal annals mention only two military expeditions by Adad-nirari himself. The first, in 805, was directed against Syria, where he collected tribute from the king of Damascus and other local rulers. The second took him to Babylonia, where he attacked Der.

Adad-nirari is described as having made an effort to restore peace and order in Babylonia by bringing back deportees and abducted statues of gods. Although he maintained the borders of the empire as they had been under SHALMANESER III, towards the end of his reign Assyria began a period of decline.

His building projects centred on Calah and other important cities. He repaired Fort Shalmaneser and completed the palace began by his father at Nineveh.

Grayson 1975: 119, 205–6; Grayson 1991: 200–38; Grayson 1982, in III/1: 271–6; Schramm 1972

Adad-shum-iddina

Thirty-first ruler of the Kassite Dynasty in Babylon, successor of KADASHMAN-HARBE II (c. 1222–1217). During his reign Babylon was largely under the authority of Assyria under king TU-KULTI-NINURTA I.

Brinkman 1976: 87–8

Adad-shumu-usur

1 Thirty-second king of the Kassite Dynasty in Babylonia, son of KASH-TILIASH IV (1216–1187). He ascended the throne as the result of a revolution that had unseated his predecessor, ADAD-SHUM-IDDINA. He was a contemporary of ASHUR-NIRARI I. A letter he sent to the Assyrian king is preserved on a later copy. He also features in a late Babylonian literary epic.

Brinkman 1976: 89–94; Grayson 1975

2 Assyrian scribe; personal exorcist (*ašipu*) under ESARHADDON and ASHURBANIPAL. He was the author of many letters and reports on medicine, magic and astrology. He was the father of another well-known Assyrian scholar, URAD-GULA.

Parpola 1970: 88–125; 1983: 101–58

Adad-sululi

Assyrian merchant who conducted his business affairs in the Cappadocian trade colony known as Karum Kanesh (present Kültepe), where his archives were excavated in the 19th century. He acted as agent for the wealthy businessman PUZUR-ASHUR.

Drecksen 1996: 93–166

Adasi

Assyrian king, heading the list of rulers in the Synchronistic History, in a new line of kings after the decline of the dynasty founded by SHAMSHI-ADAD I which links the better-known Middle Assyrian kings to the past.

According to the Assyrian King List he was one of the first six kings who were 'sons of nobodies', i.e., not part of a dynastic line. Like most of his immediate successors he remains little more than a name.

Grayson 1972: 31

Adda-Guppi' (or Hadad-happe)

Babylonian lady, priestess of the moon god Sin, the mother of king NABONI-DUS. After her death he put up a stele in Harran, where she had officiated. This says that she was born in the 20th year of ASHURBANIPAL (649) and that she had influence at the court of Babylon, particularly under the kings NABOPOLASSAR, NEBUCHADNEZZAR II and NERIGLISSAR. She lived to a ripe old age of at least 102 and died in the 9th regnal year of her son's reign in 547. Her position at Harran is thought to have been a contributing factor to Nabonidus' devotion to the moon god and the city of Harran.

Gadd 1958; Oppenheim in Pritchard 1969: 560ff.; Weisberg in Garelli 1974: 447–54, Mayer 1998

Addu-duri

High-ranking female official and administrator in Mari during the reign of ZIMRI-LIM (18th century), who performed many functions in secular as well as cultic matters. It appears that she was the mother of Zimri-lim, which explains her elevated position at court and the trust the king had in her.

Batto 1974: 64–72; Durand 1985b: 409

Agga (or Akka)

Early Dynastic Sumerian king of Kish. He appears in the Sumerian King list as the son of MEBARAGESI. According to a literary composition he was the enemy of GILGAMESH, who prevailed over him when Agga besieged Uruk. Like Gilgamesh he also features in the Tummal Inscriptions as having repaired the sanctuary at Nippur.

Römer 1980; Katz 1987

Agum I (Agum rabu)

Second king of the Kassite Dynasty in Babylonia, son of GANDASH. He ruled for twenty-two years (early 18th century) according to King List A. There are no contemporary records of this ruler.

Brinkman 1976: 96–7

Agum II kakrime

Kassite king of Babylon. He is only known from the Babylonian King List as well as from much later (7th-century) texts, supposedly copies of his royal inscriptions but of doubtful historical value. There he is given as the sixth king of the Kassite Dynasty, identified as the son of Urzigurumash. The same source makes the claim that he brought back the statues of the gods Marduk and Sarpanitum, which the Hittite had raided from Babylon in 1595. He may in fact have been little more than a military leader of Kassite tribes who established themselves in Middle Mesopotamia during the Old Babylonian period.

Astour 1986; Brinkman 1976: 95–9

Agum III(?)

King of the Kassite Dynasty in Babylonia (c. 17th century). According to one chronicle he was the son of KASHTILIASH I and campaigned against the Sealand.

Brinkman 1976: 98–9

Ahab

King of Israel, son and successor of OMRI (874–853). The biblical sources for his reign (I Kgs. 16:28ff.) are supplemented by contemporary records, such as the Moabite stone of MESHA and Assyrian documents. He ruled at a time when Assyrian power was steadily growing in Syria and the Levant. Local dynasts had to develop strategies to deal with this situation and Ahab's career is in many ways typical.

He began by completing the building of Samaria, the new capital founded by his father, making use of Phoenician labour, materials and techniques. Contact with the Phoenicians had become more intense since his marriage to JEZEBEL, the daughter of ETHBA'AL of Tyre. He built temples for Canaanite gods and set up pillars for Asherah. Most of the accounts in the book of Kings concern the violent reaction of the prophets against Jezebel and Ahab's idolatry.

His foreign policy, apart from the alliance with Tyre, was marked by the long-lasting war against HAZA'EL, king of Aram, who had invaded Israel on several occasions. Ahab successfully repelled these attacks and gained tactical advantage over the Arameans, who not only restored disputed territories but granted Ahab trading rights in Damascus.

According to the Assyrian annals of SHALMANESER III, Ahab supported Ben-Hadad and his coalition of Syro-Palestinian rulers, which also counted on Egyptian and Arab military support, at the Battle of Qarqar with 2,000 chariots and 10,000 men. This battle, despite being declared as a victory by the Shalmaneser, held off the advance of the Assyrians for some time. During this period Ahab may have responded favourably to advances made by JEHOSHAPHAT of Judah. They joined forces to recover Ramoth-Gilead from the Arameans. Ahab entered the chariot battle in disguise and was mortally wounded by an arrow. 1 Kgs. 22:38 reports that he died in his chariot, watching the battle until he bled to death at sunset. He was buried at Samaria and his son AHAZIAH became king.

Mitchell 1982, in CAH III/1: 466–79

Ahat-milki

Queen of Ugarit, wife of NIQMEPA, mother of AMMISHTAMRU II. She was the daughter of Du-Teshub of Amurru. A list of her jewellery, which formed part of her dowry, survived in the palace ruins. According to another source she mediated in a dispute between her sons.

Drower 1975, in CAH II/2: 141–1

Ahaz

King of Judah, son of JOTHAM (735–715). His name is the short form

of Jehoahaz. Early in his reign PEKAH, king of Israel, put pressure on him to join an anti-Assyrian alliance and attacked Jerusalem. Despite the warning of the prophet ISAIAH he appealed to TIGLATH-PILESER III for help. The latter invaded Israel, defeated Damascus, and made Judah a tribute-paying vassal state of Assyria.

Mitchell 1993, in CAH III/2: 336–8, 344–7

Ahaziah

King of Judah, son and successor of AHAB (853–852). He was the son of Ahab's Phoenician queen JEZEBEL. Most of the Biblical account concerns his clashes with the prophet ELIJAH (I Kgs. 22:51–2; II Kgs. 1, 18). He maintained the relationship with the Judean king JEHOSHAPHAT that had begun under his father and even entered into a trade agreement with him which involved a maritime expedition to Ophir (probably somewhere on the Horn of Africa). This proved a total failure since the ships sank.

He died after a two-year reign when he fell from the upper storey of his palace at Samaria. Since he was without an heir, his brother Joram became king.

Mitchell 1982, in CAH III/1: 479–81

Ahi-'antu

Babylonian scribe who is often cited in colophons as an ancestor of scribes working in the Seleucid period.

Lambert 1957: 4

Aitagama

King of Qadesh in the Amarna period. During the Syrian campaign of SUPPI-LULIUMA I his city was destroyed and he was taken prisoner by the Hittites and deported to Anatolia. However, he seems to have returned to the throne, possibly because Qadesh was under the official control of Egypt at the time. During year nine of MURSILI II he was murdered by his own son when a rebellion against the Hittites failed.

Klengel 1992: 157–9

Akalamdu(g)

Early Dynastic Sumerian king of Ur whose seal bears his name and that of his wife ASHUSIKILDIGIRA.

Sollberger and Kupper 1971: IB3a

Akhat-abisha

Assyrian princess, daughter of SAR-GON II. She was married to AMBARIS, the king of Tabal, who became an Assyrian vassal ruler. When he was deposed and taken prisoner for plotting against Sargon in 713, Akhat-abisha may have ruled the now-annexed province of Tabal.

Barnett 1982, in CAH III/1: 355; Hawkins 1982, in CAH III/1: 419

Akhuni

King of Til Barsip, capital of Bit-Adini (c. 875–855). He is first mentioned in the Assyrian sources in c. 876, when he paid tribute to ASHUR-NASIRPAL II after his destruction of Kaprabu, a fortress of Bit-Adini. Since

this did not eliminate his opposition to the Assyrians or much diminish the strength of Bit-Adini, it was the goal of further campaigns by SHALMANE-SER III. Akhuni was joined by several other local rulers who fought the Assyrians on a number of occasions. In 857 however, the Assyrians prevailed and Akhuni submitted. Til Barsip was besieged and turned into an Assyrian administrative centre called Kar-Shalmaneser. Akhuni had fled the city during the siege. He was pursued in a separate campaign in 855 to a mountain fortress across the Euphrates and defeated in a battle. He was then taken with his troops to Assyria. Nothing more was heard of this formidable opponent of the Assyrians.

Grayson 1982, in CAH III/1: 260–1; Hawkins, in ibid.: 391–2

Akizzi

King of Qatna during the Amarna period. He sent several letters to AMENOPHIS IV in which he expresses his friendship with Egypt in the face of the advance of the Hittites in Syria. In fact SUPPILULIUMA I captured the city and deported its population to Hatti; the fate of Akizzi is not known.

Klengel 1992: 156; Moran 1992: 123–7

Akkullanu

Assyrian scribe and astrologer. He held an important position at the temple of Assur during the reigns of ESARHADDON and ASHURBANIPAL. Thirty-five letters of his, concerning astrological and cultic matters, survive.

Parpola 1970: 254–69; 1983: 304–29; 1993: xxv, 64–83

Akurgal

Early Dynastic Sumerian king of Lagash, son of UR-NANSHE. He is depicted with his father on a stone plaque. He was the father of EANNATUM.

Gadd 1971, in CAH I/2: 117

Alahum

Assyrian copper merchant whose business archive was discovered at Kültepe in Cappadocia (19th century). Having conducted his affairs in Anatolia for years, he eventually returned to Assur, leaving his sons to carry on the business.

Drecksen 1996: 107–18

Alaksandu

Vassal ruler of Wilusa (said to be part of Arzawa; perhaps in the Troad). He concluded a treaty with MUWATALIS (II) (c. 1290).

Gurney 1990: 34, 57

Alexander the Great

Macedonian conqueror, son of Philip II of Macedon (356–321). He set out to challenge the Persian control over the Ionian cities and ended up with an empire that for the first time in history linked Western and Central Asia with India and Europe.

His first battle against the Persians was fought in Anatolia, at the river Granicus (334). The Persian king DARIUS III had mustered his troops from Babylonia and set out with a huge army to deal with the Greek advance. He moved through the Cilician gates and engaged Alexander at Issos (333). Although heavily outnumbered and sustaining great loss of life, the Greeks achieved victory and Darius fled to Babylon. From Issos Alexander made his way southwards to Syria and Palestine, where several cities surrendered voluntarily, with the notable exception of Tyre and Gaza. He then began the conquest of Egypt, where the satrap Mazaces surrendered. In 331 Alexander was enthroned as pharaoh.

Meanwhile Darius had assembled a formidable army in Babylonia. The two sides met in the battle at Gaugamela, some 75 miles north of Arbela (the present Erbil in Iraq). The hard-fought battle ended in another Macedonian victory, though Darius managed to escape to Media. Alexander marched to Babylon whose satrap Mazaeus surrendered. Alexander ordered the Babylonian temples to be rebuilt and reinstated Mazaeus as governor. He spent a month in the city and then pressed on for Susa, where the local satrap was confirmed in office. Although he received news about war in Greece, he was eager to march to Persepolis, the dynastic centre of the Achaemenid empire and containing a large treasury. Its seizure provided him with an almost inexhaustible source of wealth. His troops looted and burned the city, including the so-called 'palace' of XERXES, which was extensively burnt.

His next objective was to capture Darius, who was murdered by two Persian nobles. Alexander ordered his body to be taken to Persepolis and buried in the royal tombs. The brother of Darius, Oxyathres, he appointed as one of his Companions.

Then followed the conquest of the Iranian plateau and Bactria (324). To cement the links between the Bactrians and the Macedonians the vanquished king Spitamenes gave his daughter APAMA in marriage to SE-LEUCUS (I). Alexander married Roxane, daughter of Oxyartes, a ruler of Sogdiana.

Alexander then prepared for his invasion of India. He reached Pattala (Hyderabad?) in 325 and, in an arduous march, crossed the Gedrosian desert. His fleet set sail across the Arabian sea while he marched back to Persia. In 324 he celebrated the successful return of his navy and the conquest of India in a lavish feast at Susa. He also entered into marriage alliances with the royal house of the Achaemenids by taking Stateira, eldest daughter of Darius, and Prysatis, daughter of ARTAXERXES III, as chief wives. He furthermore sponsored marriages between the Macedonian nobles and Persian noble women.

After a brief rest at Ecbatana he left on a campaign to subdue nomadic tribesmen who lived in the mountains north of Susa and forced them to submit. He planned an expedition to Arabia and set out for Babylon, where he made preparations for his fleet to be transported down the Euphrates to be used in the exploration of the Arabian coastline. It was to start in early June but had to be abandoned. On 31 March he caught a fever and died towards evening on 10 June 323, not yet 33 years old. His untimely death led to a prolonged and bloody struggle among his Companions over his succession and the division of the vast territories he had conquered.

Lane-Fox 1973; Burn 1973; Hamilton 1973; Green 1991; O'Brien 1992; Briant 1996: 837–91; Bosworth 1996

Alila-hadum

Little-known ruler of Uruk in the Old Babylonian period, mentioned in a year name by SUMU-IL of Larsa.

Frayne 1990: 439

Allumari

King of Melid (modern Malatya), who paid tribute to TIGLATH-PILESER I in *c.* 1112.

Hawkins 1982, in CAH III/1: 380

Alyattes

King of Lydia, son and successor of Sadyattes (*c.* 610–*c.* 560). He was one of the most successful Lydian rulers and combined diplomatic strategies with military force to secure the greatest extent and prosperity for his kingdom. According to Herodotus (I.16ff.) he waged a war against Ionian cities that culminated in the capture of Smyrna, an event which has been confirmed by archaeological excavations in which his siege mount, complete with arrowheads, was discovered. The motive for attacking the

Ionian cities was probably to secure access to western harbours.

He also expanded his power in central Anatolia, where the Phrygians had had a wealthy kingdom based on agriculture and metallurgy; again archaeological excavations show signs of Lydian presence in most major areas, most notably perhaps in the find at Gordion of a hoard of electrum coins, a new Lydian invention.

His expansion towards the east brought him into conflict with the Medes, which resulted in a six-year-long war that ended on the battlefield on the day of a total solar eclipse on 28 May 585. Herodotus reports that the official end to hostilities was brought about by the intervention of the rulers of Cilicia and a certain Labynetus of Babylon (who some think was NABONIDUS acting on behalf of the then reigning NEBUCHAD-NEZZAR II). The pact was sealed with a dynastic marriage in which the daughter of Alyattes married Asty-gates, the son of CYAXARES. The result of this peace was increased prosperity for Lydia.

Alyattes was probably buried in the largest tumulus near Sardis, although an early grave-robber has removed any chances of historical confirmation.

Mellink 1991, in CAH III/2: 647–51; Kuhrt 1995: 569

Ama-duga

High-ranking woman mentioned in the older Mari texts as well as under ZIMRI-LIM. It appears that she was one of the wives of SHAMSHI-ADAD I and probably the mother of YASMAH-ADDU, who ruled in Mari as governor (and possibly also of his sister KUN-SHIMATUM). She took up residence in the palace of Mari where she had important administrative functions. It is also possible that the Sumerian name Ama-duga was her official name, given to her as a representative of the royal house, and that she was also known as Akatiya. She continued to play an important role after Yas-mah-Addu came of age and was married to BELTUM. After the arrival of Zimri-Lim she was in charge of the ancillary personnel of the palace, but eventually she moved to another place, some distance away from Mari.

Durand 1985b: 408–12

Amar-Sin (Amar-Suen)

Third king of the Third Dynasty of Ur (2046–2038), son of SHULGI. He built on the achievements of his father and further consolidated the sphere of influence and control exercised by the Ur III state. He fought various campaigns against the eastern border regions but seems to have concerned himself otherwise mainly with ambi-tious building projects in the capital and Nippur.

Gadd 1971, in CAH I/2: 607–8; Frayne 1997: 235–84

Amasis

Egyptian pharaoh of the 26th Dynasty (570–526), successor of APRIES. He was an Egyptian general and courtier who usurped the throne during a revolt of the army protesting against the poor organisation of a campaign against Cyrene, in which the troops sustained heavy losses. Apries was forced into exile but made two attempts to regain power; he even persuaded NEBUCHADNEZZAR II to force the issue by invading Egypt. Amasis reacted to his threat by asking the king of Cyrene for help. The ensuing battle was bitter and Apries was killed in the fight.

Amasis spent the remaining years of his long reign dealing with internal affairs and the Mediterranean enterprises initiated by his predecessors. In the face of the growing power of the Persians under CYRUS II, he concluded a treaty with CROESUS of Lydia and with the Babylonians. This proved ultimately fruitless, as Egypt was conquered by CAMBYSES II after the death of Amasis. According to Herodotus, Cambyses ordered his body to be exhumed and desecrated.

James, T.G.H. 1991, in CAH III/2: 718–20; Kuhrt 1995: 644–6

Amat-Mamu
Female scribe appointed to serve the needs of the cloistered *nadītu* women at Sippar. She enjoyed a long career, serving during the reigns of HAMMUR-ABI, SAMSU-ILUNA and ABI-ESUH (c. 1764–1711).

Harris 1975: 196–7

Amat-Shamash
Sister of ILTANI, queen of Karana, daughter of Samu-Addu. She served as a *nadītum* of the god Shamash in Sippar. Like her colleague ERISHTI-AYA,

princess of Mari, her official function was to pray for the life of her father.

Dalley 1984: 104–5

Amaziah
King of Judah, son and successor of JEHOASH (796–767). He sought to profit from the effects of ADAD-NIRARI III's campaigns in Syria and launched an attack against Edom. He achieved victory near the Dead Sea and took an Edomite fortress. Perhaps overconfident after the success against Edom and seriously annoyed with the behaviour of the mercenary Israelite soldiers he had hired and not deployed, he challenged JOASH of Israel to battle. This proved to be his undoing. Joash won a victory at Beth Shemesh, took Amaziah captive and plundered Jerusalem. According to II Kgs. 14:21 and II Chron. 26:1, 3 the people of Jerusalem made his son UZZIAH king of Judah; he may have acted in a co-regency with Amaziah the remaining fifteen years of his life. He died in an assassination plot and was buried in Jerusalem.

Mitchell 1982, in CAH III/1: 498–503

Ambaris
King of Bit-Burutash (Tabal), son of KHULLI under SARGON II (713). He was married to the Assyrian king's daughter AKHAT-ABISHA and became his vassal. He was involved in an anti-Assyrian plot with RUSA I of Urartu and MITA of Mushki. For this breach of loyalty Sargon had him arrested and taken in chains to Nineveh. Tabal

then became part of the Assyrian empire.

Barnett 1982, in CAH III/1: 352, 355–6; Hawkins ibid: 419

Amel-Marduk (= biblical Evil-Merodach)

Babylonian king, son and successor of NEBUCHADNEZZAR II (561–560). According to Berossus he 'managed affairs in a lawless and outrageous fashion', and a fragment of a historical Babylonian epic also describes a king who did not listen to his counsellors and paid little attention to the temples in Babylon. There is not much evidence to support either claim, and the few brick inscriptions from his reign show that he continued building works in Babylon. He was deposed, and perhaps murdered, by his sister's husband NERIGLISSAR.

Sack 1972

Amenophis II

Egyptian pharaoh of the 18th Dynasty (c. 1428–1397), son and successor of TUTHMOSIS III. He campaigned in North Syria where he faced a serious rebellion against Egypt that he ruthlessly suppressed, executing all the leaders responsible for the insurrection. This show of strength probably led to a rapprochement with the kingdom of Mitanni.

Klengel 1992: 95–6; Kuhrt 1995: 193

Amenophis III

Egyptian pharaoh of the 18th Dynasty, son and successor of TUTHMO-SIS IV (c. 1387–1350). He married two Near Eastern princesses, first Giluhepa, the daughter of Shattarna II, king of Mitanni, and then the daughter of TUSHRATTA. These kings also sent a miraculous statue of the goddess Ishtar to the pharaoh when he fell ill on two occasions.

Klengel 1992: 97

Amenophis IV (= Akhnaton)

Egyptian pharaoh, son and successor of AMENOPHIS III (1376–1379). He built for himself at el-Amarna a new capital, which he named Akhetaten, an expression of his devotion for the sun god Aten. The royal court used this city only briefly but the site has become synonymous with an era of international communication across the Near East. The letters contained in the famous archive found there, written by the various rulers of the Egyptian-controlled territories in the Levant, as well as kings of neighbouring states, are full of warning about double dealings.

In spite of the popular image of Akhnaton as a rather effete personality, mainly concerned with religious affairs and his family, there is evidence that he campaigned in Syro-Palestine. He also ordered a campaign against Nubia and deported rebellious peoples from Damascus to Nubia where he had some of them executed by impaling. The sculptors of his splendidly appointed new capital left numerous, apparently life-like, portraits of this eccentric pharaoh, as well as of his beautiful wife Nefertiti. He was buried in a rock-tomb near el-Amarna. Soon afterwards the city was abandoned as the court was moved back to Thebes and the memory of Akhnaton was erased from the official records of imperial Egypt.

Kuhrt 1995: 194–204

Ammi-ditana

King of Babylon in the Old Babylonian period, son and successor of ABI-ESUH, he reigned for 37 years (1683–1646). The few surviving inscriptions record building activities.

Frayne 1990: 411–24

Ammi-saduqa

King of Babylon during the Old Babylonian period, son and successor of AMMI-DITANA (1646–1626). He is mainly remembered for a royal decree or edict that cancelled certain debts and relieved bond-slavery. He also commissioned astronomical observations of the planet Venus to be recorded.

Kraus 1958, 1984; Finkelstein 1961; Frayne 1990: 425–35

Ammishtamru I

King of Ugarit at the time of AMENOPHIS III, father of NIQMADU II. The Amarna tablets contain one letter sent by Ammishtamru to the pharaoh asking him for assistance against an unspecified enemy.

Klengel 1992: 130–1; Drower 1975, in CAH II/ 2: 133; Moran 1992: 117

Ammishtamru II

King of Ugarit, son of NIQMEPA. He ruled as a Hittite vassal during the reigns of HATTUSILI III and TUDHALIYA IV. He was married to the daughter of BENTESHINA of Amurru whom he later divorced, possibly for political reasons. The details of this case are preserved in a number of tablets written in Ugaritic and Akkadian. He also faced problems in connection with a plot by his two brothers against their mother, AHAT-MILKI, also a princess of Amurru. He maintained good relations with his Hittite overlord after Tudhaliya and INI-TESHUP of Amurru had intervened in these affairs. He was relieved of his military obligation to help the Hittites against the Assyrians, although he was forced to pay a heavy sum in compensation.

Klengel 1992: 139–44; Kuhrt 1995: 309–13; Kühne 1973

Ammuna

Hittite king of the Old Kingdom, son and killer of his predecessor ZIDANTA I (c. 1550–1530). According to the Edict of TELEPINU his long reign was not blessed by the gods since none of his campaigns were successful and the lands rebelled against him. He seems to have died a natural death and was succeeded by HUZZIYA.

Kuhrt 1995: 246

Ammurapi

King of Ugarit, last ruler of this city. He is not explicitly named as son of an Ugaritic king but appears in some ritual texts that connect him with other royal predecessors. He ruled as a vassal of SUPPILULIUMA II and his viceroy at Carchemish, TALMI-TESHUP, and was married to a Hittite princess, Ehli-Nikkal, whom he divorced. He was probably still king when Ugarit was destroyed, perhaps because of an earthquake, perhaps through an attack, during the general upheavals of the time.

Klengel 1992: 147–51; Kuhrt 1995: 314

Amon

King of Judah, son and successor of MANASSEH (642–640). The Old Testament II kgs 21:18) claims that he continued the evil cult practices of his father and that he was assassinated by his own retainers in a palace coup.

Mitchell 1993, in CAH III/2: 382

Amos

Hebrew prophet (*c*. 760), who lived as a sheep-farmer in Judah at the time of kings UZZIAH and JEROBOAM II. He prophesied in the kingdom of Israel, stressing the moral basis of the worship of Yahweh and invoking a stern ethical and social code as an essential function of his covenant with Israel. He also railed against social inequalities and the exploitation of the poor, as well as the lax religious observation among the populace.

Kuhrt 1995: 462; Comay 1993: 30–2

Amutpi'el

King of Qatna, often mentioned in the Mari letters as an ally of ZIMRI-LIM (18th century). He was an influential and powerful ruler in his time, on a par with HAMMURABI of Babylon and RIM-SIN of Larsa. He established better relations between Qatna and its traditional enemy Yamhad, under its ruler YARIM-LIM I.

Kupper 1973, in CAH II/1: 22–3; Klengel 1992: 67–70

Amytis

Lydian princess, wife of CYRUS II of Persia, daughter of ASTYAGES.

Brosius 1996: 36, 43–5

Anam

King of Uruk in the Old Babylonian period, successor of Ilum-Gamil. A royal inscription records his restoration of the Gipar at Uruk.

Frayne 1990: 471–7

Andarim (previously read as Meshigirru)

Official from Early-Dynastic Mari whose inscribed statue dedicated to Ishtar was discovered at her temple.

Braun-Holzinger 1977: 70, Gelb and Kienast 1990: 6

Anitta

Anatolian king of Kussara, son of PITHANA. His name is mentioned in the Assyrian documents discovered at the trade colony of Kültepe in Anatolia (18th century). An iron dagger inscribed with the words 'Palace of Anitta the Prince' was found in the nearby town of Kanesh. Contemporary records of his military exploits are not preserved but he figures very prominently in the later Hittite sources, where he is regarded as an ancestral royal figure who successfully gained control over much of central Anatolia, laid waste the city of Hattusa and established himself as suzerain of the Anatolian principalities.

Dyson 1973, in CAH I/2: 714; Kuhrt 1995 I: 226–9; Neu 1974

Annubanini

King of Lullubi (probably the region of the valley of Shahrazur in modern northern Iraq) of the (early?) Sargonic period. He immortalised himself in a monumental rock-inscription written in Akkadian, near Sar-i-Pul.

Sollberger and Kupper 1971: IIIG1; Drower 1973, in CAH I/2: 444; Frayne 1990: 704–6

Antigonus Monophthalmos

Macedonian general, chief of cavalry and one of the *Diodochi* of ALEXANDER THE GREAT, satrap of Phrygia *c.*, later king (321–301). He was called the Cyclops (*monophthalmos*) because he had lost an eye in a battle. In the struggles amongst Alexander's generals after the latter's death, he eventually managed to set himself up as ruler of all Asia, supported by PTOLEMY I. He dislodged SELEUCUS I from Babylon, and when the latter came back from his Egyptian exile in 312, launched a war that was to ravage the country for four years, as described in a Babylonian *Chronicle of the Diadochi*. His brutal behaviour towards the native population resulted in Babylon's strong support

for Seleucus. He was finally defeated and killed in the battle of Ipsus in Phrygia in 301, at the age of 81.

Will 1984, in CAH VII/1: 39–61; Joannès 1979–80; Kuhrt and Sherwin-White 1987: 12–14; Kuhrt in Sherwin-White and Kuhrt 1993: 9–11

Antiochus I Soter

Seleucid king, successor of SELEUCUS I, his son by his Persian wife APAMA (281–261). After his father's murder, he had to struggle for some ten years to regain control over rebellious territories and to keep the vast empire of Seleucus together. Babylon remained loyal and he asserted his rule in Iran and Syria, but the situation in Anatolia proved highly problematic. Not only did various states fight tenaciously for independence, but the influx of Celtic warrior tribes further destabilised the country. He managed to defeat these Galatians in the Battle of the Elephants, so named because of his use of the beasts in combat. The Greeks expressed their relief by giving him the title *soter* ('saviour'). In 276 he had to deal with an offensive by PTOLEMY II, who occupied Damascus. Although he could dislodge him, the south of Syria remained under Ptolomaic control. These two victories allowed for a time of peaceful consolidation. Like his father he was a great builder of cities. In Babylonia he restored the temples of Esagila and Ezida, commemorated in a famous inscription (incidentally the last royal inscription to be written in Akkadian), where he calls himself, like the traditional kings of Babylon 'the provider of Esagila and Ezida'. In the same text he asks for the gods' blessings for his wife Stratonice and their son and his co-regent, Seleucus, who was later executed.

Sherwin-White and Kuhrt 1993: 28–37 and *passim*; Heinen 1984, in CAH VII/1: 413–18

Antiochus II

Seleucid king, son and successor of ANTIOCHUS I, who promoted him after the designated co-regent Seleucus had proved unreliable. In Babylon he was remembered by a land-grant to his wife Laodice and her sons, who passed it on to the Babylonians. He fought the second Syrian War against the Ptolemies who had occupied southern Syria. This ended in 253 when he concluded a peace treaty with Egypt, sealed by a dynastic union. He married Berenice, the daughter of PTOLEMY II. He was poisoned by his former wife Laodice, whom he had to repudiate in order to marry Berenice.

Heinen 1984, in CAH VII/1: 418–20; van der Spek, in Kuhrt and Sherwin-White 1987: 62

Antiochus III the Great

Seleucid king, younger brother and successor of SELEUCUS II (223–187). He was faced with serious problems in Anatolia and Iran. In 198 he forced his domination on the Carian towns but achieved a brilliant victory over PTOLEMY III, largely aided by the use of fighting elephants introduced by Hannibal. Other wars in the east and against Egypt resulted in a gain of territories which extended Seleucid rule beyond the area controlled by

SELEUCUS I. However, when he supported the Macedonians in their invasion of Greece, he was disastrously defeated by the Romans at Thermopylae. He was forced to retire to Asia Minor, where the Romans pursued him and inflicted another defeat at Magnesia. As a result he lost control over his previous conquests in Anatolia.

Heinen 1984, in CAH VII/1: 433–45; Sherwin-White and Kuhrt 1993: 188–216

Antiochus IV Epiphanes

Seleucid king, son and second successor of ANTIOCHUS III (175–164). He reconquered Palestine where he made attempts to repress Judaism. His persecutions caused the Maccabean rebellion. He launched a sea and land attack against Egypt. The Romans, anxious to maintain a balance of power in the Mediterranean, forced him back and furthermore ordered his combat elephants to be destroyed.

Antiochus fostered the spread of Hellenic culture in Syria, Media and Babylon, although the idea that he turned the latter city into a Greek *polis* has been rejected.

Musti, in CAH VII/1: 197–8 ; van der Spek, in Kuhrt and Sherwin-White 1987: 66ff.

Antiochus VII Sidetes

Seleucid king, successor of Antiochus VI (Epiphanes) (138–129). He campaigned against the Parthians and reconquered Babylonia and Media for a brief period, to the apparent delight of the Greeks residing in Mesopotamia. The Parthians under their youthful king PHRAATES II were numerically inferior and were prepared to sue for peace. However, the conditions imposed by Antiochus were too harsh, and the unruly behaviour of his soldiers caused the residents of the Mesopotamian garrison cities to support the Parthians. They all revolted against their occupiers simultaneously in a surprise attack which proved effective. Antiochus died in the ensuing fighting. His death signalled the end of the Seleucid power east of the Euphrates.

Schippmann 1980: 26–8

Anu-aba-uter

Babylonian scribe and astronomer in the Seleucid period, nephew of Anu-Belshunu, and a member of the famous family of scholars descended from SIN-LEQQE-UNNINNI. His name appears in colophons as owner and author of astronomical tablets.

Neugebauer 1955: 13

Anum-muttabil

Governor of Der, a contemporary of BILALAMA of Eshnunna. He left an inscription in which he claims to have 'smitten the heads of Anshan, Elam and Simashki and captured Warakh-shi'.

Hinz 1971, in CAH III/2: 633, 661

Apama

A native Bactrian, she was queen and wife of SELEUCUS I, mother of ANTI-OCHUS I. For her role in mediating with the ambassadors of Miletus during Seleucus' campaign in her homeland, Bactriana-Sogdiana, she was publicly honoured by decree.

Sherwin-White and Kuhrt 1993: 24–5

Apil-kin

Ruler (šakkanakku) of Mari during the Ur III period (c. 2126–2091). According to dynastic lists from Mari he was the son of ISHGUM-ADDU, also commemorated on an inscribed foundation brick.

Durand 1985: 151; Frayne 1997: 440

Apil-Sin

Fourth king of the First Dynasty of Babylon (1830–1813), son of SABIUM. Like his predecessors, he was kept busy strengthening the defences of his domain by building walls and fortresses and increasing the economic potential of the land by digging new waterways and canals. As there is no mention of warfare with neighbouring states at his time, he may have enjoyed a period of stability and peace.

Edzard 1957: 15; Frayne 1990: 330

Aplahanda

King of Carchemish, frequently mentioned in the Mari texts as contemporary with YASMAH-ADDU, as well as ZIMRI-LIM of Mari, YARIM-LIM I of Yamhad and HAMMURABI of Babylon, (18th century). He was on good terms with Yasmah-Addu to whom he delivered substantial quantities of wine. At the time Carchemish was also profiting from trade with horses and tin that passed through the area from

Mesopotamia to Anatolia. The texts from the period of Zimri-Lim's reign point to the prestige and influence of Aplahanda. A seal of his was discovered in Anatolia.

Klengel 1992: 70–2

Appuwashu

Anatolian king of Cilicia (then called Piriddu) (c. 557). According to Babylonian sources NEBUCHADNEZZAR II fought a successful campaign in Cilicia and conquered Piriddu. However, NERIGLISSAR had to go there again in 557 after Appuwashu had made an attack on Syria. He was defeated but escaped.

Hawkins 1982, in CAH III/1: 434

Apries

Egyptian pharaoh of the 26th Dynasty, successor of Psammetichus II (589–570). He had to come to terms with the Babylonian presence in the Levant and seems to have steered a cautious course between defending Egyptian interests (and allies) and not provoking the Babylonians renewed attacks on Egypt. When NEBUCHADNEZZAR II was besieging Jerusalem, he intervened on the side of Judah and, as reported in 2 Kgs. 24:7, suffered a defeat. However, while he could not prevent the fall of Jerusalem, he took advantage of the Babylonian engagement in Judah to attack Tyre and Sidon, which were then subject to the Babylonians, who had then to undertake a lengthy campaign to recover these important ports.

When after an abortive campaign his army officers rebelled and the general, AMASIS, usurped the throne, Apries still had considerable support in Egypt. He went into exile and pleaded with Nebuchadnezzar to invade Egypt in 567 in order to win back the kingship. The latter complied with this request, but Apries was killed in the ensuing battle and Amasis retained his position.

James, T.G.H. 1991, in CAH III/2: 718–19; Kuhrt 1995: 644

Aqba-hammu

Ruler of Karana, son-in-law of Samuaddu. An influential Amorite ruler, he became the 'servant' of HAMMURABI of Babylon, as his inscribed seal proclaims. His correspondence with his wife ILTANI and other officials is preserved in archives discovered at Tell al Rimah.

Dalley et al. 1976; Dalley 1984: 211f.

Arakha (= Nebuchadnezzar IV)

Armenian, son of Haldita, who rebelled against DARIUS III in 521 in an attempt to win independence for Babylonia from Persian rule. He took the name Nebuchadnezzar like the other ill-fated rebel NIDINITI-BEL. The rebellion was quickly squashed by the Persian troops led by Vindafarnah. Arakha was taken prisoner and impaled, together with his nobles, in Babylon.

Barnett 1982, in CAH III/1: 365; Kuhrt 1988, in CAH IV: 129–30

Arame (= Aramu)

Urartian king (858–844), the first known political leader of this state, which became an important power in the mountainous regions between Lake Van and Lake Urmia in the 9th century.

Arame was a contemporary and adversary of SHALMANESER III who led several successful campaigns against Urartu. The series of defeats suffered at the hands of the Assyrians may have galvanised the Urartians, especially under Arame, to reorganise their defences, army and administration. He is likely to have founded the capital city Tushpa (modern Van), as well as other fortified settlements, in which Assyrian architectural techniques can be observed.

Barnett 1982, in CAH III/1: 334–7

Arda-Mulissu

Assyrian prince, son of SENNACHERIB (c. 694), thought to have been at the head of a conspiracy against Sennacherib, which ended in his murder on 20 October 681. A possible reason for the assassination was resentment against the preferential treatment of one of his younger siblings, ASHURBANIPAL.

Mayer, in Dietrich and Loretz 1995: 326–7

Ardys

King of Lydia, son and successor of GYGES (c. 652–c. 630). He suffered much from the recurrent raids of Cimmerians, and as Herodotus (I,15) records, Sardis was captured and looted during his reign. Otherwise he continued the hostilities against Greek cities in Ionia. Assyrian records show that he was on good terms with ASHURBANIPAL.

Mellink 1991, in CAH III/2: 647; Kuhrt 1995: 568

Argishti I

King of Urartu, son and successor of MENUA, (c. 786–764). He continued his father's policy of expanding the Urartian empire towards the north-eastern Caucasus regions as well as towards the west, especially into Phrygia. He recorded his deeds and campaigns in annal form, one of the longest known Urartian inscriptions.

SHALMANESER IV sent his field marshal SHAMSHU-ILU to deal with the increasingly powerful Urartian, and he claims to have defeated Argishti in the region of Mannea. Despite set-backs such as this, Argishti continued to expand his kingdom and captured new territories until the empire of Urartu covered the whole territory of Armenia, including the metal-rich shores of the eastern Black Sea. It controlled vital trade routes to Anatolia, Syria and Mesopotamia. Near modern Erevan he built a strong fortress called Erebuni, in which he settled thousands of prisoners taken on previous campaigns. Another new fortification was Argishtihinili, the modern Armavir-Blur, on the middle Araxes river. Argishti constructed irrigation canals to extend the agriculturally productive land, built vast granaries to store the harvest, planted vineyards, and ensured an efficient administration of his empire. He was buried in a rock-cut tomb in the citadel at Van.

Barnett 1982, in CAH III/1: 344–7

Argishti II

King of Urartu, son and successor of RUSA I (714–680). Not much is known about this king, who was a contemporary of SARGON II, SENNACHERIB and ESARHADDON. Although by his time the territory of Urartu had lost out to renewed Assyrian power, he was able to expand his area of influence further east, as inscriptions in the Iranian Azerbaijan have shown. Like his forebears he built fortresses and canals, this time around the lakes Urmia and Sevan. In one rock-inscription in Van he boasts that he could shoot an arrow as far as 470 metres.

Barnett 1982, in CAH III/1: 357–8

Arik-den-ili

Assyrian king, son and successor of ENLIL-NIRARI (1319–1308). One Assyrian Chronicle reports that he fought in the mountainous regions of the north and east, possibly to pacify semi-nomadic tribes that threatened the border area.

Grayson 1972: 54–7; 175; 1975, in CAH II/2: 32–3

Ari-shen (Atal-shen)

Hurrian king of Urkesh and Nawar (c. 21st century); the earliest Hurrian king attested so far. He left an inscription recording building activities at the temple of Nergal.

Wilhelm 1989: 9

Arnuwanda I

Hittite king of the empire period (c. 1390–1380/1370–1355), son and successor of Tudhaliya II and father of TUDHALIYA III. His Egyptian counterpart and enemy AMENOPHIS III concluded a treaty with the king of Arzawa, a kingdom west of the Hittite empire. His reign was also troubled by raids on the part of the Gasga people, who may have destroyed the Hittite capital Hattusa at this time.

Kuhrt 1995: 252

Arnuwanda II

Hittite king of the empire period, son and successor of SUPPILULIUMA I (1330/1322–1321). He may have died prematurely after a very brief reign in the epidemic that swept the country at this time.

Kuhrt 1995: 254

Arnuwanda III

Hittite king of the empire period , son and successor of TUDHALIYA IV (1215–1210/1209–1205). During his brief reign the Hittite empire began to disintegrate, especially in the western provinces where the kings of Ahhiyawa and Arzawa made common cause to break away from Hittite rule.

Gurney 1990: 38–9

Arsaces I (= Parthian Arshak)

Parthian king, from the Iranian, no-madic tribe of the Parni, founder of the Arsacid dynasty (*c*. 247/238–217). His history is mainly known from classical sources, although his name appeared on coins and ostraca from the period.

Against the background of an inter-necine Seleucid war in the west, some of the eastern provinces of the Seleu-cid empire rebelled. When the satraps of Parthia and Bactria revolted, Ar-saces took advantage of the situation. He removed the Parthian satrap, occupied the province, and further extended his territory into Hyrcania. Although SELEUCUS II campaigned in the area, Arsaces could consolidate his position, and may have come to some agreement with the Seleucid king, who was militarily engaged in the west.

Arsaces reorganised his army, built fortifications and founded cities such as Dara, which became the Parthian capital. In later Parthian records, his reign is used as the beginning of their chronology.

Schippmann 1980: 14–20; Colledge 1967: 24ff.; Wiesehöfer 1996: 130–3

Artashumara

Hurrian king of Mitanni, son and successor of Shattarna (14th century). He was murdered and his assassin installed TUSHRATTA on the throne.

Wilhelm 1989: 30

Artatama

Hurrian king of Mitanni (beginning of the 14th century). According to the Amarna correspondence, he sent one of his daughters to become a wife of the Egyptian pharaoh TUTHMOSIS IV, thus initiating peaceful relations be-tween the two powers.

Klengel 1992: 97; Moran 1992: 70, 93

Artaxerxes I

Achaemenid king, son and successor of XERXES (465–424/423). His father, as well as his older brother and designated crown-prince, Darius, were killed in a palace revolt. Arta-xerxes' involvement in these events is unclear, but at any rate he quickly established himself on the throne and executed the assassins. He was faced with revolts on his western frontiers: one in Egypt, which was subdued by his general Megabazos in 460, the other in the Levant, where the Athe-nians had been stirring up rebellions. New fortresses were set up to provide strongholds against the rebellious population. While he was able to hold on to the Levantine area, the Greek attack on Cyprus was not successfully countered. Problems with the Greeks continued until the Peloponnesian War.

It is probable that the activities of NEHEMIAH and EZRA should be dated to his reign.

Briant 1996: 586–629; Kuhrt 1995: 671–2

Artaxerxes II

Achaemenid king, son and successor of DARIUS I (405–359). He was the longest reigning of all Persian kings. His position was initially threatened by a revolt started by his younger brother, Cyrus, who had gathered support among Persian nobles to challenge his succession. As reported by Xenophon (*Anabasis*), he marched with an army that included Greek mercenaries into northern Babylon, where they met the army of Artaxerxes at Cunaxa. The rebels were defeated and Cyrus was killed in battle. He was less successful in dealing with the Egyptian bid for independence, where revolts had broken out between 401 and 399. In Syria-Palestine and Asia Minor he maintained Persian control. Plutarch (*The Life of Artaxerxes*) portrays him as a popular ruler, a warrior and also a family man. In the Persian inscriptions of his reign he includes the gods Mithra and Anahita, and a later reference indicates that he introduced a cult of Anahita in the various centres of his realm. He was also responsible for extensive building projects in Ecbatana and Babylon.

Briant 1996: 631–99; Kuhrt 1995: 673–4

Artaxerxes III

Achaemenid king, son and successor of ARTAXERXES II (359–338). According to Plutarch his succession was the result of a violent struggle with several of his brothers. The most important event of his reign was the re-conquest of Egypt, which had rebelled against Persian rule during his father's lifetime. He first subdued a revolt of Cyprus and the Phoenician cities that was supported by a large contingent of Greek mercenaries. A Babylonian chronicle reports that the leading city, Sidon, was captured and part of its population deported. He then went on to Egypt where he reimposed Persian rule after a protracted struggle. He and most of his family died in a violent palace coup organised by the eunuch BAGOAS.

Briant 1996: 699–709, 795; Kuhrt 1995: 674–5

Artaxerxes IV

Achaemenid king, son and successor of ARTAXERXES III (338–336). He was the youngest son of Artaxerxes and raised by the eunuch BAGOAS, who was said to have been responsible for his father's death. He was originally called Arses but took the throne-name of Artaxerxes. After two years on the throne he was murdered by Bagoas, who now supported another claimant to the throne, Artashata (=DARIUS III).

Briant 1996: 794–6; Kuhrt 1995: 675

Artystone (Elamite Irtashduna)

Persian princess, daughter of CYRUS II, wife of DARIUS I. According to Herodotus (7.69.2) she was his favourite spouse. She is well known from Elamite contemporary sources, where letters sealed with her personal seal record transactions on her estates.

Brosius 1996: 50f.; Briant 1996: 460

Asa

King of Judah, son and successor of ABIJAH (911–870). According to the books of Kings and Chronicles, Asa was a great reformer of religious practices. He removed pagan cult objects and statues and fought a continuous battle with his northern counterpart BAASHA of Israel. He enlisted the support of the king of Damascus, Ben-Hadad I, who had originally been allied to Baasha. Together they raided Israel and destroyed several cities. He gained control over Dan and especially the strongly fortified Mizpah, which from then on marked the northern border of Judah. He is also said to have fought a victorious battle against an invading army from Nubia under the leadership of Zerah. In his old age he suffered from a foot ailment and he declared his son JEHOSHAPHAT his co-regent. When he died he was buried in Jerusalem.

Mitchell 1982, in CAH III/1: 462–5, 473

Ashared-apil-Ekur

Assyrian king, son and successor of TIGLATH-PILESER I, eighty-eighth in the Assyrian King List (1075–1740). Nothing else is known of this king.

Grayson 1976: 45–6

Asharedu

Two individuals bearing this name are known as Babylonian scholars and astronomers who sent omen reports to the Assyrian court between 679–65.

Hunger 1992: 183–202

Ashlultum

Wife of SARGON OF AKKAD, mentioned on a votive inscription.

Sollberger and Kupper 1971: IIA1c

Ashur-ahhe-iddina see Esarhaddon

Ashurbanipal (Assyrian Ashur-ban-apli)

Assyrian king, son and successor of ESARHADDON (668–627 (?)). Although the sources for his reign are the richest for any Assyrian monarch, with state annals and royal inscriptions being supplemented by administrative records, legal and scholarly correspondence, astrological reports, few of these sources can be reliably dated, and therefore the internal chronology of his reign is difficult to establish.

Ashurbanipal succeeded to the throne when Esarhaddon was killed on campaign in Egypt. Esarhaddon's death caused the pharaoh TAHARKA to launch a counter-offensive against the Assyrian garrison stationed at Memphis, which was retaken by a force sent promptly by Ashurbanipal. Four years later, when Taharka's nephew Tantamnni had become pharaoh, the Egyptians renewed attempts to regain control over Memphis and the Delta, which was governed by Assyrian vassal rulers. Ashurbanipal reacted with another invasion that culminated in the fall of Thebes. After this victory over the Kushite rulers he consolidated his hold over the provinces of Syro-Palestine, where Tyre proved the only persistently obstreperous city in spite of intermittent alliances.

In the north he fought a successful war against the Mannaeans, who had made inroads into his territories. Ashurbanipal maintained friendly relations with a number of buffer states in Anatolia, which were hard pressed by the continuing encroachments from the Cimmerians. The annals only report one expedition against the Medes. The Urartians pursued a policy of non-involvement, only interrupted by the attack on the city of Ubumu, which provoked swift retribution by Assyrian troops.

Relations with Elam and Babylonia proved to be more difficult to resolve. While Ashurbanipal had begun his reign by preserving the existing friendly terms with Elam that his father had established, the Elamites took advantage of the Assyrian army's Egyptian campaign and staged an invasion of Babylonia which was repressed by quickly dispatched troops. When in the following years Elam experienced a dynastic struggle that brought TEPTI-HUMBAN-INSHUSHINAK (= Teumman) to the throne, a rival faction found asylum at the court of Ashurbanipal. Hostilities between Assyria and Elam resumed when Teumman invaded the east Tigris region. Ashurbanipal's troops pursued the Elamites, who were finally beaten at the battle on the banks of the river Ulai. Ashurbanipal followed up the victory by attacking the buffer state of Gambulu, which had taken part in the earlier Elamite attack on Babylonia. He sacked the capital, took the ruler captive and showed him to the people of Nineveh in chains, with the head of Teumman hanging from his neck.

The most serious and traumatic confrontation of Ashurbanipal's reign was the rebellion of his brother SHAMASH-SHUMA-UKIN, who had been chosen by Esarhaddon to be king of Babylon under Ashurbanipal's suzerainty and whom Ashurbanipal installed in office. Though the Assyrian records stress the efforts made by Ashurbanipal to maintain good relations and to continue the restoration of Babylon which had suffered from SENNACHERIB's destruction, there was clearly resentment against the Assyrian supremacy and rivalry between the two brothers. Ashurbanipal tried to influence the leading circles of Babylonian citizens by diplomatic means, but this could not stop the outbreak of hostilities that led to a four-year war. It involved Elamites and Arabs fighting for Babylonia, as well as troops led by NABU-BEL-SHUMATI, the ruler of the Sealand and son of MERODACH-BALADAN. He brought the Babylonian alliance some success, but then a mutiny broke out in the Elamite camp. After the Sealand had been subdued, the Assyrians besieged Babylon, which fell after two years of deprivation and famine.

Relations with Elam continued to be problematic, and Ashurbanipal's attempts to secure the position on the throne of the Elamite prince TAMMAR-ITU, who had fled to Nineveh, were ultimately frustrated by HUMBAN-HALTASH III, who managed to hold on to the Elamite throne. In retaliation the Assyrian king concentrated all efforts in a war which was meant to deal with this long-standing enemy once and for all. As depicted on the reliefs from his Ninevite palace, his army stormed one city after another, finally sacking and despoiling the capital Susa, which was desecrated and symbolically devastated by sprinkling salt on the ruins to render it uninhabitable for future generations.

He also defeated the Arabs, who had helped Shamash-shuma-ukin in his rebellion and who had established themselves in Syria.

The events of the final years of Ashurbanipal's reign are still unknown and even the length of his rule remains disputed due to a lack of sources from this period, which constitutes a minor Dark Age in Assyrian history. According to some, Ashurbanipal abdicated in 631 and retired to Harran where an inscription records the installation of one of his brothers to a high priestly office. An alternative view holds that he ruled in Assyria until his death in 627, to be succeeded by his son ASHUR-ETIL-ILANI.

Despite his shadowy end amid growing internal and external threats to the Assyrian empire brought about by rebellions, as well as mounting pressure on the borders, Ashurbanipal was the last great Assyrian soldier king, and he also left a considerable cultural legacy, most famously epitomised by his library at Nineveh. He was proud of his education, which seemed to have included some literacy and scribal learning, and took a personal interest in the collection of tablets. His building activities were mostly concentrated on Nineveh, in particular the palace, though he was also responsible for the restoration and rebuilding of major temples in Babylonia. The visual arts under Ashurbanipal reached an unprece-dented degree of refinement, as the numerous sculpted reliefs recovered from the palace at Nineveh testify. They show the king in his traditional role as chief of the armed forces, leading them to victory, as the fearless protector of his people dispatching wild beasts in the famous lion-hunts and, most unusual, relaxing with his queen in a luxuriant garden, with the severed head of a vanquished enemy as the one reminder of the fragility of royal power.

Grayson 1980; 1991, in CAH III/2: 143–61; J. Oates, in ibid.: 162–71; Parpola 1970; 1983; Bauer 1933; Grayson 1980; Cogan and Tadmor 1981

Ashur-bel-kala

Assyrian king, son of TIGLATH-PILESER I, brother and successor of ASHUR-APIL-EKUR (1073–1056). After his brother's short reign, Ashur-bel-kala took on the challenge of safeguarding the huge territory his father had assembled. His annals record numerous punitive expeditions against the raiding Arameans, as well as campaigns into Anatolia where Urartu posed a threat.

He made a peace treaty with the Babylonians which was sealed by his marriage to the daughter of ADAD-APLA-IDDINA, whom he had appointed as king over Babylonia. The Egyptians made an official gift of exotic animals, which demonstrates Assyria's international standing at the time. A long inscription on the so-called Broken Obelisk, discovered at Nineveh, describes the king's prowess in hunting wild animals and his acquisition of a wide variety of fauna and records his numerous building projects, including work on palaces.

Grayson 1976: 46–62; 1975: 208–9; 1991: 86–112

Ashur-bel-nisheshu

King of Assyria (1417–1409); according to the Assyrian King List he was the son of ASHUR-NIRARI II. The Synchronistic History reports that he made a treaty with his Babylonian counterpart, KARAINDASH. His numerous inscriptions found at Assur record the building of a new city-wall.

Grayson 1972: 38–9

Ashur-dan I

Assyrian king, son and successor of NINURTA-APIL-EKUR (1179–1134). According to the Synchronistic History he went to Babylonia and captured and plundered various smaller cities.

Grayson 1972: 141–3; 1975: 209–10; Drower 1973, in CAH II/2: 451–2

Ashur-dan II

Assyrian king, son and successor of TIGLATH-PILESER II (934–912). The beginning of the Neo-Assyrian empire is associated with this king, who ended the long period of decline suffered by the country after the days of TIGLATH-PILESER I. Royal inscriptions, which had been absent for a long time, once more become abundant. The king's annals are only partially preserved but it is possible to reconstruct the main events of his reign.

He began by turning against his neighbours to the north who had inflicted much damage on his border area. He defeated the king of Kadmuhu, had him flayed and his skin draped over the city wall of Arbail. He also took rich booty of bronze, tin and precious stones. In the west he took on the ever-menacing Aramean tribes and restored land and possessions that they had taken from the Assyrians. He pacified the eastern border region to secure the trade with the Iranian plateau and beyond.

His main concern then was to reactivate the ravaged economy. He resettled displaced populations, constructed new towns and villages and put large tracts of uncultivated land under the plough to 'pile up more grain than ever before'. Hand in hand with these efforts to secure the agricultural bases he invested in the chariotry and the armed forces. The inscriptions also speak of large hunting expeditions, where scores of lions and wild bulls were killed. He also undertook various building projects, mainly restoration work on the palaces, temples and gates of the capital Assur.

Grayson 1976: 74–81; 1982, in CAH III/1: 2468–9; 1991: 131–41

Ashur-dan III

Assyrian king, son and successor of SHALMANESER IV (772–755). Very little is known about this king, who ruled in one of Assyria's times of decline. Most inscriptions from his reign belong to powerful officials.

Grayson 1996: 245; 1992, in CAH III/1: 276–9; 1996: 245

Ashur-etel-ilani

Assyrian king, son and successor of ASHURBANIPAL (*c.* 627–623). The dates and length of his reign, as well as the circumstances surrounding it, is still a matter of debate amongst historians since the sources after the death of Ashurbanipal became both scarce and contradictory. On the basis of exemption grants it is likely that he succeeded to the throne after his father's death in 627 when he was still a minor. It seems that SIN-SHUMU-LISHIR, a high ranking official and eunuch at the Assyrian court, used both his influence and his private army to secure the throne for the young prince and to ensure loyalty to his sovereignty. Ashur-etel-ilani fought in Babylonia, with a measure of success, against NABOPOLASSAR, who declared himself king of Babylonia. Throughout his brief reign he had to defend his position against the claims of his elder brother SIN-SHARRA-ISHKUN, who ultimately succeeded in claiming the throne for himself in 623. It is not known what happened to Ashur-etel-ilani after that.

von Soden 1967; Na'aman 1991: 243–67; Oates 1991, in CAH III/2: 162–78; Kataja and Whiting 1995: 36–45

Ashur-iddin

Assyrian official who rose to the highest position (*šukallu rabū*) under TUKULTI-NINURTA I (12th century). He began his career towards the end of the reign of SHALMANESER I and rose in rank under his successor. He was active in Washshukanni, but he is best known from the texts found at Dur-Katlimmu (modern Tall Sheik Hamad on the Habur), then capital of the province of Hanigalbat. He was probably the son of another important official, Ili-ipadda, and his own three sons also occupied high positions in the Assyrian imperial organisation. He enjoyed the confidence of the king and was given considerable freedom in making decisions.

Cancik-Kirschbaum 1996

Ashur-ketti-lesher

Ruler of the dynasty of Tabetu (in the land of Mari) during the time of TIGLATH-PILESER I. He built a city on a previously uninhabited site in the Habur valley which he called after himself, Dur-Ashur-ketti-lesher. His dynasty had a degree of independence from Assyria and he used this freedom to expand his territory, which in turn prompted Tiglath-Pileser to intervene and curb his ambition.

Kühne 1995: 74

Ashur-mukin-palua

Assyrian prince, younger and sickly brother of ASHURBANIPAL. His precarious health is referred to in several letters.

Parpola 1970 and 1983: *passim*

Ashur-mutakkil

Assyrian ruler and eponym in the reign of ERIBA-ADAD I. He was governor of the fortress of Qabra on the Lesser Zab.

Lewy 1971, in CAH III/2: 742

Ashur-nadin-ahhe I

King of Assyria, son and successor of ASHUR-RABI I (mid-15th century). He wrote to the Egyptian pharaoh TUTHMOSIS III, congratulating him on his victories in Syria and Palestine.

He was deposed by his brother ENLIL-NASIR II.

Grayson 1972: 37; Kuhrt 1995: 349; Drower 1973, in CAH II/1: 443, 464

Ashur-nadin-ahhe II

Assyrian king, son of ASHUR-RIM-NISHESHU (1400–1391). He received gold from the Egyptian pharaoh (either TUTHMOSIS IV or AMENOPHIS III). In the capital Assur he built a palace, as his only preserved royal inscription reports. It remained the residence of Assyrian kings for centuries.

Grayson 1972: 40

Ashur-nadin-apli

Assyrian king, son and successor of TUKULTI-NINURTA I (1207–1204). According to an Assyrian chronicle he conspired with senior court members to dispose of his father, who was held responsible for the political weakness of the empire at that time.

Not much else is known of his short reign but there is a well preserved inscription which reports that when the Tigris had altered its course and threatened to flood Assur, the king erected shrines and prayed to the gods. It proved successful.

Grayson 1972: 134–6; Wiseman 1975, in CAH II/2: 449–50; Mayer 1988

Ashur-nadin-shumi

Assyrian king of Babylon, son of SENNACHERIB (699–694).

As the crown-prince he was appointed to the Babylonian throne when his father deposed BEL-IBNI. During his reign Babylonia experienced a brief period of peace.

In 694 Sennacherib launched a naval attack against the Elamite marshland to root out Chaldaean refugees. In a surprise act of retaliation the Elamite king HALLUSHU-INSHUSHINAK marched against northern Babylonia, captured Sippar and carried off Ashur-nadin-shumi, who was betrayed by a group of Babylonians. He was taken to Elam and probably killed.

Brinkman 1972; 1984: 60–1

Ashur-nasir-apli

One of the sons of the Assyrian king TUKULTI-NINURTA I who, according to the Chronicle P, was involved in the palace plot that resulted in the assassination of his father in 1208. He may have held the throne for a short time.

Grayson 1972: 134

Ashurnasirpal (Assyrian Ashur-naṣir-apli) I

Assyrian king, son of SHAMSHI-ADAD IV (1049–1031). As with the other successors of ASHUR-BEL-KALA, there are no sources referring to this king other than entries in lists and chronicles, although some scholars attribute a stone stele known as the White Obelisk to his reign.

Grayson 1976: 66–8; Grayson 1991: 122–3; Reade 1983:16

Ashurnasirpal (Assyrian Ashur-nasir-apli) II

Assyrian king, son and successor of TUKULTI-NINURTA II (883–859). The royal inscriptions of this king are more numerous and more detailed than those of any of his predecessors.

He built on the successes of his father and grandfather (ADAD-NIRARI II) in making Assyria one of the dominant powers in the Near East, defended by a formidable army and administered by a large apparatus of civil servants. The king undertook fourteen campaigns, several of which were directed against the north (Anatolia) where previous vassal states had rebelled. He was also successful in pacifying the eastern regions of the Zagros region. He forged his way westwards and ceremoniously washed his weapons in the Mediterranean Sea, accepting presents from the Phoenician cities. This assured good relations with the economically important Levantine states and gave him access to the timber resources of the Lebanon mountains. Relations with his southern neighbour and ally Babylonia remained stable, although he did not hesitate to deal with Suhean tribespeople, who, incited by Babylon, had caused problems in the mid-Euphrates region.

His overall policy was to repress any rebellion and to punish severely the populations of disloyal states by public displays of cruelty against leaders, by mass executions and by razing cities to the ground. This was only made possible by means of a mobile and well equipped army that could be effectively deployed at short notice. However, he also built new settlements (for instance Al-Ashur-nasir-apli, Dur-Assur, etc.) and had them strongly fortified and populated with peoples from other parts of the empire. Such demonstrations of ruthless retribution assured that the majority of subject nations preferred to pay their taxes and tribute rather than risk invoking the wrath of the Assyrian king. He also accepted daughters of local rulers for his royal harem to cement friendly relationships and was ready to defend loyal subjects by lending them military aid. All these measures ensured that enormous resources were available to finance campaigns and grandiose building projects. Ashur-nasir-apli's annals record the works undertaken for the new capital Calah (modern Nimrud), where not only an enormous palace was being built, but a whole city, with temples and barracks and residential quarters where he resettled people deported from various parts of the empire, as well as people who had flocked to the new capital. He laid out parks and gardens, well stocked with trees, flowering plants and exotic animals. The furnishings and architectural appointment of the palace building, as far as they have been recovered by archaeological excavation, show the contributions of craftsmen and materials from various parts of the empire, in particular North Syria, and display the command over huge resources. The so-called Banquet Stele describes the inaugurating party where he entertained and feasted 69,574 people for ten days. He also restored and enlarged the temple of Ishtar at Nineveh, as well as other temples. Undoubtedly, Ashur-nasirapli II presents a high point of the might of Assyria, an indefatigable campaigner, but also resourceful diplomat, able to inspire loyalty as well as fear, and not least a cultivated patron of arts and letters.

Grayson 1976: 113–211; 1982, in CAH III/1: 253–9; 1991: 189–397; Paley 1976; Kuhrt 1995: 483–7

Ashur-nirari I

Assyrian king, son of Ishme-Dagan II, (c. 1500). According to the Assyrian King List he ruled for twenty-six years. Only a few short building inscriptions found at Assur survive.

Grayson 1972: 33

Ashur-nirari II

Little-known Assyrian king (1424–1418), who according to the Assyrian King List was the son of ENLIL-NASIR II.

Grayson 1972: 37

Ashur-nirari III

Assyrian king. According to the Assyrian King List, he was the son of ASHUR-NADIN-APLI (1203–1198). The only document known from his reign is a fragment of an extraordinarily insulting letter sent to him by the Babylonian king ADAD-SHUMA-USUR.

Grayson 1972: 137–8

Ashur-nirari IV

Assyrian king, son of SHALMANESER II (c. 1018–1013).

Grayson 1976: 70

Ashur-nirari V

Assyrian king, son and successor of ASHUR-DAN III (754–755). Very few sources survive from his reign. The king of Urartu, SARDURI II, claimed in one of his inscriptions to have defeated him and there is a fragmentary copy of treaty with the king of Arpad.

Grayson 1982, in CAH III/1: 276–9; 1996: 246–7

Ashur-rabi I

Assyrian king in the early 15th century. According to the Assyrian King List he was the son of ENLIL-NASIR I. He disposed of ASHUR-SHADUNI, who was probably a usurper.

Grayson 1972: 37

Ashur-rabi II

Assyrian king, son of ASHUR-NASIR-APLI I (1012–972). Although he seems to have ruled for a long time, there are no records from his reign apart from the basic entries in the lists.

Grayson 1976: 70–1

Ashur-resha-ishi I

Assyrian king, son of MUTAKKIL-NUSKU, eighty-sixth in the Assyrian King List (1132–1115). He managed to reverse the ill fortunes of Assyria during his reign by taking decisive action against pastoralist tribes on the eastern and western borders of the realm, such as the Lullume, the Guti and the Arameans.

His other inscriptions record the reconstruction of the tower gates of the Ishtar temple at Nineveh, which had been damaged by an earthquake, and the foundation of a new palace at Apku (modern Abu Maryam).

According to an Assyrian chronicle fragment he marched to Arbail where he faced the Babylonian king NI-NURTA-NADIN-SHUMI, while according to the Synchronistic History he fought against NEBUCHADNEZZAR I, who had made incursions into Assyria, and defeated him.

Grayson 1972: 147–53

Ashur-resha-ishi II

Assyrian king, son of ASHUR-RABI II (971–967). The only inscription of his reign found so far is on a cylinder found at Assur and commemorates the building works on a canal by a local ruler in the Habur area.

Grayson 1976: 71–3

Ashur-rim-nisheshu

Assyrian king. According to the Assyrian King List he was the son and successor of ASHUR-BEL-NISHESHU (1408–1401). A single building inscription on a clay cone records the restoration work on the inner city wall at Assur.

Grayson 1972: 39–40

Ashur-shaduni

Little-known Assyrian king in the late 16th/early 15th century who, according to the Assyrian King List, succeeded NUR-ILI and held the throne for 'one complete month' before he was deposed by ASHUR-RABI I.

Grayson 1972: 37

Ashur-sharrat

Assyrian queen, wife of ASHURBANI-PAL. A letter sent by Sheru'a-eterat, the daughter of ESARHADDON, mentions animosities between the two women. She may be the woman depicted on the famous relief from Nineveh which shows the royal couple in a garden.

Grayson 1991, in CAH III/2: 160; J. Oates, ibid.: 176

Ashur-uballit I

Assyrian king, son and successor of ERIBA-ADAD I, (c. 1365–1245). During his lifetime Assyria became a power to be reckoned with, primarily as the result of the defeat of the neighbouring kingdom of Mitanni, following the campaign of the Hittite king SUPPILU-LIUMA I, who established his son

SHATTIWAZA on the Mitanni throne. Ashur-uballit could therefore extend his territory to the east and extend his influence. This rise in eminence and self-confidence is well illustrated in the letters that he sent to the pharaoh AMENOPHIS IV; as opposed to an earlier missive sent with the offer of an introductory gift, a later letter explicitly emphasises his diplomatic equality. His relations with Babylonia were close since he married his daughter, MUBALLITAT-SHERUA, to KARAINDASH, son of BURNABURIASH II. When the son born of this union, KARAHARDASH, was killed in a palace revolt, Ashur-uballit interfered. He killed NAZI-BUGASH, who had taken over the Babylonian kingship, and placed KURIGALZU II on the throne.

He also left several building inscriptions referring to projects in Assur, and in one interesting foundations document, written by a scribe who had built himself a house near the temple of Marduk, he is described as 'king of the universe', a title that reflects the increased power of the monarch.

Grayson 1972: 42–50; 1975: 211–12; 1975, in CAH II/2: 23–31; Kuhrt 1995: 349–52; Moran 1992: 37–41

Ashur-uballit II

Last attested Assyrian king, successor of SIN-SHARRA-ISHKUN (*c.* 611–610). He survived the sack of Nineveh by the combined forces of the Medes and Babylonians in 612. According to the Babylonian Chronicle he fled to Harran, where he tried to establish an Assyrian government in exile. When NABOPOLASSAR attacked Harran in

610 he abandoned the city and is not heard of again.

Oates, J., 1991 in CAH III/2: 180–2

Ashusikildigira

Early Dynastic Sumerian queen, wife of AKALAMDU, king of Ur.

Sollberger and Kupper 1971: IB3a

Asqudum

Diviner at Mari during the period of ZIMRI-LIM. He was married to Yamama, a sister of Zimri-Lim, and held a high rank in the palace organisation. His personal archive was recovered in the ruins of the palace.

Charpin and Durand 1985b: 453–62

Astyages

King of the Medes, son and successor of CYAXARES (585–550). According to Herodotus he was married to the daughter the Lydian king ALYATTES following six years of warfare between the two rulers. He eventually lost his kingdom in 550. A Babylonian Chronicle reports that he marched against CYRUS (II), when his army rebelled against him. They took him captive and handed him over to Cyrus who then marched against the Median capital Ecbatana and seized it.

Briant 1996: 25–6, 34–8; Cuyler-Young 1988, in CAH IV: 24; Storck 1989; Kuhrt 1995: 657

Atarshumki (= Bar-Gush)

King of Bit-Agusi (= Arpad), son of ARAME (805–796). He was a contemporary of SHAMSHI-ADAD V and ADAD-NIRARI III and like his father active in fomenting rebellion against Assyrian supremacy. According to the Assyrian records he had incited his neighbours to rebel and withhold tribute. The revolt was not put down before c. 796, when Adad-nirari led a campaign that resulted in the pacification of Arpad.

Grayson 1982, in CAH III/1: 272; Hawkins, ibid.: 400–3, 407–8

Athaliah

Israelite princess, ruler of Judah, (841–835). She is usually designated as daughter of AHAB and granddaughter of OMRI, but she was perhaps Omri's daughter. She grew up in Ahab's household, where she came under the influence of JEZEBEL, the Phoenician princess who introduced the worship of Baal to the royal family of Israel. She married JEHORAM OF JUDAH in a dynastic marriage. She had considerable influence and status as the mother of the crown-prince who became king AHAZIAH in 841. The chroniclers make her responsible for the founding of a temple of Baal in Judah. When Ahaziah died in the wave of assassinations following the revolt of JEHU in Israel, she seized power in Jerusalem, murdering in turn any descendants of the Davidic royal family, from which only JEHOASH escaped. She ruled for six years, until the high-priest Jehodiah produced the child he had hidden and had him proclaimed king by the courtiers and the officers. Athaliah, courageous like Jezebel, came to meet her enemies

who put her to death outside the Temple.

Mitchell 1982, in CAH III/1: 488, 490, 492

Atossa

Persian queen, daughter of CYRUS II, wife of DARIUS I, mother of XERXES I. She is only known from Greek historiography, where she is said to have had great power and instigated Darius' invasion of Greece.

Sancisi-Weerdenburg in Cameron and Kuhrt 1983: 23–6; Brosius 1996: 48–51; Briant 1996: 144–6

Atta-hamiti-Inshushinak I

Elamite king, son of HUTRAN-TEMTI, cousin and successor of TEPTI-HUMBAN-INSHUSHINAK (653–648). He was set up as rightful king of Elam by ASHURBANIPAL, who had just won a decisive battle against his predecessor. He left some inscribed stelae which suggest that the territory under his control had shrunk considerably. He kept out of international politics and was succeeded by his son.

Hinz 1972: 156–7

Atta-hamiti-Inshushinak II
(Persian Attameta)

Elamite ruler who rebelled against DARIUS I in 519 and had himself declared king. He was defeated by officers of Darius and executed.

Hinz 1972: 160

Attahushu

Elamite regent of Susa, 'sister-son' of king SILHAHA (beginning of 18th century). His surviving inscriptions, written in Akkadian, report mainly building works on Susa's temples. He finished the temple of the moon god begun by his predecessors. He also built fortifications at the city. In the market place of Susa he erected a stele which served as a public price index.

Hinz 1972: 93–4

Attar-kitah

Elamite king, brother and successor of PAHIR-ISHSHAN (1310–1300). He called himself 'king of Anshan and Susa', the old Elamite royal title which had not been used for half a millennium. According to some inscriptions on votive objects he took plunder, which he deposited in the temple of Inshushinak in Susa.

Hinz 1972: 112

Azi

Public servant and scribe at Ebla, head of the school and chief archivist of the government (c. 2500).

Pettinato 1986: 91

Aziru

King of Amurru during the Amarna period, when he ruled in precarious semi-dependence under Hittite and Egyptian overlordship (mid-14th century). His career reflects the precarious situation of Syrian petty kings, who had to manoeuvre between two powerful foreign states as well as being subject to rivalries and enmities between themselves.

At some point he attacked and eventually conquered the city of Sumur, held by an Egyptian garrison, with the help of Habiru troops. His activities were reported to the pharaoh, AMENOPHIS IV. This event may have led to his official recognition as king by Egypt. His relationship with the Hittites was also tenuous. He asked the Egyptians for help against the Hittites during the Syrian campaign of SUPPILULIUMA I. Following the conquest of Nuhashshe by the Hittites he made a treaty with the Hittite king. His greatest rival was RIB-ADDI of Gubla (Byblos) who later had to go into exile where he was killed. The pharaoh then sent for Aziru to demonstrate his loyalty to the Egyptian crown. On his return he made a treaty with NIQMADU II of Ugarit.

Klengel 1992: 161–5; Waterhouse 1965: 102–43; Moran 1992: *passim*

Azitiwatas

Syro-Hittite king of Aziwataya (modern Karatepe) (after 705). He left an inscription in hieroglyphic Luwian which reports that he had built the city he named after himself, how he was promoted by the king of Adana, and that he exercised great power there. He represents his reign as exemplary for its peace and prosperity. He may have been involved in a rebellion against SENNACHERIB.

Hawkins 1982, in CAH III/1: 429–3; 1986; Hawkins and Morpurgo Davies 1978: 114–18

Azuzum

Governor of Eshnunna, successor of USSUR-AWASSU (*c.* 2000). His name is inscribed on bricks found at the Governor's Palace at Eshnunna, parts of which he rebuilt.

Frayne 1990: 505–8

B

Baal I

King of Tyre at the time of ESARHAD-DON and ASHURBANIPAL of Assyria (7th century). He made a vassal treaty with Esarhaddon concerning the trading rights of Tyre and to assist him in his fight against ABDI-MILKUTTI of Sidon. When Esarhaddon began his war against Egypt in 671, however, Baal sided with TAHARKA, against Assyria. Esarhaddon besieged Tyre, and although the fall of the city is not recorded (and may not have happened), Baal was forced to pay tribute.

Grayson 1991, in CAH III/2: 125–6

Baal II

King of Tyre (c. 587–572). He was defeated by NEBUCHADNEZZAR II, who besieged the city and eventually incorporated it into the province of Kadesh as part of the Babylonian realm.

Wiseman 1991, in CAH III/2: 235

Baasha

King of Israel, founder of its second dynasty (909–886). He was from the tribe of Issachar, the son of a certain Ahijah, and gained the throne by assassinating the incumbent NADAB, son of JEROBOAM I. He was embroiled in continuous warfare with his southern neighbour, king ASA of Judah, and the Arameans in the north, with little success. His erstwhile ally BEN-HADAD II of Damascus switched loyalty to Asa and Baasha lost valuable territories to both. The chroniclers of the Bible accuse him of persisting in idolatrous practices. (I Kgs. 15:16–16:6) He was buried at Tirzah and succeeded by his son ELAH.

Mitchell 1982, in CAH III/1: 462, 464–5

Baba-aha-iddina

Babylonian king, successor of MAR-DUK-BALASSU-IQBI, who had been taken to exile in Assyria by SHAM-SHI-ADAD V. He was not related to his predecessor and only ruled briefly in the year 812. He was to suffer exactly the same fate as his predecessor when the Assyrian king launched a further anti-Babylonian campaign.

Brinkman 1968: 210–13

Babu-aha-iddina

Assyrian high-ranking official (13th century). He served under ADAD-NIRARI I, SHALMANESER I and perhaps also under TUKULTI-NINURTA I. His archive, comprising some ninety tablets, was found in a tomb underneath a house in Assur.

Pedersen, in Hrouda *et al.* 1992

Bagoas

Persian courtier, eunuch, and official under ARTAXERXES IV. According to Diodorus and the Babylonian 'Dynastic Prophecy' he had Artaxerxes assassinated and helped DARIUS III to the throne. Darius eventually disposed of him. During a difficult time in Persian history, Bagoas seems to have held the balance of power for a short while.

Briant 1996: 286–8; 789–800

Balasi

Assyrian scribe, teacher of the crown-prince ASHURBANIPAL, later a personal friend and favourite of the king. Forty-three of his letters, mainly concerning magic and medicine, have survived.

Parpola 1970: 24–37; 1983: 38–64; 1993: 29–48; Hunger 1992: 47–58

Baranamtara

Wife of the Early Dynastic Sumerian ruler LUGALANDA of Lagash, identified as such on a seal (*c.* 24th century). She seems to have fulfilled an important ritual function since other texts refer to her lavish funeral, celebrated by the succeeding ruler URUINIMGINA, involving some 300 people.

Gadd 1971, in CAH I/2:120; Sollberger and Kupper 1971: IC10d; Lambert, M. 1949: 14–15

Bardiya

Persian prince, brother of CAMBYSES II (522). He was the legitimate successor of his brother but died in mysterious circumstances. In a story told by Herodotus, who calls him Smardis (3.30; 61–7), Cambyses had given orders to have him murdered secretly and a 'magus' took on his identity to have himself declared king. This seems to go back to the version of events as proclaimed by DARIUS I, who says that he killed the magus (called GAUMATA by Darius) in revenge. It is now thought not unlikely that 'Gaumata' was in fact Bardiya and that he was killed by Darius.

Briant 1996: 102–5, 109–18, 125–6; Kuhrt 1995: 664–5; Cuyler-Young 1988, in CAH IV: 53–7

Bar-Rakib

King of Sam'al (modern Zincirli), son of PANAMMU II (733–732). He was installed on the throne by TIGLATH-PILESER III. Under Assyrian protection he reigned for quite a long time (though exact dates are not available), commissioning buildings and leaving inscribed monuments. One of these concerns the dynastic feud that led to the death of his grandfather, Bar-sur.

Hawkins 1982, in CAH III/1: 402, 408, 416; Orthmann 1971: 63ff., 199ff.

Bartatua (in Greek sources Protothyes)

King of the Scythians, successor and perhaps son of Ishpaka (c. 678–c. 645). He may have married the daughter of the Assyrian king ESAR-HADDON, to cement a treaty which made him a vassal of Assyria. According to Herodotus, his reign was prosperous, and under his rule the Scythians became the dominant force in Western Asia, though this story raises chronological problems. After his death in c. 645 he was succeeded by his son Madyes.

Sulimirski and Taylor 1991, in CAH III/2: 564–5

Baya

Assyrian prophet from Arbela who sent oracles to the Assyrian court. The name is written with a female determinative on one text; perhaps this is indicative of ritual self-castration, a practice not unheard of among ecstatic followers of the goddess Ishtar.

Parpola 1997: IL, 7

Belakum

Governor of Eshnunna in the Old Babylonian period, successor, perhaps

brother, of WARASSA (late 20th century).

Frayne 1990: 534–8; Yuhong 1994: 38

Bel-harran-beli-usur

Assyrian official. He occupied the office of palace herald (nāgir-ēkalli) for a very considerable period, from the reign of ADAD-NIRARI III onwards (782–727). He also held several other important offices, such as eponym and governor of Guzana. In a stele discovered north of Hatra his name appears before that of the king, which demonstrates that his power in the area was greater than the king's. He also mentions in the text that he had founded a new city, called Dur-Bel-harran-beli-usur.

Grayson 1982, in CAH III/1: 279; 1993: 19–52

Bel-ibni

King of Babylon (703–700), he was a commoner, brought up at the Assyrian court, and installed by SENNACHERIB on the throne as a puppet ruler under Assyrian control. When he rebelled against Sennacherib, he was replaced by the Assyrian crown-prince ASHUR-NADIN-SHUMI.

Brinkman 1983; 1991, in CAH III/2: 34–5; Brinkman and Dalley 1988; Dietrich 1998

Bel-re-ushu see Berossus

Bel-shar-usur (biblical Belshazzar)

Babylonian prince, son of NABONI-DUS. During his father's absence in the oasis city of Teima (c. 553–543) he was in charge of all aspects of the administration of the kingdom. His fate after the capture of Babylon in 539 by the Persians is unknown.

Wiseman 1993, in CAH III/2: 246–9; Dougherty 1929

Bel-shimanni

Babylonian rebel leader who started a revolt against XERXES in *c.* 484 which was repressed soon afterwards.

Briant 1992

Bel-tarsi-iluma

Assyrian official, governor of Calah and eponym in 797 during the reign of ADAD-NIRARI III. His archives and inscribed statues were discovered in Calah.

Grayson 1982, in CAH III/1: 274, 275

Beltum

Daughter of ISHKI-ADAD, king of Qatna (early 18th century). She married the son of SHAMSHI-ADAD I, YASMAH-ADDU, who was governor of Mari. According to the Mari letters she lived in the Royal Palace and was unhappy. In one letter Shamshi-Adad warns his son of the consequences of neglecting his wife and admonishes him to keep her in Mari. It is not certain whether she remained at Mari after her husband's flight from the city after ZIMRI-LIM's coup. It is possible that she stayed in the vicinity of the capital and went back to Qatna at the beginning of the latter's reign.

Klengel 1992: 65–6; Durand 1985b: 398–407

Bel-ushezib

Babylonian scholar who served during the reigns of SENNACHERIB and ESAR-HADDON whom he reminds in one missive that he had correctly predicted his succession to the throne. He seems to have had a keen interest in politics and some of his reports form the basis of present understanding for certain events of his time, particularly Esarhaddon's Mannean campaign in 675.

Starr 1990: xxxiv; Parpola 1993: 85–101

Ben-Hadad II (Assyrian Adad-idri)

King of Damascus (mid-9th century). He was one of the main leaders of the great anti-Assyrian coalition which united twelve kings against SHALMANESER III. In 853 he took part in the battle at Qarqar, where some 40,000 soldiers and 4,000 chariots met the Assyrian army. Shalmaneser claimed victory but in fact he had to face the coalition several times more. He may be identical with the Ben-Hadad who is mentioned in the Bible as the enemy of AHAB. He was killed by HAZA'EL, who usurped the throne between 845 and 841. Ben-Hadad is sometimes identified with HADAD-EZER.

Grayson 1982, in CAH III/1: 261–2; Hawkins, ibid.: 392

Benteshina

Ruler of Amurru, vassal of the Hittite kings SUPPILULIUMA I and MUWA-TALLI II, son of DUPPI-TESHUP. In the conflict between the Egyptian pharaoh RAMESSES II, which culminated in the Battle of Qadesh (*c.* 1275), he was on the side of Egypt. As the result of this treachery he was captured when the Hittite king returned, deported to Hakpish in Anatolia and replaced by another vassal. He was later rein-stalled by HATTUSILI III, who con-cluded a treaty with him that obliged him to protect the Hittite royal family like his own. To cement the special relation, he was given GASHULIYAWA, daughter of the Hittite royal couple, Hattusili III and PUDUHEPA, in mar-riage to be his queen, while one of his daughters married Nerikkaili, son of Hattusili. From this period of his second reign dates a letter from the Babylonian king KADASHMAN-ENLIL II sent to the Hittite king, in which he accuses Benteshina of having insulted Babylonia in connection with the murder of some Babylonian mer-chants.

Klengel 1992: 116–19, 169–72

Berossus (Babylonian Bel-re'ushu)

Babylonian scholar, priest of Marduk. About 280 he wrote a History of Mesopotamia (*Babyloniaka*) in Greek, of which only fragments sur-vive as quotations in much later Greek and Roman writers. The work was apparently in three volumes. The first contained a geographical descrip-tion of Babylonia and the origin of human life and civilisation. The sec-ond was about the ten kings before the flood and various later dynasties down to NABU-NASIR (8th century). The last covered the period of Assyr-ian domination and the conflict with Babylon from TIGLATH-PILESER III to the defeat of the Assyrians, the reign

of NEBUCHADNEZZAR II, the fall of Babylon to the Persians and their rule down to ALEXANDER THE GREAT. He dedicated this work to ANTIOCHUS I. Later Classical tradition also claims that he introduced astronomy to the Greeks.

Jacoby 1958; Burstein 1978; Kuhrt in Kuhrt and Sherwin-White 1987: 32–56

Bilalama

Governor of Eshnunna, son of KIR-IKIRI (mid-21st century). He was a contemporary of IDDIN-DAGAN and SHU-ILISHU of Isin and reigned for at least twenty years. He is mainly remembered for the marriage of his daughter MEKUBI to the son of the Elamite king Indattu I. Year names from the time of his reign mention battles against Amorites and that he restored public buildings at Eshnunna. Letters from Amorite chiefs supply further details of his wars against some of them.

Hinz 1971, in CAH I/2: 660–1; Frayne 1990: 491–9; Yuhong 1994: 14–21

Burnaburiash I

Kassite king of Babylonia according to the Babylonian King List (16th cen-tury). According to a later chronicle he made a treaty with Assyria. He was probably only a military leader of the Kassites at the time of SAMSU-DITANA of Babylon.

Brinkman 1980, in RlA V: 467; Saggs 1995: 116

Burnaburiash II

Kassite king of Babylon, successor and possibly son of KADASHMAN-ENLIL I (1359–1333). He corresponded with the pharaoh AMENOPHIS IV (AKHNATON), asking for gold and other royal prestige gifts. He reigned for at least twenty-seven years. Numerous building inscriptions found at Nippur and elsewhere record his architectural projects.

Brinkman 1976: 100–21; Moran 1992: 12–37; Boese 1982

C

Cambyses I

Achaemenid king, son of CYRUS I
(c. 585–559). No records survive from
his reign but he is called a 'Great King
of Anshan' in the Cyrus Cylinder.

Hinz 1976–80, in RlA 5: 328; Briant 1996:
34–5

Cambyses II

Achaemenid king, son and successor
of CYRUS II (530–522). His father
declared him to be King of Babylon
after his conquest of the city in 539,
an office which he only filled for one
year.

He inherited the throne when Cyrus
died in battle in July 530. After he
buried his father's remains at Pasargadae he embarked on the conquest of
the last remaining power in the Near
East – Egypt – for which Cyrus had
already made preparations. He started
in 525 with a great army and defeated
the Egyptian troops at Pelusium. The
pharaoh fled to Memphis. When the
capital fell also, Egypt capitulated and
Lybia and the Cyrenaica submitted
voluntarily.

Although Egypt was apparently
won easily, the consolidation of
Persian rule proved more difficult.
According to Herodotus the attempt
to subdue Nubia almost ended in
disaster, as did an attempt to conquer
Siwa oasis, due to the great loss of life
during the desert march south. There
were revolts in Egypt, which he
suppressed brutally and ordered the
pharaoh PSAMMETICHUS III to be
executed. In 522 he had intelligence
about the revolt of GAUMATA in the
Persian heartland and hastened back.
According to Herodotus, he had an
accident on the way, wounding himself with his own sword. This gave
him blood-poisoning and he died on
the way east, near Hamath in Syria.
He left no sons and may have been
succeeded by his brother BARDIYA. In
the event DARIUS I became the next
king on the Achaemenid throne.

Hinz, 1976–80, in RlA 5: 328–9; Kuhrt 1995:
662–5; Cuyler-Young 1988, in CAH IV: 47–52;
Briant 1996: 60, 73–4, 144–6 and *passim*;
Dandamaev 1976: 144–52

Croesus

King of Lydia, son and successor of
ALYATTES (c. 560–540s). His reign saw
the fulfilment of Lydian ambitions to
dominate western Asia Minor and to
have effective control over trade
routes between Greece and Asia
Minor. The main source for his reign
is Herodotus (I, 26ff.), who reports
that under Croesus the old hostilities
between Ionian Greeks and Lydians
came to an end. His proverbial wealth
attracted craftsmen from all parts of
Greece and he made spectacular donations to Greek temples, as well as
undertaking building projects such as
the Artemis temple at Ephesus. He
changed the Lydian coinage from
electrum to gold and silver to stimu-
late trade. He bestowed lavish gifts on
other rulers in an attempt to win allies
in the face of the growing power and
expansionist moves of the Persians.
He made overtures to the Spartans
and other Greek city-states, the Egyptians and the Babylonians. He set out
to challenge king CYRUS THE GREAT,
the Persian leader who had defeated
the Medes, by marching eastwards
across the river Halys, to the old
Hittite heartland in eastern central
Anatolia. A battle was fought, though
the outcome was indecisive. However,
Croesus retreated to his capital Sardis,
awaiting the arrival of his allies. Cyrus
did not wait for this to happen but
attacked and besieged the city, which
was taken after a fortnight. According
to Herodotus Croesus survived, but
other Greek traditions suggest he was
executed. This was the end of Lydian
independence; the state was incorporated into the Persian empire.

Mellink 1991, in CAH III/2: 651–3; Storck
1989; Kuhrt 1995: 569–72

Cyaxares (Babylonian Umakishtar)

King of the Medes, son of Madyes
(c. 625–585). Sources for his reign are
the largely fictional history of the
Median royal house supplied by Herodotus, and the Babylonian Chronicle. It appears that Cyaxeres did unite
the Medes and achieved some impressive military victories. In 614 he
attacked Nineveh and captured Ashur
and Tarbisu. Soon afterwards the
Babylonian king NABOPOLASSAR arrived in Assyria and made a formal
alliance with Cyaxares. Two years
later their combined troops attacked
Nineveh, which was taken and destroyed after a three-month siege.
According to Berossus, the connection
with the Babylonians was sealed by a
dynastic marriage; NEBUCHADNEZZAR
II married Cyaxares' daughter.

By 585 he was active in Anatolia,
where he fought against the Lydian
king CROESUS on the bank of the
Halys, which became the border
between their countries.

J. Oates 1991, in CAH III/2: 179–80; Cuyler-
Young 1988, in CAH IV: 21; Kuhrt 1995: 654

Cyrus I (Babylonian Kurash)

King of Persia, son of TEISPES of
Anshan, (c. 620–590). He is mentioned
as the grandfather of CYRUS II THE

GREAT in the Cyrus Cylinder and his name also appears on seal impressions on tablets discovered at Persepolis. He ruled in the area of Fars (Anshan).

Briant 1996: 102–3, 122; Miroschedji 1985

Cyrus II the Great

King of Persia, son and successor of CAMBYSES I, grandson of CYRUS I, founder of the Achaemenid empire (559–530). His childhood and education became a literary topic in Greek tradition (e.g. Xenophon's *Cyropaedia*), but there is no historical evidence for it. Sources for his reign are Herodotus and Ctesias, as well as contemporary Babylonian records, especially the Babylonian Chronicle and his own inscriptions, such as the Cyrus Cylinder.

He began his career by defeating the Median king, ASTYAGES. In 550, the Median army rebelled against their king, took him prisoner and handed him over to Cyrus. Cyrus sacked Ecbatana and is said to have taken Astyages into his court. Having thus gained control over most of Iran, he set out to extend his dominions further west, where he encountered the resistance of the Lydian king CROESUS in a battle on the river Halys which ended in a draw. However, Cyrus made a surprise attack on Croesus' capital Sardis and took the city. In the following five years he incorporated most of Anatolia into his empire.

The next stage was the conquest of Babylon, where king NABONIDUS had returned from his campaigns in Arabia. In 539 Cyrus crossed the Diyala river and took and looted Opis on the Tigris, massacring the inhabitants, after he had vanquished the defending Babylonian troops. Soon afterwards Sippar surrendered and Babylon was taken by his commander, Gibryas, on 12 October. Nabonidus was taken and deported to Persia. Cyrus entered Babylon on 29 October. He declared his son CAMBYSES II to be king of Babylon, while he himself took the traditional Mesopotamian title 'King of the Lands'. According to the Old Testament Book of Ezra, he issued the decree that allowed the deported Jews to return to Palestine and rebuild the temple in Jerusalem.

He made efforts to extend his realm further east, and it is likely that he controlled most of Afghanistan and south central Asia. Within thirty years he had made a small kingdom into a vast empire. He died, probably on the battlefield, in 530, while fighting against a Central Asian tribe. His body was taken to Pasargadae, his new royal foundation, and buried in a stone-built tomb. A funerary cult continued there down to the end of the Achaemenid empire.

Dandamaev 1976: 152–67; Hinz 1980–3, in RlA 6: 401–2; Kuhrt 1995: 656–61; Cuyler-Young 1988, in CAH IV: 28–46; Briant 1996: 41–60

D

Dada-ahhe

Assyrian wealthy citizen (*c.* 681–653), whose large archive detailing his various transactions was discovered at Assur.

Fales and Rost 1991; Fales, in Waetzold and Hauptmann 1997: 31–7

Dadusha

King of Eshnunna during the Old Babylonian period, son of IPIQ-ADAD II (19th century). He ruled for about nine years. Like his father he adopted the official title 'king' (*lugal*). His name also appears on the seals of his dependants in many cities.

Frayne 1990: 562

Daiian-Ashur

Eponym and field marshal (*turtānu*) in the reign of SHALMANESER III (*c.* 853–826). He held office during the entire length of the king's reign and seems to have had extraordinary prestige and influence, and he is repeatedly mentioned in the king's annals as leading campaigns.

Grayson 1993

Dam-hurashi

Wife of ZIMRI-LIM, king of Mari. It appears that she was his main wife before SHIBTU, princess of Aleppo, became the main wife and queen of Mari. From the letters in the Mari archives it is clear that she was in charge of the lesser women of the royal harem in the capital. She herself was probably installed at the palace at Terqa, where she was also partially responsible for the cult. The letters also suggest that she was linked to the king with strong ties of mutual affection.

Batto 1974: 21–3; Dossin 1967; Durand 1985b: 408

Damiq-ilishu

King of Isin, son and successor of SIN-MAGIR (*c.* 1816–1794). He left some building inscriptions on clay cones. He was the last independent ruler of the Isin dynasty. He lost his kingdom to RIM-SIN of Larsa in a protracted struggle that took several years.

Gadd 1971, in CAH III/2: 642–3; Sollberger and Kupper 1971: 182–3; Frayne 1990: 102–6

Dannaya

Assyrian official, ESARHADDON's chariot driver, a position that had great prestige. His numerous investment transactions, such as a large-scale land purchase, are well documented from economic sources of the period.

Fales and Postgate 1992: 189–95

Dannum-tahaz

Ruler of Eshnunna in the Old Babylonian period. His place in the chronological sequence is not certain, but it is possible that he occupied the throne before or after NARAM-SIN of Eshnunna and was a contemporary of ZIMRI-LIM of Mari (18th century). He is only known from servant seals found at the neighbouring cities of Shaduppum and Neribtum.

Frayne 1990: 557–8; Yuhong 1994: 87–91

Darius I

Achaemenid king, son of Hystaspes, grandson of Arsames, descendent of ACHAEMENES (522–486). He was from a minor line of the Achaemenian clan and took the throne by force in circumstances that are far from clear. According to Herodotus he was one of the courtiers of his predecessor, CAMBYSES II. He is said to have killed the alleged impostor GAUMATA and had himself declared king. New research

suggests that he may have actually killed the legitimate successor of Cambyses, BARDIYA, and concocted a genealogy that linked the ancestors TEISPES and Achaemenes. At any rate, his accession to the Achaemenid throne was not easily accepted; there were revolts in the Persian heartland which prompted most dependent states, from Central Asia to Egypt, to rebel against Persian rule. Darius reacted quickly and decisively, supported by a group of influential Persian nobles and their troops; in just over a year he managed to suppress all revolts in an unremitting series of battles fought throughout his empire. He executed the ringleaders and their supporters and repressed any uprisings brutally. He ordered a record of his triumph to be carved on the rock-face at Behistun with an inscription in Old Persian, Elamite and Babylonian.

With such measures the imminent disintegration of Cyrus' and Cambyses' world empire was converted into a convincing show of strength by the Achaemenid king. He went on to add new territories to this vast realm, including north-west India in the east and various Aegean islands in the west, although progress there was more difficult when the Ionian cities revolted. The pacification of the Greek border took four years and ended in the Persian defeat at Marathon in 490.

In Egypt he consolidated his control, as documented by various stelae and monuments that he ordered to be set up.

In his home-land he built a new

capital at Persepolis, a vastly ambitious project for which he employed thousands of workmen from all provinces of his huge empire. He also built new palaces at Susa and he had his tomb cut from the rocks near Naqsh-i-Rustam, in which he was eventually buried. He was succeeded by his son XERXES.

Kuhrt 1995: 664–70; Cuyler-Young 1988, in CAH IV: 53–71; Stronach 1990: 197ff.; Koch 1992; Briant 1992; 1996: *passim*

Darius II

Achaemenid king, son and successor of ARTAXERXES I (423–405). He was not in line for the direct succession, being an illegitimate son, but prevailed in a struggle with two other brothers. According to Greek sources he had to fight against a new enemy, the still mysterious Cadusians who lived in northern Media, south-west of the Caspian Sea. In Asia Minor he levied tribute from the Ionian cities and had to send his younger son Cyrus to intervene in a quarrel between his governors who were charged with the collection of tribute.

Kuhrt 1995: 673; Briant 1996: *passim*

Darius III

Achaemenid king, cousin and successor of ARTAXERXES IV (336–330). When Artaxerxes IV was murdered by the eunuch BAGOAS the latter supported his claims to the throne as a member of the royal family. He changed his name from Artashata to Darius. He had to face the rise of ALEXANDER THE GREAT and met his

advance in a series of battles, most memorably at Issos and Gaugamela. He was defeated both times but managed to escape, though his family was taken hostage by Alexander. In the face of Alexander's victories and the loss of Babylonia, Susa and Fars he was murdered after the fall of Ecbatana by one of his own generals, Bessus. Alexander had his body taken to Persepolis and buried with royal honours.

Kuhrt 1995: 675; Briant 1996: *passim*

David

King of Israel, son of Jesse, successor of SAUL (*c.* 1000). The only extant sources for his life are the Second Book of Samuel and 1 Kings in the Bible, historically plausible narratives although with legendary elements.

He is said to have been a talented military commander under Israel's first monarch, king SAUL. In reaction to the latter's personal animosity he set up his own army to become a mercenary for the Philistines. Saul's hostility never ceased, but his son Abner made overtures to David by marrying his sister Micah to him. David continued to increase his influence and had Abner assassinated. When Saul's other son, Ishbaal, was killed by the Canaanites, David was crowned king at Hebron. He was careful to eliminate all able-bodied males of Saul's lineage. He made Jerusalem, which he captured from the Canaanites, his royal city. It lay on the boundary between Judah and Israel, where he was accepted as king soon afterwards. He needed to defend his kingdom, especially against its western neighbours, Ammon, Moab and Edom, over which he is said to have triumphed. He also defeated the Arameans in the north, and elsewhere forged strategic alliances, such as with the Philistines and perhaps Tyre. In religious matters he strove to centralise the cult.

Eissfeldt 1975, in CAH II/2: 580–6

Dudu

1 King of Akkade (c. 2195–2174). After a troubled period following the death of SHAR-KALI-SHARRI, with increasingly frequent incursions by the Gutians, Dudu seems to have established some stability in what was left of the Akkadian empire. He directed a campaign against the regions of Girsu, Umma and Elam. He is also known from inscriptions on seals and votive offerings. He was succeeded by his son SHU-TURUL.

Gelb and Kienast 1990: 121; Frayne 1993: 210–13

2 Early Dynastic high-priest (en) of Ningirsu at Lagash, a contemporary of ENMETENA (c. 2400). He is known from several inscribed votive objects.

Gadd 1971, in CAH I/2: 105

Dugdamme (Greek Lygdamis)

Cimmerian general whose troops, formidable fighters accompanied by fierce dogs, terrorised Asia Minor in the 7th century. He was a contemporary of ASHURBANIPAL, who defeated him at the Cilician Gates in 636.

Barnett 1982, in CAH III/1: 361–3; Kuhrt 1987–90, in RlA VII: 186–9

Dunnasha-amur

Prophetess from Arbela who makes references to a highly ascetic life-style in one of the oracle reports she sent to king ASHURBANIPAL.

Parpola 1997: xxi, l, 40–2

Duppi-Teshup

King of Amurru during the Amarna period, although he is only known from Hittite sources (late 14th/early 13th century). He was the son of Ari-Teshup who succeeded AZIRU for a brief reign. The treaty agreed between SUPPILULIUMA I and his grandfather Aziru was updated by MURSILI II, with new stipulations asking Duppi-Teshup to protect the Hittite royal house and pay a tribute to Hatti while forcibly forbidding him to continue paying any tribute to Egypt. His sister, AHAT-MILKI was married to NIQMEPA of Ugarit.

Klengel 1992: 167–8; Moran 1992: 256

E

Ea-mukin-zeri

Second king of the Second Sealand Dynasty (*c.* 1009). He gained the throne for some five months after the assassination of his predecessor SIM-BAR-SHIPAK (1009). His name suggests that he came from a Babylonian priestly family.

Brinkman 1968: 155–6

Eannatum

Early Dynastic Sumerian king of Lagash, son of AKURGAL and brother of his successor ENANNATUM I (*c.* 2400).

Eannatum was probably his official throne-name; he was also known as Lumma, an Amorite name. He pursued expansionist policies, attacked Kish, Ur and Mari, and also campaigned further afield, in Elam in the east and Subir in the north. Closer to home he was involved in a longstanding but ultimately successful conflict with the neighbouring city of Umma. This war is described in great detail on a unique monument, the so-called Stele of Vultures, which depicts the victorious army of the Lagashites trampling over the fallen foes, while vultures pick their bones.

Gadd 1971, in CAH I/2: 117–19, Sollberger and Kupper 1971: IC5a–d, 11q1; Cooper 1986: 47–53

Ebarti *see* Eparti

Ebarti II *see* Eparti II

Ebih-il (also read as Abih-il)

Official from Mari whose inscribed statue dedicated to the god Ashtar was found in the Early Dynastic III levels of the city (25th–24th century). The statue (now in the Louvre) depicts a seated man wearing a long woollen skirt, his hands clasped before his chest, with an expression of cheerful expectancy.

Braun-Holzinger 1977: 69; Gelb and Kienast 1990: 5

Ebrium (or Ibrium)

Ruler of Ebla who is thought to have introduced an absolute monarchy in the kingdom, (mid-3rd millennium). He concluded the so-called 'Treaty with Ashur', which offered the Assyrian king (Tudia?) the use of trading posts officially controlled by Ebla.

Pettinato 1980: 82–3; 1986: *passim* and 229–37; Klengel 1992: 27

Egibi

Family of Babylonian businessmen, active for some 100 years, from NEBUCHADNEZZAR II to the beginning of the reign of XERXES. Five generations of the family are known. They became wealthy through land-leasing and short loan transactions, and left the largest private archive of this period (see also ITTI-MARDUK-BALATU, NABU-AHHE-IDDIN, NUPTAYA and SHU-LAYA).

Ungnad 1941–44; Krecher 1970; van Driel 1985–86; Wunsch 1995/6

Ehli-Nikkal

Hittite princess, probably the daughter of SUPPILULIUMA II. She married the king of Ugarit, possibly AMMUR-API, who later divorced her, which caused the Hittite viceroy at Carchemish, TALMI-TESHUP, to intervene and negotiate a compensation. She may have got married for a second time, to the king of Habishe, Tanhu-watasha.

Klengel 1992: 148

Ekur-zakir

Babylonian scribe and exorcist who appears as the founder of a prolific scribal family in colophons of various astronomical tablets.

Neugebauer 1955: I, 13; Lambert 1957: 4–5

Elah

King of Israel, son and successor of BAASHA (886–885). According to I Kgs. 16:6–14 he had a weak character, and was inclined to drunkenness and idolatry. He was killed in a palace coup by one of his chariot commanders, ZIMRI, who usurped the throne.

Mitchell 1982, in CAH III/1: 465

Elijah

Prophet of Israel, active during the reign of AHAB and AHAZIAH of Israel (9th century). According to I Kgs. 17–19 and II Kgs. 1–2 he spoke out against the preferment of Canaanite cults and their priesthood over that of Yahweh in Israel. This was seen as the result of Ahab's marriage with the Phoenician princess JEZEBEL. She disliked the prophet and persecuted him so that he fled to Mount Horeb. After his return he spoke out again in connection with the queen's conduct in the Vineyard of Naboth affair (I Kgs. 21). He witnessed the revolt of JEHU, whom he was said to have anointed as rightful king of Israel. He also anointed the Aramean king, HAZA'EL, who like Jehu, was a usurper.

Mitchell 1982, in CAH III/1: 473, 485–6

Elulu (or Elulmesh)

King of Akkade, fourth of the Gutian Dynasty (*c.* 22nd century). His name survives on some bronze and copper implements.

Sollberger and Kupper 1971: 113 ; Gadd 1971, in CAH I/2: 113, 457

Enanedu

Babylonian *entum* priestess of the moon god at Ur, daughter of KUDUR-MABUK, sister of WARAD-SIN and RIM-SIN. The latter restored her cloister (*Gipar*) after he had won the war against Isin. An inscription by her, written in poetic Sumerian, survives. The text was discovered by NABONI-DUS in the 6th century when he rebuilt the old temple precinct at Ur.

Gadd 1951; Reiner 1985: 2–5

Enannatum I

Early Dynastic Sumerian king of Lagash, brother of EANNATUM (*c.* 2460). His votive inscriptions record works on temples. During his reign Umma, led by its king URLUMMA, revolted against the conditions imposed by EANNATUM and successfully attacked Lagash.

Gadd 1971, in CAH I/2: 119, Sollberger and Kupper 1971: IC6a–f; Cooper 1986: 47–53

Enannatum II

Early Dynastic Sumerian king of Lagash, son of ENMETENA (24th century).

Sollberger and Kupper 1971: IC8a; Cooper 1986: 68

Enannatum

Daughter of ISHME-DAGAN of Isin. She became *entum* priestess of the moon god at Ur (20th century).

Gadd 1971, in CAH I/2: 634

Enentarzi

Early Dynastic Sumerian governor of Lagash and former priest (24th century). He is mainly known as the recipient of a letter from another priest who had managed to scare off 600 marauding Elamites.

Sollberger and Kupper 1971: IC9a; Gadd 1971, in CAH I/2:137, 276: Cooper 1986: 68

Enheduanna

Daughter of SARGON OF AKKAD, *entum* priestess of the moon god at Ur. A limestone disc with a short dedicatory inscription and a depiction of her officiating has been discovered at Ur. She may have been the first of a long line of royal princesses who were installed as *entum* at Ur, a prestigious and influential position. Enheduanna is also held to be the author of two literary compositions written in Sumerian, which mainly deal with her relationship to the goddess Inanna of Uruk.

She is the first-known female author in the history of literature. Her name and portrait and some of her probable work have survived nearly four millennia.

Hallo and van Dijk 1968; Asher-Grève 1985; Winter 1987; Frayne 1993: 35–6, 38–9; Zgoll 1997

En-hegal

King of Lagash (*c.* 26th century). He is only known from an administrative text about a purchase of land.

Gadd 1971, in CAH I/2:116

Enlil-bani

1 King of Isin (c. 1860–1837). He is said to have been installed as a 'substitute king', but survived and took the place of the previous ruler. Several royal hymns were written in his honour.

Edzard 1957: 138–42

2 Assyrian businessman active in the period of the great trading ventures between Assyria and Asia Minor (19th century). He carried on the family business that was apparently founded by his father Ashur-malik, a contemporary of PUSHU-KENU, and his own sons continued the tradition. All appear often in the tablets from Kültepe, the site of an Assyrian colony in Anatolia, during the second period of colonisation (*c.* 1910–1840).

Orlin 1970; Larsen 1976

Enlil-kudur-usur

Little-known Assyrian king, son of TUKULTI-NINURTA I, successor of ASHUR-NIRARI III, who was deposed by NINURTA-APIL-EKUR, descendent of ERIBA-ADAD I (1197–1193). According to the Synchronistic History he did battle with the Babylonian king ADAD-SHUMA-USUR.

Grayson 1972: 138–9

Enlil-nadin-ahi

Thirty-sixth and last king of the Kassite Dynasty in Babylon (*c.* 1157–1155). He is mentioned on a boundary stone and in the king lists, otherwise only in later literary and historical texts. According to these he led a campaign against the Elamite king KUDUR-NAHHUNTE, in which he was defeated and carried off as a prisoner to Elam, while important cities were destroyed and people deported. This crushing defeat brought the Kassite Dynasty to an end.

Brinkman 1968: 88–9; 1976: 122–5

Enlil-nadin-apli

Fifth king of the Second Dynasty of Isin, son and successor of NEBUCHAD-NEZZAR I (1104–1101). He probably came to the throne as a minor and died after a brief reign without issue, possibly during a coup staged by his uncle and successor MARDUK-NADIN-AHHE. A few kudurrus record land transfers, otherwise nothing is known about this king.

Brinkman 1968: 116–18

Enlil-nadin-shumi

Twenty-ninth king of the Kassite Dynasty of Babylon who occupied the throne during the period when the Assyrian king TUKULTI-NINURTA I had control over Babylon. He was probably not a member of the Kassite royal family.

Brinkman 1976: 125–7

Enlil-nasir I

Little-known Assyrian king of the 16th century, son and successor of PUZUR-ASHUR III. According to the Assyrian King List he ruled for thirteen years. He left two inscribed clay cones recording building works.

Grayson 1972: 36–7

Enlil-nasir II

Assyrian king (*c.* 1430–1425). According to the Assyrian King List he was the brother and successor of ASHUR-NADIN-AHHE I, whom he removed from the throne to rule for six years.

Grayson 1972: 37

Enlil-nirari

Assyrian king, son and successor of ASHUR-UBALLIT I (1329–1318). The Synchronistic History reports a conflict with the Babylonians that resulted in a battle between Enlil-nirari and KURIGALZU II, in which the Assyrians retained the upper hand. The Babylonian Chronicle P, however, states that the Assyrian king involved was ADAD-NIRARI I and that the Babylonians won the battle. He also issued a palace decree to regulate what was to be done if someone of the royal household should die during the king's absence.

Grayson 1972: 51–4; in CAH II/2: 31–2

Enmenana

Akkadian princess, daughter of NARAM-SIN who installed her as *entum*-priestess of the moon god Nanna at Ur. Her name is also preserved on seals and other objects.

Sollberger and Kupper 1971: IIA4g–i; Gelb and Kienast 1990: 41

Enmerkar

Legendary early Sumerian ruler, referred to in the Sumerian King List as the grandson of the sun god Utu and *en* priest of Eanna, a district of Uruk. He also features prominently in several literary compositions about the early Uruk kings. These texts describe him as having a special and intimate relationship with the goddess Inanna. She helps him to achieve cultural as well as military superiority over the possibly legendary eastern kingdom of Aratta, with whose ruler Enmerkar engages in a series of contests.

Kramer 1952; Alster 1973: 101–9; Cohen 1973; Berlin 1979

Enmetena (previously read as Entemena)

Early Dynastic king of Lagash, son of ENANNATUM I (*c.* 2450). He defeated URLUMMA king of Umma, and restored the previously agreed frontier between the rival cities. In his inscriptions he records that he embellished and built various temples. A beautiful silver vase with an engraved image of the mythical Imdugud bird and a statue of the king were found at Tello. All this points to a state of prosperity in Lagash at the time, which may be due to Enmetena's major enterprise, the building of a canal that linked the Euphrates and the Tigris. He also decreed an annulment of debts for the citizens of Lagash which freed them from bond slavery.

Gadd 1971, in CAH I/21: 19–120; Cooper 1986: 54–67

En-nigaldi-Nanna

Babylonian princess, daughter of NA-BONIDUS (556–539). She became *en-tum* priestess of the moon god at Ur, an office which he claims had been forgotten at his time. Ancient records of previous incumbents were discovered during repairs to the Gipar and she kept them in a kind of museum.

Kuhrt 1995: 598–600

Enshakushana

Sumerian king of Uruk, son of Elili of Ur (*c.* 24th century). There is an inscribed vase dedicated to Enlil that records his victory over Enbi-Ishtar of Kish and his restitution of votive goods pillaged from the temple.

Sollberger and Kupper 1971: IH1a–c; Gadd 1971, in CAH I/2: 113–14

Entemena *see* Enmetana

Eparti (also Ebarti)

Elamite king who in about 1890 founded a new dynasty, 'the kings of Anshan and Susa'. Nothing is known about his origins. Numerous tablets inscribed in Akkadian were discovered in Susa and other places. They deal mainly with legal matters. Unusually Eparti wrote his name with the

determinative for gods, a practice that was abandoned again after his death.

Hinz 1971, in CAH I/2: 661–2; 1972: 87, 91–3; Carter and Stolper 1984

Eparti (also Ebarti) II

Third ruler of the Dynasty of Simashki (*c.* 2200–*c.* 1900), according to a king list from Susa dating to the Old Babylonian period. He is probably to be identified with the *sukkalmah* Ebarat who ruled Susa during the reign of SHU-SIN.

Stolper: 1982

Epir-mupi

Ensi of Susa by appointment of the Akkadian king NARAM-SIN (2213–2230). He later became governor (*sukkal*) of Elam.

Gadd 1971: CAH I/2:445; Hinz ibid: 650; Frayne 1993: 305–7

Eriba-Adad I

Assyrian king, son of ASHUR-BEL-NISHESHU, according to the Assyrian King List (*c.* 1390–1364). Only a couple of fragmentary building inscriptions survive from his reign.

Grayson 1972: 40–2

Eriba-Adad II

Assyrian king, son and successor of ASHUR-BEL-KALA (1055–1054). Only fragments of his inscriptions survive.

Grayson 1976: 62–4; Grayson 1991: 113–15

Eriba-Marduk

Babylonian king, member of the Bit-Yakin tribe of the southern part of the country known as the Sealand (c. 770). He was a strong tribal leader and, taking advantage of Assyrian weakness after the death of ADAD-NIRARI III, assumed control as legitimate 'king of Babylon'. This is the title given him in contemporary inscriptions. He checked the incursions of nomadic tribes and restored peace and prosperity to Babylonia. He was much admired by later Babylonian kings, some of whom, like MERODACH-BALADAN, traced their lineage back to Eriba-Marduk and acknowledged his reverence for the Babylonian gods and their rites.

Brinkman 1968: 221–4

Erishti-Aya

Previously believed to have been a daughter of ZIMRI-LIM of Mari; now it is thought that she was either a sister of YASMAH-ADDU or a daughter of YAHDUN-LIM. She lived in the *Gipar* section of the temple at Sippar as a *nadītum* woman, dedicated to the god Shamash and his consort Aya. Her function was to pray for the king's life. Her letters have survived in the Mari archives. They contain demands for servants, various commodities and complaints about neglect by her father.

Batto 1974: 93–102; Harris 1962; Dossin 1967; Durand 1985b: 400

Erishum I (also Irishum)

Old Assyrian ruler (*iššiākum*) at Assur, son of ILUSHUMA (1934–1900).

He appears in the commercial texts discovered in the trading colony Karum Kanesh in Anatolia. He confirmed the important decision of his father to exempt Ashur's trading partners from commercial taxes. Otherwise he is known for his building activities in the capital city, such as the temple of Adad and the court building.

Landsberger and Balkan 1950; Larsen 1976; Grayson 1987: 19–40

Erridupizir

King of Gutium, son of Enridapizir. He is not mentioned in the list of Gutian kings in the Sumerian King List but several important inscriptions, some of them later copies, survive that describe military campaigns against the Lullubi and other peoples in the eastern mountains. Stylistically the texts resemble those of his possible contemporary, the Akkadian king NARAM-SIN.

Kutscher 1989: 52–66; Gelb and Kienast 1990: 303–16; Frayne 1993: 220–7

Esagil-kin-apli (= Saggil-kinam-ubbib)

Babylonian scribe under NEBUCHADNEZZAR I and ADAD-APLA-IDDINA (11th century), probably writer of the literary composition known as the *Babylonian Theodicy*, where his name appears in an acrostic formed by the initial signs of each line. He is mentioned in the Seleucid *List of Sages and Scholars* and also credited as the compiler of an important collection of omens, known as SA.-GIG.

Lambert, W.G. 1960: 63–91; Finkel, in Hunger 1996: 143–60

Esarhaddon (Assyrian Ashur-ahhe-iddina)

Assyrian king, son and successor of SENNACHERIB (680–669). The circumstances of his accession are still unclear; according to his own inscriptions his father had destined him to be his heir in view of the fact that the eldest son, ASHUR-NADIN-SHUMI, had died in Elamite exile. Esarhaddon was the youngest, a son of the Aramean woman NAQI'A-ZAKUTU. Some sources attributed the murder of Sennacherib to one of his sons, now thought to have been ARDA-MULISSU, Esarhaddon's elder brother. At any rate, the murder of Sennacherib unleashed serious civil disorder while his sons were fighting for the throne. Esarhaddon prevailed and was crowned in March 681.

Sources for his reign are plentiful. In addition to the usual royal inscriptions there are numerous letters and reports from diviners and astrologers, as well as two Babylonian chronicles. Even so, the chronology of events is not always easy to determine.

The main event of Esarhaddon's career was the invasion of Egypt, which had changed its policy from being pro-Assyrian to fomenting revolts along the border ever since SARGON II's foray into southern Palestine. In 674 Esarhaddon led an abortive campaign to Egypt. In 671 he made a more concerted effort, crossed the desert of Sinai with the help of Arab camels carrying water for the troops and fought three victorious battles against the Egyptians. He took Memphis and captured the son of pharaoh TAHARKA, who had managed to escape. Although he appointed Assyrian governors, the country was not easily subdued.

Apart from the Egyptian venture he had to face rebellions by various dependent states, such as Sidon, where king ABDI-MILKUTTI had rebelled in 677. Events in Anatolia were also worrying, especially with respect to the Cimmerians and the Scythians, and Esarhaddon was forced to deal with the situation. Towards Babylonia he pursued a policy of appeasement and began a programme of reconstruction and redevelopment; he also resettled exiled inhabitants and restored to them their property. He was at pains to rebuild the temple precinct that had been damaged by his father's troops and allowed some of the deported gods to return to their shrines.

Perhaps wary about the difficulties of a peaceful transition of power, he drew up a document which affirmed the succession of his sons ASHURBANI-PAL to rule Assyria and the crown-prince SHAMASH-SHUMA-UKIN to rule Babylonia. His vassals and nobility were sworn to respect this document.

In 669 Esarhaddon again led his troops against the Egyptians. It was to be his last campaign, for he died on the way.

Esarhaddon built the main arsenal at Nineveh, and restored the Ashur temple at Ashur, in addition to his care for despoiled Babylon.

In spite of his tireless campaigning, he has the reputation of a superstitious and anxious person, who was forever seeking reassurance by consulting countless oracles. He reintroduced the ritual of the substitute king who would officially occupy his place during inauspicious times. Many letters have survived that were sent to him by his diviners, astrologers and physicians. In his correspondence to his learned advisers he also reveals personal feelings, such as worry over the health of his family, which are not usually attested for Assyrian monarchs.

Grayson 1991, in CAH III/2: 122–41; Weippert 1981; Wiseman 1958; Parpola 1970/83; 1980; Parpola, in Alster 1980; Watanabe 1987; Hunger 1992; Porter 1993

Esharra-hamat

Assyrian queen, wife of ESARHADDON. She was a Babylonian and the mother of the crown-prince SHAMASH-SHUMA-UKIN, who became king of Babylonia. She built herself a mausoleum where she was buried in 673.

Grayson 1991, in CAH III/2: 139

Eshpum

Elamite ruler, *ensi* of Susa and viceroy of Awan. He left an inscribed stone figure of the Akkadian king MANISH-TUSU at Susa in which he recommends his overlord to the goddess Narunte. A seal of his, with figures of naked priests, has also been found.

Gadd 1971, in CAH I/2: 437; Hinz, ibid.: 650; Frayne 1993: 304

Ethba'al (= Ittobaal)

King of Sidon, (*c.* 887–856). He belonged to the priestly elite of Tyre and was perhaps also related to the dynasty of HIRAM I. According to the Bible he was the father-in-law of AHAB of Israel, who had married his daughter JEZEBEL.

He may be the unnamed ruler of Sidon/Tyre who sent tribute to the Assyrian king ASHURNASIRPAL II, when he campaigned in Syria and perhaps was invited to attend the inauguration banquet at the new royal residence of Calah.

According to the Jewish writer, Josephus, he founded a Phoenician colony in Libya and another near Byblos.

Klengel 1992: 204–5; Katzenstein 1973: 135ff.

Eulmash-shakin-shumi

Babylonian king from the Bazi tribe that ruled for three generations after the close of the Second Sealand Dynasty. He established peace and reigned for seventeen years (1005–989).

Brinkman 1968: 161–2

Evil-Merodach *see* Amel-Marduk

Ezekiel

Hebrew prophet who was deported to Babylonia after the fall of Jerusalem in 597. He is said to have settled with other exiles along the Kabaru canal, and delivered messages to the Jews that warned them not to place their hopes on an early return to Judah. He predicted the final destruction of Jerusalem of 588/7, of which the exiled Jews only heard three years later. However, he also communicated other visions which concerned the restoration of Israel and in his final revelation, dated to 573, he saw the Temple refashioned as a sign of God's forgiveness.

Mitchell 1991, in CAH III/2: 422–3

Ezra

Jewish leader and writer who was active during the Achaemenid period under ARTAXERXES I. His writings cover the period from the conquest of Babylonia by CYRUS II to the restoration of the temple under DARIUS I. He was put in charge by the Persian king to oversee the observance of the Jewish law in Palestine. His book, which takes the form of a personal memoir, forms a valuable source for the Jewish history of the 5th and early 4th centuries, although some scholars have expressed doubts as to its authenticity.

Mitchell 1991, in CAH III/2: 426–9; Myers 1965; Grabbe 1992

G

Gabbar

King of Sam'al, (*c.* 920). As stated in an inscribed stele by one of his descendants, KILAMUWA, he founded a dynasty that was to last for several generations.

Hawkins 1982, in CAH III/1: 382, 397

Gandash

According to the Babylonian King List he was the first king of the Kassite Dynasty, which ruled in Mesopotamia for some 400 years. He may have been a Kassite ruler or military commander at the time of SAMSU-ILUNA, in the 18th century, but his historicity is doubtful as there are no contemporary inscriptions that mention his name. In a document from the first millennium he is given all the prestigious titles of Mesopotamian monarchs and referred to as king of Babylon. This is probably an attempt to create an illustrious founder of the dynasty retrospectively.

Weidner 1957–71, in RlA 3: 138–9

Gashuliyawa

Hittite princess, daughter of HATTU-SILI III and his wife PUDUHEPA. She was married to BENTESHINA, king of Amurru, a vassal of the Hittite king. In a letter her mother reports her intention to visit her daughter in Syria but it is not known whether that ever took place or not.

Klengel 1992: 172

Gaumata

A Persian priest (magus) who is said to have rebelled against CAMBYSES II while the latter was in Egypt. According to the Behistun inscription of DARIUS I and Herodotus (3.30; 61–7) he acted after Cambyses had ordered that his brother BARDIYA be murdered in secret. Gaumata is said to have used this cover-up to pretend that he was Bardiya and have himself proclaimed king, gaining the support of many Persians. According to Herodotus, Cambyses set out to deal with the matter as soon as he heard of it but died en route, although not before he had disclosed the fratricide and warned his courtiers against the impostor. They then discovered and killed him. However, in the inscriptions of Darius I he claims that he was aware of Gaumata's trickery and disposed of him personally. This version of events may have been propaganda by Darius as several factors, not least the reported striking resemblance between Bardiya and Gaumata, point to the possibility that Gaumata was in fact none other than the brother of Cambyses and that Darius invented the imposture to make his own usurpation less obvious.

Balcer 1987; Kuhrt 1995: 664–5

Gedaliah

Governor of Judah, appointed to this position by NEBUCHADNEZZAR II after the deportation of ZEDEKIAH in 587. Since the city of Jerusalem had been badly damaged he moved the residence to Mizpah. He managed to restore order and some stability to the conquered land and seems to have been a man of moderation. He was murdered by a certain Ishmael ben Nethaniah, who claimed rights to the throne for himself.

Mitchell 1991, in CAH III/2: 410–13

Geme-Enlila

Wife and queen of IBBI-SIN, fifth king of the Third Dynasty of Ur (2029–2006). It has been suggested that she was his sister, but it is more likely that there were several royal ladies with the same name at the Ur court.

Michalowski 1982

Geme-Ninlila

Royal lady at the court of Ur. She bore the still enigmatic title *lukur*; which may signify a secondary wife of the king. She was buried along with SHULGI and queen, SHULGI-SHIMTI, in the royal mausoleum at Ur.

Michalowski 1982

Gigitu

Babylonian princess, daughter of NERIGLISSAR. She was married off to an important official at the Nabu temple in Borsippa.

Weisberg, in Garelli 1974: 448

Gilgamesh

Sumerian king of the Early Dynastic period who was later deified and became the protagonist in several literary compositions. There is as yet no contemporary evidence for his reign but he appears in the Sumerian King List, as well as in the so-called Tummal text which concerns repairs to his Nippur temple by successive rulers. One Sumerian narrative concerns his fight against AGGA of Kish, which fits in well with the struggle for supremacy in the Early Dynastic period.

Gadd 1971, in CAH I/2: 110–11; Leick 1991: 68–77; Kovacs 1989

Girnamme

Elamite king of the dynasty of Shi-mashki, contemporary of SHU-SIN of Ur. In 2037 he sent an ambassador to Ur who escorted a daughter of Shu-Sin back to Anshan, where she was to marry the local prince who may or may not have been Girnamme himself.

Gadd 1971, in CAH I/2: 657; Carter and Stolper 1984: 20, 22

Gubaru (= Gobryas)

Governor of Babylonia under CYRUS II and (probably) under CAMBYSES II (535–522). He had the powers of a satrap and his name is mentioned in several legal tablets. There is also some evidence for his personal finan-cial dealings and his family in the contemporary Babylonian tablets.

Kuhrt 1988, in CAH IV: 125–8

Gudea

Sumerian ruler (*ensi*) of Lagash, son-in-law and successor of UR-BABA (*c.* 22nd century). The dating of Gudea's reign is still uncertain: some place it after the defeat of the Gutians, others put him within the period of Gutian rulership, contemporary with Puzur-Sin. He left numerous inscribed stone statues of himself, most of which were placed in the temple of Ningirsu. According to these and other dedica-tory inscriptions, Gudea's reign brought peace and prosperity. He embarked on ambitious building pro-jects (especially the temple Eninnu) for which he had to import raw materials and luxury goods from distant parts. One successful military expedition

eastwards (to Anshan and Elam) also yielded substantial booty. Within Su-mer and Akkad Gudea seems to have maintained independence and re-frained from attempts to extend his sphere of influence by military means.

Gudea's fame for posterity lies primarily on his fostering of the arts. His monumental statues combine powerful concentration of masses with delicate modelling of details. The language of his inscriptions counts as the epitome of classical Sumerian.

Gadd 1971, in CAH I/2: 459–461; Jacobsen 1987: 386–444; Johansen 1978; Steible 1991; Wilson 1996; Edzard 1997: 26–180

Gungunum

First king of the Larsa dynasty (1932–1906). He took over titles of hegemony that for the previous fifty years had been held by Isin; even the *entum*-priestess of Ur, the daughter of LIPIT-ESHTAR, declared her alliance to him rather than the ruler of Isin. Having achieved control over Ur, he could assure the financially profitable basis of the Gulf trade.

Edzard 1957: 100–3

Gyges

King of Lydia, son of Dascylium, founder of the Mermnad Dynasty (*c.* 680–*c.* 652). Sources for his reign come from later Greek tradition in Herodotus, as well as from contem-porary Assyrian records. Archaeolo-gists have furthermore discovered proof for the famous wealth of his kingdom at Sardis and other sites. He had access to the gold deposits of the

Pactolus river and the silver mines in Anatolia. Herodotus speaks with admiration of the gold and silver vessels that he was reputed to have sent to Delphi.

According to Herodotus he usurped the throne with the help of his allies in neighbouring Caria. He made overtures to Egypt and procured mercenaries for pharaoh PSAMMETICHUS I. He was also a contemporary of ASHURBANIPAL, to whom he appealed for help against the Cimmerians who were a continuous menace to his kingdom. This was granted, though Ashurbanipal records his astonishment at the strangeness of land and language of the people. At some point Gyges dispatched Cimmerian prisoners to Nineveh to prove his loyalty, but when Ashurbanipal discovered his dealings with the Egyptian pharaoh he accused him of supporting the latter's revolt against Assyria. He therefore cursed him as a traitor, presumably withheld his support, and the Cimmerians did indeed eventually overrun Gyges' kingdom.

Mellink 1991, in CAH III/2: 643ff.; Kuhrt 1995: 567–9; Cogan and Tadmor: 1977

H

Hadad-ezer

1 King of Zobah and Rehob in the 10th century. He is so far only known from accounts in the Bible (2 Sam. 8) which describe his wars against DAVID, in which David proved victorious.

Pitard 1987; Malamat 1983

2 King of Damascus (*c*. 853–841), known to the Assyrians as Adad-idri. Together with the kings of Hama and Israel he led an alliance against the Assyrians during the reign of SHALMANESER III which proved difficult to defeat for several years. He is usually thought to be identical with BEN-HADAD.

Wiseman 1972–5, in RlA 4: 38; Klengel 1992: 209; Pitard 1987: 132–8

Hadad-yis'i (Assyrian Adad-it'i)

Governor of the Assyrian province of Guzana, either in the mid-9th or during the middle to late 8th century. His almost life-size statue of black basalt was discovered in 1979 at Tell Fekheriye (north-eastern Syria). It has an inscription in Aramaic and Assyrian which states that he dedicated the statue to the local god Hadad. His father, who bore the Akkadian name of Shamash-nuri, may have served as an Assyrian eponym official in the year 866.

Abou Assaf *et al.* 1982; Fitzmayer and Kaufman 1992: 36ff.; Bordreuil, in Cluzan *et al.* 1993: 260–3

Hallushu-Inshushinak

Elamite king, brother of SHUTRUK-NAHHUNTE II, whom he displaced in a violent palace coup (699–693). Only one Elamite inscription remains, in which he calls himself 'expander of the kingdom'. The events of the last year of his reign are better known, since he was dragged into the conflict between SENNACHERIB and MERO-DACH-BALADAN. When Sennacherib, in a great naval expedition, pursued his Babylonian arch-enemy into the marshes of the Persian Gulf, Mero-dach-baladan and a number of his supporters had escaped to the Elamite side. The Assyrians sailed across the Gulf where they attacked and destroyed a number of Elamite coastal cities. While they were thus engaged, Hallushu-Inshushinak entered northern Babylonia, took Sippar and captured the Assyrian crown-prince ASHUR-NADIN-SHUMI, whom Sennacherib had appointed as king of Babylonia. He had him deported to Elam and put the Babylonian NERGAL-USHEZIB on the throne instead. In ensuing confrontations between the Babylonian faction and the Assyrians he was successful at first, but in September 693 Sennacherib overcame the Elamite and Babylonian troops at Nippur. Hallushu-Inshushinak managed to get back to Susa but was killed by his own people upon arrival, as the Babylonian Chronicle reports. His son KUDUR-NAHHUNTE became king after him.

Hinz 1972: 147–9; Levine 1982; Carter and Stolper 1984: 47

Hallutush-Inshushinak

Little-known Elamite king (1205–1185). He may have originated from the south-east of Anshan; but there are as yet no sources from this period of Elamite history.

Hinz 1972: 121; Carter and Stolper 1984: 39

Halparuntiyas II
(=Assyrian Qalparunda)

Neo-Hittite king of Gurgum, son of Muwatalis (855–830). He was a contemporary of SHALMANESER III, to whom he submitted in 855. He commissioned a colossal figure to be carved in his memory, bearing an inscription in hieroglyphic Luwian, of which only the lower part remains.

Hawkins 1982, in CAH III/1: 383, 392, 396; Orthmann 1971: 288

Halparuntiyas III (Assyrian Qalparunda)

Neo-Hittite king of Gurgum, son of Palalam, contemporary of ADAD-NIRARI III (805–780). He left an inscription in Luwian hieroglyphics that lists his genealogy on a sculpted lion, discovered at Maras. He probably joined the anti-Assyrian coalition led by ATARSHUMKI, the king of Arpad, which led to a battle with Adad-nirari. As a result Halparuntiyas lost territories to the ruler of Kummuh.

Hawkins 1982 in CAH III/1: 383, 400, 401

Hammurabi of Babylon

Amorite king of Babylon, son of SIN-MUBALLIT, consolidator of the First Babylonian Dynasty and famous legislator (c. 1792–1750).

At the time of his accession to the throne, Mesopotamia was largely controlled by two experienced and powerful kings, SHAMSHI-ADAD I of Assyria and RIM-SIN of Larsa. Initially, Hammurabi controlled only a rather small territory around the city of Babylon, including Kish, Sippar and Borsippa. Year names from the beginning of his reign mainly record building activities and dedications to religious institutions. Early military campaigns were probably waged as an ally of his overlords. It was not before his thirtieth year (1763) that he defeated his great-est rival, Rim-Sin of Larsa. A year later he also gained control over Eshnunna – important for the eastern trade routes leading to Iran and beyond. In 1761 he conquered Assyria. Mari, which had been an ally of Babylon for a long time, was taken in 1760, which secured the western regions of the Euphrates. Hammurabi's empire by 1755 was as substantial as that of the Third Dynasty of Ur had been, and he was the undisputed ruler over all of Mesopotamia. The administration and organisation of the state is well documented. It was not as revolutionary as had once been assumed and followed in many respects earlier practices and procedures: as far as southern Mesopotamia is concerned, heavily relying on regulations laid down by Rim-Sin of Larsa. The redistribution of new crown land that resulted from conquest was strictly controlled under the so-called *ilku* system.

Hammurabi is widely known for his 'law-code', inscribed on a large stone stele, which was found in Susa where it had been taken by Elamite raiders. At the top it bears a scene of the god Shamash investing the king with the insignia of royal power. The lengthy prologue and epilogue describe the divinely approved functions of the king as the protector and shepherd of his people, upholder of justice and peace. The function and actual application of the laws are still much debated but the Code remains one of the most important documents in Mesopotamian social history. Hammurabi's letters and royal inscriptions were much admired by subsequent generations and copied in the scribal training centres.

He remains one of the great kings of Mesopotamia: an outstanding diplomat and negotiator who was patient enough to wait for the right time and then ruthless enough to achieve his aims without stretching his resources too far; an able and far-seeing administrator; a ruler with a strong sense of justice and order. His legacy was to provide inspiration for many generations to come.

Kuhrt 1995, I: 108–17; Frayne, 1990; Kärki 1984; Westbrook 1989; Yoffee 1977; Postgate 1992; Kraus 1984; Schmökel 1971; Gadd 1973, in CAH II/1: 176–220; Kupper, ibid.: 28–9

Hammurapi I

King of Aleppo, son of YARIM-LIM I (*c.* 1765–1761). He was on friendly terms with ZIMRI-LIM of Mari, whom he met in person, and the ruler of Ugarit, who was interested in visiting Zimri-lim's by then famous palace. Relations with HAMMURABI OF BABYLON were also good. It seems generally that this king enjoyed a relatively peaceful reign; even the old rivalry with Qatna had abated.

Klengel 1972–5, in RlA 4: 73; 1992: 58–9

Hammurapi II

King of Yamhad, son of YARIM-LIM II (18th century). He is also known from the Hittite tradition.

Klengel 1992: 64

Hanne

Elamite ruler at the time of SHUTRUK-NAHHUNTE II. He was a vassal king over the mountain province of Ayapir. He is well known because he left a number of sculpted rock monuments, some with Elamite inscriptions. They reiterate his loyalty to his overlord, his devotion to the gods, and also commemorate his wife and ministers.

Hinz 1972: 143–5; Carter and Stolper 1984: 45, 171

Hantili I

Hittite king of the Old Kingdom, brother-in-law and successor of MURSILI I, whom he had assassinated (1590–1560). According to the Edict of TELEPINU his reign was troubled by revolts and invasions by the Hurrians. His son and designated successor, Piseni, was the victim of a palace intrigue and was murdered by ZIDANTA.

Otten 1972–5, in RlA 4: 110; Kuhrt 1995: 145

Hanun-Dagan

Ruler (*šakkanakku*) of Mari during the Ur III period, son of PUZUR-ESHTAR (*c.* 2016–2008). His name appears on votive gifts and in dynastic lists.

Durand 1985: 151–2

Harapsili

Hittite princess, sister of king MURSILI I. According to the Edict of TELEPINU she was married to HANTILI. Together with ZIDANTA they planned a palace coup and had Mursili killed.

Otten 1972–5, in RlA 4: 113; Kuhrt 1995: 245

Hattusili I

Hittite king of the Old Kingdom, (*c.* 1650–1620). He was the first Hittite ruler to leave extensive documents. He reports in his annals that he waged war in central Anatolia, as well as further afield in northern Syria, to extend and stabilise Hittite control in spite of challenges by the growing power of Mitanni to the south. He claimed the protection and help of the sun goddess of Arinna, who was to remain the divine protectress of Hittite kings throughout the empire's history. Hattusili I used the enormous booty from his successful campaigns to enrich the great shrines of the gods of Hatti and he compares himself to the great king SARGON OF AKKAD. Apart from annals, he also left an extraordinary document, a 'political testament', in which he refers to internal strife and intrigues at the court and justifies his decision to nominate MURSILI I, his grandson, to be his successor, instead of his nephew, who, with his mother, had plotted against him.

Otten, 1972–5, in RlA 4: 173–4; Kuhrt 1995: 238–43; Gurney 1990; Houwink ten Cate 1983/4

Hattusili III

Hittite king of the Empire period, brother of MUWATALLI II (1275–1245/1264–1239). While his brother still reigned as Great King of Hatti, Hattusili was entrusted with establishing order in the northern Anatolian provinces, which suffered from frequent incursion by the Gasga people. To this purpose he set up a province with its centre at Hakpis and was eventually able to liberate the capital Hattusa. When his nephew URHI-TESHUP acceded to the throne his power gradually diminished, as he reports in a long text, the so-called 'Apology of Hattusili III'. He states that the goddess Shaushga had declared her support for him and promoted his bid to become Great King of Hatti himself, thus contravening the traditional sequence of succession laid down by TELEPINU. Once his rival was exiled to Syria and his accession to the Hittite throne was recognised by the other political powers of the age, he concluded a peace treaty with RAMESSES II of Egypt, to whom he also gave a daughter in marriage.

Kuhrt 1995: 258–64; Otten 1972–5, in RlA 4: 173–4; 1981

Haza'el

King of Damascus (c. 844/42–800), officer of BEN-HADAD II, whom he assassinated and succeeded on the throne as a usurper. He faced SHAL-MANESER III in 841, after the anti-Assyrian coalition led by Damascus had disintegrated. In 838 Shalmaneser returned and defeated Haza'el, although he did not succeed in capturing the capital. He expanded his territory westward into Israel during the reigns of JEHU and JEHOAHAZ. He captured Gad and only the costly gifts

sent by king JEHOASH could prevent him from attacking Jerusalem.

Hawkins 1982, in CAH III/1: 393–4; Klengel 1992: 209–10; Pitard 1987; Lemaire, A. in Charpin and Joannès 1991: 91–108

Henti

Hittite queen, wife of SUPPILULIUMA I. Her name is found on two seals from Hattusa and also occurs in temple lists that detail offerings for dead queens.

Otten 1972–5, in RlA 4: 325

Hepattarakki

Hurrian woman who appears as the author of an incantation ritual discovered in the archives of the Hittite capital Hattusa.

Szabo 1972–5, in RlA 4: 329

Herodotus

Greek writer and historian (born in Halicarnassus, south-west Turkey, according to later tradition around 484). He incorporated an account of his visit to Babylonia in his *Histories*. He provides accounts of the country and the city of Babylon, which many think reliable, while others doubt this. He also includes scanty and hearsay reports on history and social customs that are subject to misunderstandings, such as the alleged practice of the requirement of prostitution for all women. He is also one of the major sources for the history of the Medes, the Persians, the Egyptians, the Lydians and other Anatolian people.

Saggs 1972–5, in RlA 4: 332–3; Rollinger 1993; Dalley 1996

Hezekiah

King of Judah, son and successor of AHAZ (715–687). In the Book of Chronicles he is particularly praised for his religious reforms, which not only did away with innovations introduced by his father but generally purified the Israelite cult from syncretistic elements. He was an Assyrian vassal and exercised his rulership at a difficult time, when the northern kingdom had ceased to exist after the fall of Samaria and the deportation of Israelites under SARGON II. According to II Kgs. 18:7 he received an embassy from the Babylonian king MERODACH-BALADAN, in the early years of SENNA-CHERIB's reign. The Babylonian was involved in a rebellion against Assyria and was perhaps looking for an ally. He began preparations for a confrontation with Assyria by strengthening his defences around Jerusalem and digging a channel for water, the well-known Siloam tunnel. According to his annals, Sennacherib marched west in his third campaign to deal with the west Syrian provinces. He defeated the Egyptian army and conquered forty-six fortified Judean cities, including Lachish. According to the account in the Book of Kings, he then sent his general or *turtānu* to begin the siege of Jerusalem. From the camp opposite the city, the Assyrian commander addressed the king and the citizens of Jerusalem urging them to surrender.

According to the biblical account the Assyrian army was slain during the night by an 'angel of God'. Whatever may have been the reason, Sennacherib did not continue his siege in 701 and Judah remained an autonomous state, attached to the Assyrian empire. Hezekiah may have shared the kingship with his son MANASSEH during his last years. He was buried in the royal cemetery.

Mitchell 1993, in CAH III/2: 344–73

Hiram I

King of Tyre, son and successor of ABIBA'EL (*c.* 969–936). According to the Bible he had a close relationship with the Israelite king, DAVID, and especially with his successor, SOLO-MON, with whom he made an alliance, sending him timber and skilled workers for the temple and helping him build a fleet in the Red Sea.

Röllig 1972–5, in RlA 4 :418; Klengel 1992: 203–4; Katzenstein 1973

Hishep-ratep

Elamite king, son of LUH-ISHSHAN, whom he first succeeded as king of Anshan. When RIMUSH of Akkad became king, he revolted against him, together with his ally, ABALGA-MASH of Warakhshi. They were defeated in a great battle and his country was despoiled by Rimush. Vessels inscribed by Rimush have been discovered at Nippur which refer to his successful Elamite campaign. Hishep-ratep's own fate is not known.

Hinz 1972: 73

Hita

Elamite king of Awan, contemporary of NARAM-SIN of Akkad, who concluded a treaty with him *c.* 2280, probably to form an alliance against the Gutians. This is the first historical text to be written in Elamite; and it was deposited in the Inshushinak temple in Susa, where it was discovered by French archaeologists. It appears that a daughter of Hita was married to Naram-Sin.

Hinz 1971, in CAH I/2: 651–2; 1972: 75–7

Hitlal-Erra

Ruler (*šakkanakku*) of Mari during the Ur III period, son of PUZUR-ESHTAR, brother of HANUN-DAGAN (*c.* 2024–2008). He is only mentioned in dynastic lists.

Durand 1985: 155

Hosea

Hebrew prophet in the kingdom of Israel, during the reign of king JEROBOAM II (*c.* 740). He attacked the lax morals of his time, particularly in sexual matters, which is thought to relate to his marriage to a promiscuous wife. He also criticised the synchretistic cult practices of the Israelite priesthood, and warned Israel not to meddle in international affairs and attract the attention of powers such as Egypt and Assyria.

Donner 1972–5, in RlA 4: 476; Comay 1993: 139–40

Hoshea

The last king of Israel (732–722), he succeeded PEKAH, whom he had killed. He was an Assyrian vassal and paid tribute to TIGLATH-PILESER III, who had confirmed his rule over a much reduced kingdom. When SHALMANESER V acceded he stopped paying the tribute and sought protection from Assyrian attack in an alliance with Egypt. The Assyrians besieged Samaria and captured it after a three-year siege. According to II Kgs. 17:4 Hoshea had been imprisoned before the fall of the city. His end is not recorded.

Mitchell 1993, in CAH III/2: 338–9

Humban-haltash I

Elamite king, successor and brother of HUMBAN-NIMENA (687–681). He died from a stroke in October 681.

Hinz 1972–5, in RlA IV: 492

Humban-haltash II

Elamite king, successor and probably son of HUMBAN-HALTASH I (681–675). According to the Babylonian Chronicle he raided Sippar in 675 and died 'without having been ill'.

Hinz 1972–5, in RlA IV: 492; Carter and Stolper 1984: 48–9

Humban-haltash III

Last known Elamite king, who supplanted his predecessor in *c.* 648–642. No Elamite records of his time exist, but Assyrian sources describe two campaigns against Elam, in which Susa fell (646). After this Humban-haltash tried to secure a position in the mountains north of Susa. He sought to win Assyrian favour by offering to surrender the Babylonian rebel NABU-BEL-SHUMATE, who killed himself at the news. Internal trouble forced him to flee to Luristan, where local people captured him and handed him over to Ashurbanipal, who forced him and another Elamite ruler, Tammaritu (II?) to pull the Assyrian king's triumphal chariot to the Ishtar temple. Nothing further is known of his fate.

Hinz 1972: 157–9; 1972–5, in RlA IV: 492; Carter and Stolper 1984: 51–3

Humban-nikash I (Assyrian Ummanigash)

Elamite king, son and successor of HUMBAN-TAHRAH (c. 743–711). No Elamite records survive from his reign, but the Babylonian Chronicle records that he defeated SARGON II in the battle of Der in 720. MERODACH-BALADAN, the Babylonian king, arrived with auxiliary troops only to find that the battle was already over.

Hinz 1972: 138–9; 1972–5, in RlA IV: 492; Carter and Stolper 1984: 45

Humban-nimena (Assyrian Umman-menanu)

Elamite king, successor and younger brother of KUDUR-NAHHUNTE (692–689). In 691 he mustered an army against SENNACHERIB in support of the Babylonians, who had sent him gold and silver from the treasury of the temples of Marduk, as the annals of Sennacherib report. He mustered an army that included Persian auxili-

aries as well as Arameans. The Assyrian king claims that the battle, fought in the plain of Halule on the river Tigris, was a victory and that he spared the lives of the Elamite and Babylonian kings when they tried to escape. However the Babylonian Chronicle states he suffered defeat. Humban-nimena died in 689 following a stroke.

Hinz 1972: 149–51; 1972–5, in RlA IV: 493; Carter and Stolper 1984: 48

Humban-numena

Elamite king, son and successor of ATTAR-KITAH (c. 1275). He was apparently a successful monarch, presiding over a domain which he had probably extended further east and south to include Liyan. A later inscription commemorates his building of the Inshushinak temple at Susa; his own texts record buildings within the sacred precinct of Humban and Kirisha at Liyan. He is shown praying for his throne and the life of two women, presumably his mother and wife.

Hinz 1972: 112–13; 1972–5, in RlA 4: 493; 1975, in CAH II/2: 384; Carter and Stolper 1984: 36–7

Humban-tahrah

Elamite king, founder of the last Elamite dynasty, father of HUMBAN-NIKASH I (760?–743), only known from later genealogies.

Hinz 1972: 138

Hurbatila

Elamite king (*c.* 1330), only known from Babylonian sources. An inscription by king KURIGALZU II on a statue that he put up at Susa marks him as the 'tyrant of Susa and Elam'. According to Chronicle P he fought against Hurbatila and defeated him.

Hinz 1972: 111; Carter and Stolper 1984: 35; Kuhrt 1995: 370

Huttelush-Inshushinak
(= Huteludush-Inshushinak)

Elamite king of the Shutrukide dynasty (*c.* 1120–1110). According to an official inscription he claimed descent from three 'fathers': SHUTRUK-NAHHUNTE, the founder of the dynasty, KUTIR-NAHHUNTE, and SHILHAK-INSHUSHINAK, who were brothers. Genealogies are notoriously difficult to establish for Elamite royal families. Huttelush-Inshushinak may have been the son of Kutir-nahhunte and his wife/sister NAHHUNTE-UTU. He dedicated numerous sanctuaries to her memory. According to later Babylonian sources he was supposed to have murdered his father with an iron dagger but there is little evidence to support this claim. He managed to maintain the vast realm bequeathed to him by his forebears and presided over a relatively prosperous and stable realm as the administrative documents suggest. However, in the middle of his reign the Babylonian king NEBUCHAD-NEZZAR I launched an attack against Elam, claimed a resounding victory, plundered the land, and triumphantly brought back the cult statue of Marduk. Huteludush-Inshushinak was reported to have 'hidden himself in the mountains', which may signify that he met his death. After this the fortunes of Elam changed drastically, and the historical sources fall silent for the next 300 years.

Kuhrt 1995: 373; Stolper 1984; Hinz 1972: 133–7; 1972–5, in RlA 4: 525–6; Vallat 1985; Grillot 1988

Hutran-temti (= Hutran-tepti)

Elamite king of the dynasty of Shimashki mentioned as one of the illustrious ancestors of SHILHAK-INSHUSHINAK. This enduring fame has been ascribed to the possibility that he was the king who defeated Ur in 2006 and carried king IBBI-SIN to Elam, where he died in exile.

Hinz 1971, in CAH 1/2: 659; Carter and Stolper 1984: 132 n.401

Huzziya I

Hittite king of the Old Kingdom (*c.* 1530–1525). He followed AM-MUNA on the throne as a result of a bloody palace intrigue. According to the Edict of TELEPINU he also had murderous designs on his brother-in-law Telepinu, who learned about the plot and sent Huzziya and his brothers into exile.

Kuhrt 1995: 246

Hystaspes

Satrap of Parthia in the Achaemenid empire, father of DARIUS I. When his son usurped the throne in 522 and revolts broke out all over the Persian empire, he dealt with an uprising in his satrapy. The revolt was only put down in 521/20 when Darius sent reinforcements. According to Ctesias he died when he went to inspect the rock-tomb of Darius at Naqsh-i-Rustam.

Cuyler-Young 1988, in CAH IV: 60–1; Hinz 1972–5, in RlA IV: 548–9; Briant 1996: ch. 34

I

Iaubi'di (= Yaubi'di)
King of Hamath during the reign of
SARGON II, who calls him 'an evil
Hittite', since he led a revolt against
Assyria, with the help of newly sub-
jugated rulers. He and his allies were
defeated at Qarqar and Iaubi'di was
taken to Assyria where he was flayed,
as a relief in the Khorsabad palace
shows.

Hawkins 1976–80, in RlA 5: 272–3

Ibal-pi-El I
Governor of Eshnunna in the Old
Babylonian period, son and successor
of BELAKUM

Frayne 1990: 539–43; Yuhong 1994: 39

Ibal-pi-El II
King of Eshnunna in the Old Babylo-
nian period, son of DADUSHA (18th
century). During a time of intense
political rivalry in Middle Babylonia,
Eshnunna was an important power.
Ibal-pi-El was instrumental in driving
YASMAH-ADDU, the son of SHAMSHI-
ADAD I, from Mari and took several

other strategically important towns.
His son Silli-Sin was eventually defeated by HAMMURABI OF BABYLON,
who brought Eshnunna's independence to an end.

Gadd 1971, in CAH II/2: 17; Frayne 1990:
573–86; Yuhong 1994

Ibbi-Sin (=Ibbi-Suen)
Fifth and last king of the Third
Dynasty of Ur, son of SHU-SIN
(2026–2004?).

His reign is well documented, since
the standard forms of historical information in Mesopotamia, date-
formulae, votive inscriptions and
omen texts with historical allusions,
are supplemented by letters that throw
a vivid light on the volatile situation in
Ibbi-Sin's time. He had to face rebellions as well as the expansion of
pastoralist tribes. Ibbi-Sin undertook
several military expeditions, some of
them temporarily successful, and also
made use of alliances and other
diplomatic means to secure peace.
This policy secured some twenty years
of relative stability until the downfall.

This was probably the result of many different factors, not least natural calamities, such as a great flood, and the emergence of many smaller political units who would form short-lived alliances to maximise short-term gains. Delegating power to governors, as practised by all Ur III kings, was another element that weakened central control, as individuals, notably ISHBI-ERRA of Isin, were quick to exploit the situation to achieve independence. Finally, the eastern states of Elam and Shimashki attacked and devastated the city of Ur and many other towns of Mesopotamia. The king was taken captive and died in Anshan.

A Sumerian literary text, called 'A Lamentation over the Destruction of Ur', describes the cruel fate of the city and her inhabitants.

Gadd 1971, in CAH I/2: 611–17; Edzard 1957: 44–50; Sollberger 1976–80, in RlA 5: 1–8; Michalowski 1989; Kuhrt 1995: 70–2; Frayne 1997: 361–92

Ibbi-Sipish

Fifth and last king of Ebla of the period documented by the great archive (middle of the 3rd millennium). He was the son of Ebla's most powerful king, EBRIUM, and the first to succeed in a dynastic line, thus breaking with the established Eblaite custom of electing the ruler (*en*) for a fixed term of office lasting seven years. It has been proposed that the catastrophic fall of the city may have been due to an internal revolt protesting against this new concept of absolute and dynastic kingship. During his reign he visited cities abroad, such as Kish in Mesopotamia, and concluded a treaty with Armi, as Aleppo was called in this time.

Pettinato 1986: 51–2, 72–7, 135

Ibbit-Lim

Ruler of Mari in the Middle Bronze Level I period of the city, contemporary with the end of the Third Dynasty of Ur (*c.* 2000). A fragment of an inscribed votive statue of this king, discovered in AD 1968, allowed the site of Tell Mardikh to be identified with Ebla.

Pettinato 1986: 16–24; Gelb and Kienast 1990: 367; Klengel 1992: 41

Ib-Damu

Ruler of Emar at the time covered by the archives of Ebla (*c.* 2500).

Pettinato 1986: 141

Ibdati

Ruler of the Mediterranean port of Gubla (later: Byblos) at the time of AMAR-SIN of Ur (2045–2037).

Sollberger 1959: 120–2

Ibiranu

King of Ugarit, son of AMMISHTAMRU; probably a vassal of the Hittite king ARNUWANDA III and answerable to the local viceroy at Carchemish, INI-TESHUP, (*c.* 1230). There are some doubts about his succession, as his brother Utri-Sharruma was the eldest. He also received a missive from the Hittite Great King, who accused him of not appearing before him in person and for neglecting to send messengers.

Klengel 1992: 144–6

Iblul-Il

Early Dynastic king of Mari, whose inscribed stone statue was found in the Ishtar temple. His name was also mentioned on other votive offerings, such as on the statuette of the singer UR-NANSHE. He also appears in the texts from Ebla archive, where Iblul-Il was a contemporary of IRKAB-DAMU. A chronicle reports that he was defeated by an Eblaite commander, Enna-Dagan. Iblul-Il was captured and allowed to remain on the throne, but no longer as king but as governor by Ebla's grace. This ended a long conflict. Iblul-Il had apparently formed a powerful coalition in an attempt to limit Ebla's expansion of its business interests.

Parrot 1956: 208, Gelb and Kienast 1990: 12–14; Pettinato 1986: 115–17; 237, 241; Edzard 1981

Idaddu I (= Idaddu-Inshushinak; Indattu)

Elamite king of the dynasty of Shimashki, son of Pepi and 'sister-son' of HUTRAN-TEMTI, possibly grandson of Kindattu. His extensive reconstruction work in Susa is commemorated on an inscribed limestone basin. He became king of Shimashki around 1970 when he appointed his son Tan-Ruhuratir as governor of Susa and had him marry

MEKUBI, daughter of BILALAMA of Eshnunna in Babylonia.

Hinz 1971, in CAH I/2: 660–1; 1972: 85; 1976–80, in RlA 5: 28

Idaddu II (= Idattu)

Elamite king, son of TAN-RUHURATIR and the Babylonian princess MEKUBI, grandson of IDADDU I (c. 1925–1870). During the reign of his father he was governor of Susa, where he was engaged in substantial building work on the temple perimeter walls. The picture of this king survives on a seal belonging to a high court official. With the death of Idaddu II the dynasty of Shimashki kings came to an end.

Hinz 1971, in CAH I/2: 661; 1972: 85–7; 1976–80, in RlA 5: 28

Iddin-Dagan

Third king of the Dynasty of Isin, son of SHU-ILISHU (1974–1954). He seems to have presided over a stable and peaceful period in Babylonian history, and only cultic activities are recorded in the preserved year names. He is now mainly famous for works of literature that were composed during his reign, especially the hymn to the goddess Ninisinna in which the New Year festival is described that culminates in the goddess 'marrying' the king.

Edzard 1957: 74–6; Reisman 1973

Iddin-El (=Iddin-ilum)

Ruler (šakkanakku) of Mari during the Ur III period, (c. 2090–2985). His name appears on a seal and an inscribed statue.

Durand 1985: 151; Frayne 1997: 441

Iddin-Marduk

Babylonian businessman and entrepreneur (6th century). There has survived a substantial archive of various letters and documents about his commercial activities and those of his family who inherited the business. They had close connections by marriage with another well-known Babylonian family, the EGIBI.

Wunsch 1993

Iddin-Sin

King of Simurrum, a city in the Transtigris area, a contemporary of ISHBI-ERRA of Isin.

Frayne 1990: 708

Ididish

Ruler (*šakkanakku*) of Mari during the Old Akkadian period (*c.* 2266–2206), who was the first of the military governors bearing this title. He was appointed to the office by NARAM-SIN of Agade. He is also mentioned in inscribed votive gifts presented by his daughters.

Durand 1985: 157–8

Idrimi

King of Mukish, son of ILIMILIMMA, a predecessor of NIQMEPA (beginning of 15th century). He left a report of his life's events on an inscribed statue which was discovered in the temple of Alalakh. According to this account his father was forced to flee from Halab (Aleppo) to Emar. Idrimi spent seven years in the desert in exile, becoming king after he had sworn an oath of allegiance to the Mitanni king Barattarna. He also formed an alliance with another ruler, Pilliya of Kizzuwatna, in Cilicia.

Klengel 1992: 87–9; Dietrich and Loretz 1981: 201–69; Kuhrt 1995: 289–91

Ige-halki

Little-known Elamite king (*c.* 1320), who after the defeat of HURBATILA founded a new dynasty.

Hinz 1972: 111; 1976–80, in RlA 5: 37; 1975, in CAH II/2: 383; Carter and Stolper 1984: 36

Igrish-Halam (= Yigrish-Halam)

King (*en*) of Ebla of the period covered by the archives that were discovered in the Ebla palace (*c.* 2500).

Pettinato 1986: 66–73; Klengel 1992: 27

Ikunum

Old Assyrian ruler, son of ERISHUM I (20th century). He is known from inscriptions found in the Assyrian trading colony Kültepe, as well as in a later text by SHALMANESER III, where he is said to have restored the walls of the city Assur.

Grayson 1987: 41–4

Iku(n)-Shamagan

Early Dynastic king of Mari, attested on an inscribed stone vase and a well-preserved statuette, showing him with a long beard and shaved head and a confidently smiling countenance. His name also appears on other votive offerings and statues.

Parrot 1956: 208; Braun-Holzinger 1977: 74f.; Gelb and Kienast 1990: 9–11

Iku-Shamash
Early Dynastic king of Mari. He dedicated his statue to the god Shamash.

Kupper 1976–80, in RlA 5: 46

Ikur-Shar
King of Mari, known from the Ebla texts as independent ruler of the city and contemporary of the Eblaite king EBRIUM (c. 2500).

Pettinato 1986: 115–17

Ili-hadda
Assyrian high official (šukallu rabū) during the reign of ASHUR-NIRARI III, also known as 'king of Hanilgabat' and addressed as 'king of Assyria' in an insulting letter sent by the Babylonian king ADAD-SHUMA-USUR that was preserved on Neo-Assyrian copies.

Grayson 1972: 137

Ili-Ishar
Ruler (šakkanakku) of Mari in the Ur III period (c. 2084–2072). A brick inscription commemorates a canal building project.

Durand 1985: 151

Ilimilimma
King of Aleppo, successor (and son?) of NIQMEPA, father of IDRIMI (c. 1500).

Klengel 1992: 89; Kuhrt 1995: 290–1

Iltani
Queen of Karana, daughter of Samu-Addu, king of Karana at the time of SHAMSHI-ADAD I. She married AQBA-HAMMU, who succeeded to the throne of Karana, displacing her brother Ashkur-Addu. The palace archives of Tell al Rimah (probably Qatara, part of the kingdom of Karana) contain a large number of letters written by and to the queen, who was responsible for the running of the palace, especially textile manufacture and food provisions. During her husband's frequent absences from the city she acted as his deputy, like her counterpart and contemporary, SHIBTU at Mari. The letters suggest that she had spent some years in exile in Eshnunna.

Dalley et al. 1976: 31–162; Dalley 1984: 101–5

Ilu(a)-kabkabi
Amorite chief, ruler of Terqa (19th century), father of SHAMSHI-ADAD I. According to the Mari Eponym List he fought in the Mari region and took the town of Suprum. Another Mari letter gives details of the war between Ilu-kabkabi and YAGGID-LIM and his son YAHDUN-LIM.

Yuhong 1994: 66–70

Ilushuma

Old Assyrian ruler, son of Shallim-ahhum, contemporary of the Babylonian king SUMU-ABUM (*c*. 1960–1939). He opened trade with cities of Babylonia, especially in copper. It was probably in his reign that Assyrian commercial links with Anatolia were set up, leading to the establishment of trading colonies there. A building inscription commemorates that he restored the Ishtar temple at Assur.

Edzard 1976–80, in RlA 5: 63; Larsen 1976; Grayson 1987: 15–18

Ilussa-amur

Prophetess from Assur, probably attached to the temple there. She sent several oracles to ESARHADDON.

Parpola 1997: L, 7

Imdi-ilum

Assyrian trader in Cappacia (*c*. late 20th century) whose archive containing some 200 texts was discovered at Kültepe. He was a close associate of PUSHU-KENU.

Larsen 1982

Immerum

Ruler of Sippar (1880–1845) at a time when the city was still relatively independent of Babylon. Although he did not use the title of king (*lugal*) he assumed public responsibility in his domain, building a temple, restoring public buildings and canals. The *gagum*, the residence of *nadītum* women dedicated to the local sun god, seems to have come to prominence in his time. His diplomatic activities are mentioned in some of the Tell-ed-Der letters.

Harris 1975: 2–4; Edzard 1957: 129; Yuhong 1994: 31

Ini-Teshup

Hittite viceroy of Carchemish, son and successor of SHAHURUNUWA (13th century). He probably acceded to the throne during the reign of HATTUSILI III (*c*. 1240) and functioned under TUDHALIYA IV. He was a contemporary of BENTESHINA of Amurru and AMMISHTAMRU II of Ugarit.

Klengel 1992: 124–7

Ipiq-Adad I

Governor of Eshnunna during the Old Babylonian period, son of Ur-nimar (*c*. 1950). He used the title 'governor' (*ensi*) throughout his reign and did not prefix his name with the divine determinative. His year names mainly record building activities. His dealings with neighbouring Amorite chiefs are referred to in some of the Tell-ed-Der letters.

Edzard 1976–80, in RlA 5: 151; Frayne 1990: 522–9; Yuhong 1994: 25–8

Ipiq-Adad II

King (*lugal*) of Eshnunna in the Old Babylonian period, son and successor of IBAL-PI-EL I. He greatly enlarged Eshnunna's territory, unified the whole Diyala region, and thereafter all Eshnunna rulers called themselves 'king' (*lugal*). He was a contemporary of SHAMSHI-ADAD I.

Edzard 1976–80, in RlA 5: 151; Frayne 1990: 544–51; Yuhong 1994: 71–9

Irhuleni (= Urhilina)

King of Hamath in Syria (*c.* 853–845). He headed alliances against Assyrian attacks under SHALMANESER III and in 845 jointly with BEN-HADAD of Damascus. His name is also inscribed in Luwian hieroglyphics on votive objects found in Calah. Other inscriptions discovered in Syria record his building activities. His relations with the Assyrians after the collapse of the coalition were good.

Klengel 1992: 213; Hawkins 1972–8, in RlA IV/1: 67–70; 1982, in CAH III/1: 393, 396

Irishum *see* Erishum I

Irkab-Damu (= Yirkab-Damu)

Second of the Ebla kings who ruled over the powerful kingdom in the mid-3rd millennium. He is mentioned in the administrative texts of the city. He married his daughter to the ruler of Emar.

Pettinato 1986: 72–4; Klengel 1992: 27; Archi, in Gordon and Rendsburg 1990: 115–24

Irkabtum

King of Yamhad, son of NIQMEPA, brother of YARIM-LIM III (18th century). According to tablets found at Alalakh he conducted business there.

Wiseman 1976–80, in RlA 5: 164; Klengel 1992: 63

Ir-Nanna (= Urdu-Nanna)

1 High-ranking governor and functionary in the Third Dynasty of Ur who served under AMAR-SIN.
2 Son, who became even more influential under SHU-SIN. Originally governor (*ensi*) of Lagash, he was entrusted with the office of *sukkalmah* which gave him command of several towns and areas along the eastern borders of the realm.

Edzard, in Bottéro *et al.* 1965: 149; Goetze 1963

Isaiah

Hebrew prophet (8th century). The writings collected in the Old Testament as the Book of Isaiah combine the visions of other two other prophets from later periods; chapters 11–35 deal mainly with events from the 8th century, the prophet's lifetime.

He began his public life in the year king UZZIAH died (740). He was active under a number of Judean kings: JOTHAM, AHAZ and HEZEKIAH. He was a contemporary of the prophet MICAH and, like him, concentrated his prophetic activities in Judah and Jerusalem. He advised Ahaz against calling on the Assyrians for aid when PEKAH of Israel and Rezin of Damascus (RAKHIANU) tried to forge an anti-Assyrian alliance. His counsel was not heeded, and Judah became a vassal state of Assyria in 732. He repeated his warnings not to provoke any further retaliation when Ahaz died, and in subsequently under Hezekiah, when a Judean–Egyptian alliance was crushed by SARGON II. He urged the king not to rely on Egypt. In the account of Sennacherib's siege of Jerusalem he reassured Hezekiah's delegates that the Assyrians would withdraw without battle. His last appearance can be dated to the campaign of SENNACHERIB against Jerusalem (701 or 688).

He was married to a woman who was also active as a prophet.

Mitchell 1993, in CAH III/2: 327; Anderson 1960

Ishar-Damu

King (*en*) of Emar, known from the archive of Ebla (*c.* 2500).

Pettinato 1986: 141; Klengel 1992: 27

Ishar-Lim

Military commander of SHAMSHI-ADAD I and YASMAH-ADDU. According to the Mari texts he acted for both rulers.

Klengel 1976–80, in RlA 5: 173–4

Ishbi-Erra

Originally governor of Mari, vassal and high ranking official of the Ur III king IBBI-SIN, he was able to assert considerable influence in Middle Babylonia during the Amorite invasion. A famous correspondence between him and the king of Ur demonstrates how he could hold the capital to ransom over a shipment of grain in a period of acute food shortage in Ur while he controlled Nippur and Isin. Highly skilful at playing one party off against the other and forming alliances with Ur's other enemies, he

eventually gained control over the remnants of the Ur III empire, following the devastation of the capital. Assuming the titles of the former Ur kings, he moved the seat of government to the fortified city of Isin, where he ruled from 2017 to 1985, thus founding a new dynasty.

Gadd 1971, in CAH I/2: 613–17; Edzard 1957: 44–8, 59–66; van Dijk 1978: 189–208; Michalowski, in RlA 6: 57–9

Ishgum-Addu

Ruler (*šakkanakku*) of Mari during the Neo-Sumerian period (*c.* 2135–2127), mentioned in a dynastic list.

Durand 1985: 150

Ishmah-Dagan

Ruler (*šakkanakku*) of Mari during the period of Gutian hegemony (*c.* 2199–2154). His name is preserved on stone tablets commemorating temple building.

Durand 1985: 150

Ishki-Adad (= Ishhi-Adad)

King of Qatna, contemporary and powerful ally of SHAMSHI-ADAD I, whose son YASMAH-ADDU married Ishki-Adad's daughter, BELTUM.

Dossin 1954; Klengel 1992: 65

Ishma-Ia

Professor of mathematics, originally from Kish, who was active in the scribal school of Ebla. One of his mathematical problems was discovered among the academic texts found in the Ebla archives (*c.* 2500).

Pettinato 1986: 95

Ishme-Dagan (of Isin)

Fourth king of the Dynasty of Isin, son of IDDIN-DAGAN (1953–1935). The political stability that his father seems to have enjoyed was less assured during Ishme-Dagan's reign. He had to reinforce the walls of Isin, and there are signs that other cities, especially Larsa, considered themselves beyond his authority. Year names stress his concern with social legislation and maybe tax reforms. He features in several important literary compositions of the time, especially the long poem that commemorates the destruction of Nippur and its glorious restoration under Ishme-Dagan.

Edzard 1957: 74–90; 1976–80, in RlA 5: 194–5; Frayne 1990: 26–46; Kramer 1991

Ishme-Dagan I

Elder son of SHAMSHI-ADAD I, who appointed him as governor of Ekallatum, entrusting to him the difficult task of keeping order on the eastern border protecting Ekallatum and Assyria against the hostile powers of Elam and Eshnunna. From the letters that Shamshi-Adad sent to his other son YASMAH-ADDU (preserved in the Mari archives) we hear that Ishme-Dagan was regarded as tough, manly, reliable and competent.

Kupper 1948; 1953; 1971, in CAH II/1: 16–17; 1976–80, in RlA 5: 195–6

Ishpuini

King of Urartu, son and successor of SARDURI I (*c.* 825–810), contemporary of SHAMSHI-ADAD V, whose *turtānu* (field marshal) conducted military raids against Urartu. Ishpuini expanded Urartu's territory eastward and introduced an important innovation, namely the adaptation of the cuneiform writing system to record Urartian, a language related to Hurrian, for official and administrative purposes. He set up inscribed stelae, some with Assyrian translations. In the later part of his reign he may have associated his son and successor, MENUA, in the kingship. On a joint inscription he records that they built a new cult centre at Musasir, capital of a province near Lake Urmia, in which Ishpuini may also have created a grazing park. He built new fortifications which became the basis for further campaigns.

Barnett 1982, in CAH III/1: 338–41; Kuhrt 1995: 554–6

Ishtar-duri *see* Sarduri III

Ishtar-shumu-eresh

Assyrian scholar, son of Nabu-zeru-lishi, chief scribe (*rab ṭupšarri*) and master (*ummānu*) of ESARHADDON and ASHURBANIPAL. He was the author of seventy-two letters and reports on astrology and divination discovered at Nineveh.

Parpola 1970: 2–19; 1983: 3–33

Ishtup-ilum

Ruler of Mari, probably at the time of the Third Dynasty of Ur. Two of his inscriptions report temple building, another is on a statue.

Gelb and Kienast 1990: 361–2; Durand 1985: 152–9; Frayne 1993: 234–6

Isqimari (previously read as Lamgi-Mari)

Early Dynastic king of Mari, whose inscribed statue showing him with a long beard, parted and plaited hair wound around his head and a fringed coat leaving one shoulder bare. It was found in the Ishtar temple and enabled Tell Hariri to be identified as Mari.

Parrot 1956; Gelb and Kienast 1990: 15

Issar-shumu-eresh

Assyrian scribe and scholar who sent numerous omen reports to the Assyrian court.

Hunger 1992: 3–22

Ithi-Teshup

King of Arrapha (second half of the 15th century). He was a contemporary of SHAUSHTATAR, the king of Mitanni, to whom he paid tribute.

Cassin, in Garelli 1974: 373ff.; Wilhelm 1976–8, in RlA 5: 216

Itti-Marduk-balatu

1 Second king of the Second Dynasty of Isin, son and successor of Marduk-kabit-aheshu (1140–1133). Like his father he tried to interfere in the internal affairs of Assyria by supporting one of the contenders to the throne on the death of ASHUR-DAN I.

Brinkman 1968: 94–8

2 Babylonian businessman, of the third generation of the EGIBI family, which carried on the business to the end of the reign of CAMBYSES II (522); he was married to NUPTAYA.

Ungnad 1941–4; Krecher 1970; Roth 1991: 201.

Ittobaal see Ethba'al

Iturya

Governor of Eshnunna under SHU-SIN and IBBI-SIN during the final years of Ur III, father of SHU-ILIYA.

Yuhong 1994: 2

J

Jehoahaz I of Judah *see* Ahaz

Jehoahaz of Israel

King of Israel, son and successor of
JEHU (*c.* 814–798). During his reign
Israel came under increased pressure
from Syria, especially under HAZA'EL
and Ben-Hadad II.

Mitchell 1982, in CAH III/1: 496–7

Jehoahaz II of Judah

King of Judah, son and successor of
JOSIAH. Soon after his accession phar-
aoh NECHO II had him deported to
Egypt, where he died.

Mitchell 1991, in CAH III/3: 392

Jehoash (= Joash-ben-Ahaziah)

King of Judah, son and successor of
AHAZIAH (835–796). According to II
Kgs. 11 and II Chron. 21 he had
survived the purges of ATHALIAH,
who sought to exterminate the male
descendants of DAVID when she took
power after the death of her son
Ahaziah. Jehoash was concealed by
his aunt, Ahaziah's sister, and her
husband, the high-priest Jehoiada. He
was later supported by the army and
palace guards after being picked as
king by Jehoiada when still a child. He
ruled for forty years. The Baal temple
and other cult places built by Athaliah
were destroyed, and repairs undertaken in the main temple of Jerusalem.
When HAZA'EL of Damascus threatened to invade Judah, he bribed him
with the temple treasure, but this did
not stop Haza'el from raiding Jerusalem. Chronicles and Kings differ in
their descriptions of how he met his
death. According to the former he was
killed in his bed by retainers; the latter
says he was struck down at Beth-
Millo. At any rate he was assassinated
by his own men, perhaps because of
his handling of Haza'el's attack. He
was buried in Jerusalem and succeeded
by his son AMAZIAH.

Mitchell 1982, in CAH III/1: 489–92, 497–8

Jehoiakim

King of Judah, son of JOSIAH and
brother of JEHOAHAZ OF JUDAH,

whose place he took after his deportation to Egypt. He reigned for eleven years (609–598) until the fall of Jerusalem to NEBUCHADNEZZAR II. Jehoiakim had become a Babylonian subject in 607, although he rebelled later, much against the advice of the prophet JEREMIAH. He probably died before the capture of Jerusalem, which was defended by his son JEHOIAKIN.

Mitchell 1991, in CAH III/2: 393–400

Jehoiakin

King of Judah, son and successor of JEHOIAKIM (598–597). Only three months after he ascended the throne, the Babylonian king NEBUCHADNEZ-ZAR II besieged Jerusalem and took the Judean king, together with his family, courtiers and others, captive to Babylon. He appointed Jehoiakin's uncle, Mattaniah, to rule over Judah under the name of Zedekiah. In administrative documents from the palace of Babylon his name appears as the recipient of rations with the title 'king of Judah'. According to II Kgs. 25, 27–30 he was rehabilitated by Nebuchadnezzar's successor AMEL-MARDUK and asked to sit at his table.

Weippert 1976–80, in RlA 5: 274–5

Jehoram of Israel (= Joram ben Ahab)

King of Israel, son and second successor of AHAB (852–841). He was the last king of the Omrid dynasty. Early in his reign he fought unsuccessfully against MESHA of Moab, together with his brother JEHOSHAPHAT of Judah. He was killed by his general JEHU, who had allied himself with Jehoram's enemy, HAZA'EL of Damascus.

Weippert 1976–80, in RlA 5: 275; Mitchell 1982, in CAH III/1: 481, 482–3

Jehoram of Judah (= Joram)

King of Judah, son and successor of JEHOSHAPHAT, he married ATHALIAH, the daughter of AHAB of Israel (848–841). According to II Kgs. 8:6–24) and II Chron. 2:21 Edom revolted against Judah and became independent despite Jehoram's attempt to regain control. Other calamities, such as Philistine and Arab incursions into the southern regions of Judah, were attributed to Jehoram's deviation from Yahweh worship. All his sons except the youngest, AHA-ZIAH, were killed defending the country. Jehoram suffered from a stomach ailment from which he died. He was buried in Jerusalem, possibly without full burial rites and not in a royal tomb.

Mitchell 1982, in CAH III/1: 484–5

Jehoshaphat

King of Judah, son and successor of ASA (870–848). The biblical accounts in Chronicles (II Chron. 17, 18) and Kings (I Kgs. 22:42, 43, 46) refer to his far-reaching reorganisation of the administration by appointing judges and governors in the provincial cities of Judah, as well as priests and heads of families to deal with local issues. He fortified these cities and provided them with troops to protect Judah from her neighbours, including Israel. His religious orthodoxy was viewed favourably by the Jewish chroniclers, but they criticised his decision to form an alliance with Israel, ratified by the marriage of AHAB's daughter ATHALIAH to his son JEHORAM. With JEHORAM OF ISRAEL, the son of Ahab who was then king of Israel, he made a joint attack against MESHA of Moab, though the outcome was not conclusive. The alliance seems to have impressed the southern peoples as well; Jehoshaphat received tribute from the Philistines and Arabs. During his last year he ruled together with his son Jehoram.

Mitchell 1982, in CAH III/1: 474–5, 481–3

Jehu

King of Israel who succeeded the last Omrid king, JEHORAM OF ISRAEL, after he had assassinated him in a military coup (II Kgs. 9:21–4) (841–814). He also killed the queen-mother, the Phoenician princess JEZEBEL. According to a newly discovered fragment of the Tel Dan stele, HAZA'EL of Damascus took credit for the murder of the Omrids and the Judean king AHAZIAH who was at the court at the time. Jehu as Jehoram's general, may have joined the alliance of the twelve kings against SHALMANESER III led by Haza'el, which was defeated in 845. As a result of his vassalage to Haza'el, areas previously under Israelite control went to Damascus. The Black Obelisk of Shalmaneser III shows Jehu kissing the ground before the Assyrian king on the occasion of delivering tribute.

Weippert 1976–80, in RlA 5: 275–6; Schneider

1996; Schniedewind 1996; Mitchell 1982, in CAH III/1: 488–97

Jeremiah

Hebrew prophet who was active for some forty years, during the reigns of JOSIAH, JEHOAHAZ II, JEHOIAKIM, JEHOIAKIN and ZEDEKIAH until the fall of Jerusalem in 587. In his advice to these rulers he warned consistently against provoking the anger of the Babylonians, who had gained the upper hand in Syria-Palestine after NEBUCHADNEZZAR II's defeat of the Egyptians at Carchemish. The situation became even more serious after the first fall of Jerusalem in 597, when the royal family and the elite of the city were taken to Babylon. The appointed vassal ruler Zedekiah revolted against the Babylonians, despite Jeremiah's warnings, and the city was besieged. When the prophet urged surrender he was arrested by Zedekiah as a traitor. When the city finally fell and the king was taken prisoner, Jeremiah was released and treated well, and joined the new governor GEDALIAH. He was forced to flee to Egypt after the latter's murder, along with Baruch, his secretary. In Egypt he prophesied an attack on the country by the Babylonians, and rebuked the Jews for their idolatrous practices. Nothing is known about the circumstances of his death.

Mitchell 1991, in CAH III/2: 392–413

Jeroboam I

King of Israel, son of Nebat (931–910), of the tribe of Ephraim.

He was supervisor of forced labour for SOLOMON and became the first king to rule over the northern kingdom. According to I Kgs. 11:31, the prophet Ahija-ben-Shiloh prophesied that he would become the ruler over the northern tribes. When Solomon sought to kill Jeroboam, he fled to Egypt. The resentment felt by the north against the obligations imposed by the king led to demands for independence. On the accession of Solomon's son REHOBOAM, the situation was exploited by Jeroboam newly returned from Egypt. This led to the secession from Judah and the establishment of the northern kingdom of Israel. The invasion of the Egyptian pharaoh SHOSHENQ proved disruptive for both kingdoms and is well attested archaeologically at several sites. Since Jerusalem remained within the southern kingdom, Jeroboam developed alternative cult centres in the north, of which the Old Testament redactor of Kings disapproved. His residence was Tirzah, which served as capital until the foundation of Samaria.

Mitchell 1982, in CAH III/1: 451–2, 456–61; Kuhrt 1995: 456–7

Jeroboam II

King of Israel, son and successor of JOASH (782–753). Though little is said about him in the Old Testament, he reigned for a long period of peace and prosperity, partly as a result of ADAD-NIRARI III's pacification of the Arameans. He defeated the king of Damascus and managed to restore previously lost territories. He also profited from having gained control over the lucrative trade routes coming from the Transjordan to the Phoenician coast.

Mitchell 1982, in CAH III/1: 501–3

Jezebel

Phoenician princess, daughter of ETH-BA'AL, king of Tyre and Sidon (c. 880–841). She was married to AHAB, king of Israel, in a dynastic alliance set up by her father-in-law OMRI, who wanted to form closer links with the wealthy Phoenician neighbours. She is presented as introducing 'alien' gods, whose priests provoked the fierce condemnation from the prophet ELIJAH. Her high-handedness in assuming absolute royal prerogatives in the matter of Naboth's vineyard (I Kgs. 21) forms part of this negative image. It has been suggested that a seal inscribed 'YZBL' may have been hers. After her husband's death she held a highly honoured position as queen-mother during the reigns of her sons AHAZIAH and JEHORAM. When JEHU began his revolt and killed Jehoram, she showed no signs of fear, but mocked the usurper and met her end with courage and dignity.

Mitchell 1982, in CAH III/1: 463, 470–1, 473; Ackroyd, in Cameron and Kuhrt 1983: 245–59

Joash (= Jehoash ben Jehoahaz)

King of Israel, son and successor of JEHOAHAZ (798–782). He ruled at a time when the Assyrians under ADAD-NIRARI III were campaigning in the west with renewed vigour. A stele of Adad-nirari record that a certain

Ia-'a-su, a 'Samarian', paid tribute to him in Damascus; this probably refers to Joash. Taking advantage of Damascus' defeat, the Judean king AMAZIAH began a campaign against Edom, supported by Israelite mercenaries. He had trouble with these unruly soldiers and challenged Joash to a fight. In the ensuing war the Israelites won the upper hand. Joash captured Amaziah and took him to Jerusalem and there he plundered the palace and temple treasuries and took hostages back to Samaria.

Mitchell 1982, in CAH III/1: 497–501

Josiah

King of Judah, son of AMON (640–609). When he was only 8 years old he was put on the throne when his father was assassinated in a palace revolt. Unlike his forebears, MANASSEH and Amon, he is said by the Old Testament chroniclers to have turned back to Yahweh and to have concentrated on the official cult in the temple at Jerusalem. His long reign was relatively untroubled, for Assyria was in decline during ASHURBANIPAL's last years and under his successors Josiah may have gained independence. When the Babylonians and Medes destroyed the Assyrian city of Nineveh in 612, the last Assyrian king ASHUR-UBALLIT II, fled to Harran and the Egyptians came to his aid. According to II Kgs. 23, 29, Josiah challenged the pharaoh NECHO II near Megiddo and was mortally wounded in combat.

Mitchell 1991, in CAH III/2: 383–92

Jotham

King of Judah, son and successor of UZZIAH (740–735), with whom he shared the regency during the latter's last years as a leper. He was responsible for building the Upper Gate of the Temple and an extension to the wall of Ophel. According to the Book of Chronicles he exacted tribute from the Ammonites. Towards the end of his reign the king of Israel, PEKAH, invaded Judah with his ally, Rezin of Damascus (RAKHIANU). In his last two years his son AHAZ exercised kingship with him as official co-regent.

Mitchell 1993, in CAH III/2: 328–9

K

Kabti-ilani-Marduk

Babylonian scribe, probably a contemporary of NABU-APLA-IDDINA (9th century). He was the author of the literary work known as the *Erra Epic*, which describes the turmoil and breakdown of law and order in the wake of the Sutian invasion of Babylonia. Kabti-ilani-Marduk states that the work was revealed to him in a dream.

Brinkman 1982, in CAH III/1: 293; Foster 1993: 771–805

Kadashman-Enlil I

Kassite king of Babylonia during the Amarna period (*c.* 1374–1360). The letters from Amarna concern dynastic marriages between the ruling houses of Babylon and Egypt. One of the Babylonian princesses had already been sent to Egypt when pharaoh AMENOPHIS III demanded another daughter of Kadashman-Enlil but the pharaoh refused to reciprocate with an Egyptian princess. Cuneiform inscriptions document that he restored temples at Nippur and Larsa.

Brinkman 1976: 130–45; 1976–80, in RlA 5: 285; Saggs 1995: 117; Liverani 1979: 21–33; Moran 1992: 1–11

Kadashman-Enlil II

Twenty-fifth king of the Kassite dynasty of Babylon (*c.* 1263–1255). He engaged in various building projects, especially in Nippur, as votive inscriptions testify. He also corresponded with the Hittite king HATTUSILI III.

Brinkman 1976: 131–45; 1976–80, in RlA 5: 285

Kadashman-Harbe I

Sixteenth (?) king of the Kassite dynasty of Babylon, father of KURI-GALZU I (around 1400). Although legal texts mention his name, the chronology of his reign and its history remain unknown.

Brinkman 1976: 146–8; 1976–80, in RlA 5: 286

Kadashman-Harbe II

Thirtieth ruler of the Kassite dynasty of Babylon, successor of ENLIL-NADIN-SHUMI. He ruled for only one year (1223) during the Assyrian hegemony initiated by TUKULTI-NINURTA I.

Brinkman 1976: 148–52; 1976–80, in RlA 5: 286

Kadashman-Turgu

Twenty-fourth king of the Kassite dynasty of Babylon, son and successor of NAZI-MARUTTASH (1281–1264). He ruled for eighteen years and seems to have had a relatively peaceful time judging by the large number of votive objects inscribed with his name, quite a few of which bear the title 'king of the world' (*šar kiššati*). He repaired the ziggurat at Nippur. He was a contemporary of the Hittite king HATTUSILI III, with whom he corresponded, pledging support in case of difficulties with the Egyptians.

Brinkman 1976: 153–65; 1976–80, in RlA 5: 286

Kaku

King of Ur (late 24th century) According to inscriptions by the Akkadian king RIMUSH, he led a rebellion against Akkad and was captured when Ur was attacked.

Gadd 1971, in CAH I/2: 113, 435, 459; Sollberger and Kupper 1971: IIA2b, c; Frayne 1993: 1.2.3, 1.2.4

Kamanis

Syro-Hittite king of Carchemish (*c.* 738). He is known from some statues and monuments inscribed in hieroglyphic Luwian that were set up by himself and his predecessor YARIRIS with whom he shared the regency for some time. He mentions the Urartian king SARDURI II and was probably a contemporary of SHAMSHI-ILU, the Assyrian commander in chief.

Hawkins 1982, in CAH III/1: 406–7; 1979: 157ff.

Kamash-khalta

King of Moab, contemporary and vassal of ASHURBANIPAL. He managed to capture a chief of the Arabs whom he delivered to his Assyrian overlord.

Weippert 1976–80, in RlA 5: 328

Kandalanu

King of Babylon, successor of SHAMASH-SHUMA-UKIN (647–627). Nothing is known about his background and his reign remains equally obscure. His name is known only from king lists and chronicles; other events must be reconstructed on the basis of economic tablets. He was installed by the Assyrian king ASHURBANIPAL soon after the repression of the revolt by Shamash-shuma-ukin; under close Assyrian supervision, he presided over the gradual recovery of the country after the ravages of the civil war. Assyrian power declined towards the end of Kandalanu's reign and there was another period of unrest and civil disorder after his death in 627.

Brinkman 1993, in CAH III/2: 60–3; Oates 1993, in CAH III/2: 166–71; Kuhrt 1995: 542–4

Karahardash

Twentieth (?) king of the Kassite dynasty of Babylon who ruled briefly (1333) at the time of the Assyrian king ASHUR-UBALLIT I, whose daughter MUBALLITAT-SHERUA was Karahardash's mother. He was dethroned and probably killed in a Kassite revolt.

Brinkman 1976: 166–8

Karaindash

Kassite king of Babylonia. He ruled during the lifetime of the Assyrian king ASHUR-BEL-NISHESHU (around 1413). He built a new temple to the goddess Inanna at Uruk that shows various unusual architectural features. In his building inscriptions discovered at Uruk he calls himself 'king of Babylon, king of Sumer and Akkad, king of the Kassites, king of Karduniash'. He also corresponded with the king of Egypt as one of the Amarna letters reports.

Brinkman 1976: 169–72; Saggs 1995: 116–17

Kashshaia

Babylonian princess, eldest daughter of NEBUCHADNEZZAR II. One surviving cuneiform text reports that she received quantities of 'blue wool for a sumptuous garment'. Another tablet pertains to a donation of land to the temple of Ishtar. She was married to NERIGLISSAR, who became king of Babylon in 559.

Joannès 1980

Kashshu-nadin-ahi

Third ruler of the Second Sealand Dynasty, successor of EA-MUKIN-ZERI (1008–1006). Little is known of his brief reign, other than that the country experienced hard times and famine, which caused the regular food offerings at the Sippar temple to be suspended.

Brinkman 1968: 156–7

Kashtiliash I

According to the king list he was the third king of the Kassite Dynasty of Babylon, son and successor of AGUM I (around 1660).

Brinkman 1976: 173–4

Kashtiliash IV

Twenty-eighth king of the Kassite Dynasty of Babylon, successor and possibly son of SHAGARAGTI-SHURIASH (1232–1225). He was deposed by the Assyrian king TUKULTI-NINURTA I.

Brinkman 1976: 173–89

Katuwas

King of Carchemish (c. 880?). He left a number of inscribed statues at Carchemish and from these monuments we know that he was the fourth in a dynastic line beginning with Suhis I. He mentions military engagements, pious deeds and building works.

Hawkins 1982, in CAH III/1: 385, 387

Khaianu

King of Sam'al, successor of Gabal
(858–853). He fought on the side of
Akhuni of Bit-Adini and other local
rulers against SHALMANESER III and
submitted to him in 853.

Hawkins 1982, in CAH III/1: 391–2

Khanni see Hanne

Khelaruada

King of Melid (c. 780–750). His
territory was invaded by the Urartians
at least twice, once in 783 by the
Urartian king ARGISHTI I and then
again by SARDURI II in 750.

Hawkins 1982, in CAH III/1: 405

Khita see Hita

Khulli

King of Tabal, 'a son of a nobody', i.e.
not of royal descent, according to
TIGLATH-PILESER III, who placed him
on the throne of Tabal as a puppet
ruler to replace WASSURME (c. 730).
For some unspecified reason he was
later deported to Assyria by SHALMA-
NESER V but subsequently restored by
SARGON II.

Hawkins 1982, in CAH III/1: 415, 416, 418,
419

Kiden-Hutran

Elamite king, successor and brother of
Unpahash-napirisha, last of the
dynasty founded by IGE-HALKI
(around 1215). He was one of the
great Elamite warrior kings who
directed his attention towards Baby-

lonia, which was under the direct
control of the Assyrians. Their king
TUKULTI-NINURTA I had established
ENLIL-NADIN-SHUMI as a puppet ruler
on the Babylonian throne. Kiden-
Hutran crossed the Tigris and conquered Nippur, killing most of the
inhabitants. He also attacked Der and
destroyed its temple. The Babylonian
king fled.

In the reign of the third vassal ruler
ADAD-SHUM-IDDINA, Kiden-Hutran
struck again, this time taking Isin
and Marad and he returned victorious, laden with booty. Kiden-
Hutran's further fate is unknown.

Hinz 1972: 119–21; CAH II/2: 387–8; Kuhrt
1995: 371–2; Carter and Stolper 1984: 35–6;
38–9

Kikkia

Old Assyrian king (probably 20th
century), mentioned in the Assyrian
King List. In a much later building
inscription by ASHUR-RIM-NISHESHU
he is credited with having built the
earliest wall of the city of Assur. He
may have been the first ruler to free
Assur from the domination of the
Third Dynasty of Ur.

Grayson 1972: 39–40

Kilamuwa

Syro-Hittite king of Sam'al, a contemporary of SHALMANESER III,
(840–830). He does not feature in
the Assyrian records but he left an
inscribed stele written in Phoenician,
with an attendant portrait figure. This
gives an account of the dynasty of
Gabbar and the vicissitudes faced by a

small state in turbulent times. He claims to have 'hired' the services of the Assyrian king against the ruler of Que.

Hawkins 1982, in CAH III/1: 398–9; Orthmann 1971: 66f.; Donner and Röllig 1962–8: II, 32f.

Kirikiri

Governor of Eshnunna during the Old Babylonian period, successor and perhaps brother of NUR-AHUM. He bears an Elamite name and seems to have established amicable relations with Elam, as well as keeping up alliances with Amorite chiefs.

Frayne 1990; Yuhong 1994: 11–13

Kiru

Daughter of ZIMRI-LIM, king of Mari, she was married to Haya-Sumu, ruler of Ilansura, as part of the Mari king's dynastic alliances. She was given political authority in her own right and seems to have functioned as mayor of Ilansura, a unique occurrence in the ancient Near East. Her correspondence, recovered from the Mari archives, reveals that she advised the king on military and diplomatic matters, but also speaks of deep personal unhappiness in her marriage which was (probably) eventually dissolved.

Batto 1974: 42–8; Dossin 1967

Ku-Baba

Early Dynastic queen of Kish, known only from later sources. She is mentioned in the Sumerian King List, where she is described as 'woman of wine' (innkeeper?) who ruled for 100 years. As a legendary ruler of old she also features in later divination tablets.

Gadd 1971, in CAH I/2: 115; Jacobsen 1939; Goetze 1947: 264

Kubatum

Royal lady at the court of Ur during the Third Dynasty of Ur. The inscription on an agate pearl found at Ur identifies her as SHU-SIN's 'beloved' *lukur* but in other texts she is called his *nin* (reigning queen?). Offerings were made to her statue, a practice usually reserved for deified kings. A famous Sumerian poem celebrates Kubatum giving birth to Shu-Sin's child, an event that is juxtaposed with highly erotic praise of the king.

Steinkeller 1981; Michalowski 1982; Alster 1985: 134ff.; Leick 1994: 112–14

Kudur-Enlil

Twenty-sixth king of the Kassite dynasty of Babylon (1254–1246). His name occurs on various votive and building inscriptions, as well as on numerous economic texts.

Brinkman 1976: 190–204

Kudur-Mabuk

Old Babylonian leader of an Amorite tribe who established himself in the region of Larsa. He gained control over the city, which was then ruled by SILLI-ADAD, and appointed his own son WARAD-SIN as king instead. He is thought to have exercised considerable influence during his reign and that of RIM-SIN, his other son, who succeeded Warad-Sin.

Edzard 1957: 168–74

Kudur-Nahhunte

Elamite king, son and successor of HALLUSHU-INSHUSHINAK (693–692). He ascended the throne after his father was killed in an uprising. He was attacked by SENNACHERIB, who pursued him into the mountains until frost and snow forced him to retreat. Kudur-Nahhunte was murdered in July 692 in a revolt.

Hinz 1972: 149

Kudurru

Governor of Nippur (*c.* 745–732), businessman and one of the most influential citizens of his age. He was a contemporary of MUKIN-ZERI and NABONASSAR. Some of the letters he sent to these two, as well as other leading figures, are preserved in the governor's archive. They concern his extensive trading and business interests and document his considerable political influence.

Cole 1996

Kunshimatum

Important woman in the kingdom of Mari, well known from the correspondence found in the city. She was a daughter of SHAMSHI-ADAD I and the sister of YASMAH-ADDU, governor of Mari. The latter installed her as high priestess of the god Dagan at Terqa. She maintained this important position also under ZIMRI-LIM, who took

an interest in her welfare as the Mari letters testify.

Batto 1974: 24–5; Dossin 1967; Durand 1985b: 396–8

Kurash *see* Cyrus I

Kurigalzu I

Seventeenth (?) king of the Kassite Dynasty of Babylon, successor of KADASHMAN-HARBE I (early 14th century). He established friendly relations with Egypt, consolidated by the marriage of a Babylonian princess to the pharaoh AMENOPHIS III. This instigated the lively exchange of gifts and letters that is so well documented in the Amarna tablets. His policy of pacification seems to have been successful as under his rule, Babylon achieved the status of a major international power. He reintroduced old Mesopotamian royal titles and used the divine determinative to write his name.

He founded a new fortified city called Dur-Kurigalzu (modern Aqar-Quf, near Baghdad) to guard the trade route linking Babylonia to the Iranian plateau. The extensive ruins of the ziggurat remain to this day. The archaeological excavations of the nearby palace and temple ruins show that he made use of innovative building methods such as vaults and arches. It was the main royal residence of the Kassite kings for centuries to come.

Brinkman 1976: 205f.; Cassin, in Bottéro *et al.* 1966: II, 21

Kurigalzu II

Twenty-second king of the Kassite dynasty of Babylon, son of BURNA-BURIASH II and father of NAZI-MARUTTASH (1332–1308). According to the Synchronistic History he was installed by the Assyrian king ASHUR-UBALLIT I after he had removed the usurper NAZI-BUGASH from the Baby-lonian throne. Chronicle P records his military exploits, such as his victory over Elam and his fight against ENLIL-NIRARI of Assyria which resulted in a defeat and subsequent border align-ments. He also features in various later Babylonian 'epics'. Contempor-ary inscriptions abound, mainly con-cerning building projects, especially from the Kassite royal city Dur-Kurigalzu. He also restored the temple of Inanna at Uruk, as commemorated on inscribed bricks found at Eanna.

Brinkman 1976: 205–46; Grayson 1975: 223–4; Cassin, in Bottéro *et al.* 1966: 27f.

Kurti (previously read Matti)

Anatolian king of Atuna, a small principality (*c.* 732). He seems to have enjoyed good relations with the Assyr-ians, for in *c.* 718 he was given control over Shinukhtu by SARGON II when the latter removed the local ruler because of his treachery.

Hawkins 1982, in CAH III/1: 418, 419

Kurtiwaza *see* Shattiwaza

Kurunta

Anatolian king of Tarhuntassa, cousin of the Hittite king TUDHALIYA IV. A treaty between Tudhaliya and Kurunta

is preserved on a bronze tablet which assigns vassal status to the latter.

Otten 1988; Beal 1993

Kushtashpi

Syro-Hittite king of Kummuh (*c.* 755–732). He is known from Assyrian and Urartian sources. SAR-DURI II reports in his annals that he received rich tribute from Kushtashpi after he had taken Khalpa in *c.* 747 and that he joined the anti-Assyrian coalition headed by Urartu. He fought for this alliance against TIGLATH-PILESER III in 743 and this resulted in the rout of the Urartian army and its allies. Since Kushtashpi returned to the throne afterwards he must have been pardoned for his enforced dis-loyalty to Assyria and carried on ruling as vassal.

Hawkins 1982, in CAH III/1: 412; Barnett, in ibid.: 350

Kutik-Inshushinak (= Puzur-Inshushinak)

Elamite king, twelfth and last of the First Dynasty of Awan, probably grandson of HITA, during whose life-time he was a vassal of NARAM-SIN of Akkad and governor of Susa. His influence and power grew in the reign of Naram-Sin's successor SHAR-KALI-SHARRI. Still as a vassal of Akkad he led a successful campaign against rebellious territories in the Upper Diyala region and he added a further series of victories over hostile forces in Elam, all of which are inscribed on a limestone statue of Kutik-Inshushinak. He succeeded Hita to the throne of Awan around 2240 and henceforth his titles show that Mesopotamian political influence had disappeared and that Elam experienced a period of independence and prosperity. A fair number of inscriptions have survived from this time, some bilingual, in Elamite and Akkadian, others in a linear form of Elamite. They mainly concern the pious deeds of the king but display a strong sense of national pride. During the upheavals of the Gutians' rise to power in Mesopotamia, the dynasty of Awan also became a casualty and Elam was once again plunged into historical obscurity until the dynasty of Shimashki at the turn of the 3rd to the 2nd millennium.

Hinz 1971, in CAH 1/2: 652–4; 1972: 78–9; Carter and Stolper 1984: 16–23; Gelb and Kienast 1990: 321–38

Kutir-nahhunte

Elamite king, successor and son of SHUTRUK-NAHHUNTE, who had founded a new dynasty (1155–1150). After his father's invasion and conquest of Babylonia in which he had taken part, he was nominated regent there, though the official ruler was a Kassite ENLIL-NADIN-AHI. This caused widespread resistance in which, according to a later chronicle, the Babylonian king was implicated. In retaliation Kutir-Nahhunte swept over the land 'like a flood' and turned Babylon and her temples into a heap of ruins. Enlil-nadin-ahi, as well as the cult statue of the god Marduk, were taken away to Elam.

Elamite sources record mainly his building activities, especially at the temple of Inshushinak at Susa.

Brinkman 1968: 88; Hinz 1972: 126–7; Carter and Stolper 1984: 40–1

Kuzi-Teshub

Neo-Hittite king of Carchemish (c. 1200). On his inscribed seal he declares himself to be a direct descendent of the Hittite royal family and bears the title 'great king'. Later kings of Carchemish in turn claim him as their ancestor. He seems also to have been the ancestor of at least two kings of Melid.

Hawkins 1988

L

La'erab (previously read Lasirab)
King of the Gutians. The name of this
king appears in fragmentary form in
the Sumerian King List. An inscription
on a mace threatens any usurper of his
inscription.

Gelb and Kienast 1990: 295; Hallo, in RlA 3/9:
708–20; Frayne 1993: 228

Lamgi-Mari *see* **Isqimari**

Lipit-Eshtar
Fifth king of the dynasty of Isin, son of
ISHME-DAGAN (1934–1896). Little is
know about the political events of his
reign. He was responsible for building
in Ur, especially the Gipar, where his
daughter Enninsunzi, was installed as
entum priestess. Like his predecessor
he was concerned with social justice
and proclaimed periodic adjustment
of debts, forced labour, etc. He is
primarily remembered for his legal
and fiscal reforms contained in the
'Code of Lipit-Eshtar', which regu-
lates, among other matters, the parti-
cipation of certain parts of the
population in public works and tries
to set limits to debt enslavement.

Edzard 1957: 93–8; Steele 1948

Liqtum
Princess from Mari, sister of ZIMRI-
LIM. She married Adal-shenni, king of
Burundum, who was an important
ally of Zimri-Lim. Surviving letters by
Liqtum show that she enjoyed royal
prerogatives and was in charge of the
women of the palace, who included
the daughter of ISHME-DAGAN. It
seems that after her husband's defeat
by the hands of the king of Elulut she
ended up in the harem of the victor.

Marello 1997

Lubarna I
Anatolian king of Unqi (= Pattin)
(*c.* 870). He submitted to ASHURNA-
SIRPAL II by offering tribute, troops
and hostages.

Grayson 1982, in CAH III/1: 256

Lubarna II

Anatolian king of Unqi (= Pattin) (*c.* 831), a contemporary of SHALMA-NESER III. According to Assyrian sources he was assassinated by a usurper.

Grayson 1982, in CAH III/1: 263

Lugalanda

Early Dynastic Sumerian ruler and priest of Lagash, son of ENENTARZI (*c.* 24th century).

Sollberger and Kupper 1971: IC10a–b

Lugalannimundu

Early Dynastic Sumerian king of Adab, mentioned in the Sumerian King List as having been defeated by Mari. A long inscription from a slightly later period records a revolt of neighbouring cities which he put down successfully.

Gadd 1971, in CAH I/2: 115

Lugaldalu

Early Dynastic Sumerian king of Adab whose stone statue bearing his name was found there.

Sollberger and Kupper 1971: IF3a; Gadd 1971, in CAH I/2: 115

Lugalkineshedudu

Early Dynastic Sumerian king of Uruk, contemporary of ENMETENA of Lagash, with whom he made a treaty. The inscriptions on his votive objects claim sovereignty over Umma, Ur and Kish.

Sollberger and Kupper 1971: IEa–d

Lugalkisalsi

Early Dynastic Sumerian king of Uruk, son of LUGALKINESHEDUDU.

Sollberger and Kupper 1971: IE2a

Lugalzagesi

Early Dynastic king of Uruk (*c.* 2370). He started his career as governor (*ensi*) of Umma. He sacked the city and temples of Lagash, the traditional enemy of Umma, as URUINIMGINA deplored in his inscriptions. His own inscriptions, especially those on a number of votive bowls found at Nippur, describe him at the acme of his success, installed as king of Uruk, holding sway 'from sunrise to sunset', having secured the trade routes from the 'lower sea' (Persian Gulf) to the 'upper sea' (Mediterranean?). In a rather poetic manner he declares that 'all countries lay content in their meadows' under his shepherdship. He is also mentioned in the Sumerian King List as having reigned for twenty-five years. He was eventually defeated by SARGON OF AKKAD, who 'brought him in a yoke to the gate of Enlil' at Nippur thus ending the Early Dynastic period in Sumer and the Third Dynasty of Uruk.

Cooper 1986: 95–105; Gadd 1971, in CAH I/2: 143–4; Charvát 1978; Westenholz, A. 1987, in RlA VII/1–2: 155–7

Luh-ishshan

Elamite king, eighth ruler of the house of Peli, son (or father?) of Hiship-rashini. He is known from Elamite inscriptions and Akkadian sources. He was a vassal of SARGON OF AKKAD, who had invaded his country and carried away large amounts of booty.

Gadd 1971, in CAH I/2: 432; Hinz 1971, in ibid.: 649; 1972: 73; Carter and Stolper 1984: 11–12, 64 n.52

Lygdamis *see* **Dugdamme**

M

Maacah

Judean queen, favourite wife of king REHOBOAM, mother of ABIJAH, perhaps also the grandmother of ASA, who for some time had the position of 'Great Lady'. When she was accused of having introduced the cult practice of the Canaanite goddess Asherah, Asa had her removed from her position.

Mitchell 1982, in CAH III/1: 462, 463

Manana

Old Babylonian king of Kish, probably originating from Yamutbal, at the time of SUMU-ABUM. He is mainly known from date formulae. He founded a dynasty that was to rule Kish, as well as Babylon, for some time.

Rutten 1958–60

Manasseh

King of Judah, son and successor of HEZEKIAH (687–642). He ruled peacefully as a vassal to Assyria under ESARHADDON and ASHURBANIPAL. According to II Chron. 33 he was taken to Babylon in chains but allowed to return home. The biblical sources reproach the king for his restoration of unorthodox cult practices and the revitalisation of 'high places', for which his foreign wife Meshullemeth is made partly responsible. When he died he was buried in the garden of his palace.

Mitchell 1993, in CAH III/2: 373–81

Mandane

Median princess, daughter of ASTYAGES. According to Herodotus (I 107.1) she married the Persian king CAMBYSES I.

Brosius 1996: 42–5

Manishtusu

Akkadian king, brother and successor of RIMUSH, son of SARGON OF AKKAD (2275–2260). His name, literally 'Who is with him?' may suggest that he was Rimush's twin. The extent of his realm can be gauged from the votive gifts and statues dedicated to him by governors of far-flung places such as Susa. His own inscriptions, mainly written in Akkadian, and often copies of dedicatory texts from inscribed objects, record not only his successful suppression of widespread insurrection but also trade expeditions with military overtones to Anshan and Magan (on the gulf of Oman?) to import semi-precious stones, ivory, timber and gold. A large stone obelisk records his land purchases in the northern parts of Babylonia.

As Assyria was part of his realm, later tradition credits him with the foundation of the Ishtar temple at Nineveh. Like other kings of this dynasty he features in the omen-literature. According to one such text he was killed, like his brother, by his own courtiers 'with their cylinder seals'.

Gadd 1971, in CAH I/2: 437–40; Sollberger and Kupper 1971: IIA3a–d; Hallo and Simpson 1971: 59–60; Goetze 1947: 198; Gelb and Kienast 1990: 75–80, 220–5; Frayne 1993: 74–83; Foster 1982b

Mannu-ki-Arbail

Assyrian official and cohort commander under ESARHADDON (680–673). He is known from economic documents detailing large-scale land purchases.

Fales and Postgate 1992

Mar-biti-ahhe-iddina

Third ruler of the so-called Dynasty of E, son of NABU-MUKIN-APLI and successor of NINURTA-KUDURRI-USUR I (943–). Nothing is known of his reign, not even when it ended.

Brinkman 1968: 175–6

Mar-biti-apla-usur

Only king of the so-called Elamite Dynasty who ruled over Babylonia for five years (985–980). He may have claimed Elamite ancestry; later historical sources count him as a legitimate Babylonian king.

Brinkman 1968: 165–6

Marduk-ahhe-eriba

Ninth king of the Second Dynasty of Isin, successor of ADAD-APLA-IDDINA, he reigned for only six months in 1047 and is only known from one inscribed boundary stone, which records land grants in northern Babylonia.

Brinkman 1968: 144–5

Marduk-apla-iddina I

Thirty-fourth king of the Kassite Dynasty of Babylon, son and successor of MELI-SHIPAK (1171–1159). Several inscribed kudurrus survive which document large donations of land and tax exemptions.

Brinkman 1976: 247–52

Marduk-apla-iddina
(the Chaldean) *see*
Merodach-baladan

Marduk-balassu-iqbi

Babylonian king, son and successor of MARDUK-ZAKIR-SHUMI (c. 818–813). He was fairly old when he acceded to the throne. In his reign the long period of friendly relations with Assyria came to an end. SHAMSHI-ADAD V turned against Babylonia and in 814 and 813 despoiled many cities in the Diyala regions and captured Marduk-balassu-iqbi at Der. He was taken to Assyria where he presumably died.

Brinkman 1968: 205–10

Marduk-nadin-ahhe

Sixth king of the Second Dynasty of Isin, brother of NEBUCHADNEZZAR I, successor and uncle of ENLIL-NADIN-APLI, whom he may have deposed whilst the latter was still a minor (1100–1083).

He built on the successes of his brother Nebuchadnezzar and managed to consolidate Babylonian power in Mesopotamia despite the energetic leadership of his Assyrian contemporary, TIGLATH-PILESER I. According to Assyrian sources he led campaigns against Assyria and early in his reign captured the towns of Ekallate near Assur, carrying off the statues of the gods Adad and Shala to Babylon. A further clash, ending in possible victory for the Babylonians seems to have occurred in his tenth regnal year, according to a passage in a land grant document. The Synchronistic History reports clashes between Assyrian and Babylonian chariotry in the succeeding years when the Assyrians attacked major cities in northern Babylonia, though the outcome was undecided. The following year Tiglath-pileser launched another attack against Babylon, this time capturing Dur-Kurigalzu, Sippar, Opis and Babylon, where he destroyed the royal palace. A severe famine in the 18th year of Marduk-nadin-ahhe, which affected both countries, led to massive incursions of semi-nomadic Aramean tribes

and general unrest. Assyrian sources report that he 'disappeared' at that time and that the Babylonian throne passed to MARDUK-SHAPIK-ZERI.

Brinkman 1968: 119–30

Marduk-shakin-shumi

Assyrian scribe, chief exorcist (*rab āšipu*) of ESARHADDON and ASHURBANIPAL, writer of forty-three surviving letters, mainly concerning magic and medicine.

Parpola 1970: 126–59; 1983: 159–97

Marduk-shapik-zeri

Seventh ruler of the Second Dynasty of Isin, successor of MARDUK-NADIN-AHHE (1082–1070). During his reign the famine in Babylonia, which led to the influx of Aramean tribes seems to have abated. According the Synchronistic History Marduk-shapik-zeri concluded peace with the Assyrian king, ASHUR-BEL-KALA. The same source mentions that he died during the latter's reign.

Brinkman 1968: 130–5

Marduk-shumu-usur

Assyrian scholar, chief exorcist (*rab āšipu*) under ESARHADDON and ASHURBANIPAL, writer of five official letters to the king.

Parpola 1970: 80–4; 1983: 84–5; 1993: 135–40

Marduk-zakir-shumi I

King of Babylon, son and successor of NABU-APLA-IDDINA (*c.* 854–819). He benefited from the good relations his father had consolidated with Assyria when his younger brother Marduk-bel-usate revolted. The Assyrian king SHALMANESER III came to his assistance by attacking the cities loyal to the rebellious faction in the Diyala region. The insurrection could only be quelled after several campaigns in a combined Assyrian and Babylonian effort. In the end Marduk-bel-usate and his entourage, who had fled to the mountains, were captured and executed and Marduk-zakir-shumi was confirmed as rightful king of Babylonia. Towards the end of his reign Marduk-zakir-shumi was in a position to return the favour when a widespread revolt broke out in Assyria. A very fragmentary treaty between him and Shalmaneser's successor SHAMSHI-ADAD V has been thought to suggest that the latter's accession relied heavily on the support of the Babylonian king, who exploited Assyria's temporary weakness to force terms favourable for Babylonia, but the gaps in the text makes it possible to counter this argument. He probably died of old age and passed the throne to his son MARDUK-BALASSU-IQBI.

Brinkman 1968: 192–205; Parpola and Watanabe 1988: XXVI–XXVII, no. 1

Mar-Issar

Assyrian scholar and official under ESARHADDON, whose agent he was in Babylon. He was in charge of the reorganisation of cultic services and the rebuilding of destroyed temples in Babylonia.

Parpola 1997: 281–306

Mati'ilu

Aramean king of Bit-Agusi (8th century). He is known from Assyrian inscriptions as party to a treaty imposed on him by ASHUR-NIRARI V. According to a stele of TIGLATH-PILESER III, he was a central factor of an anti-Assyrian coalition involving SARDURI II of Urartu. He was defeated by Tiglath-pileser in 743. There is also a stele written in Aramaic which contains the terms of a treaty imposed on him by a certain *Br-g'yh*.

Hawkins 1987–90, in RlA 7: 586; 1981, in CAH III/1: 403,7; Donner and Röllig 1962–8: 222–4; Lipiński 1975: 24–57; Lemaire and Durand 1984

Matti *see* Kurti

Mattiwaza *see* Shattiwaza

Mebaragesi (previously read En-mebaragesi)

Early Dynastic king of Kish (*c.* 2700). His laconic line on an alabaster vase: 'Mebaragesi, king of Kish', found at Khafaji, is the earliest surviving Mesopotamian royal inscription. His name with the title *en* also appears in the Sumerian King List as the twenty-second ruler of the first dynasty of Kish, after the Flood. He is said to have made a military excursion into Elam and is named as the father of AGGA. The Tummal texts ascribe the building of the Enlil temple at Nippur to him.

Sollberger and Kupper 1971: IA1a; Edzard, in Bottéro *et al.* 1965, vol. 1: 59–62; Gadd 1971,

in CAH I/2: 110; Hallo and Simpson 1971: 45;
Nissen 1965

Mekubi

Babylonian princess, daughter of the
king of Eshnunna, BILALAMA. She was
married to TAN-RUHURATIR, the son of
the Elamite king NDATTU I, who
succeeded his father to the throne in
about 1945. Mekubi came well provided to Susa, where she founded a
temple to the goddess Inanna.

Gadd 1971, in CAH I/2: 660–1; Hinz 1972: 85;
Frayne 1990; Yuhong 1994: 13

Meli-Shipak

Thirty-third king of the Kassite Dynasty of Babylon, son and successor
of ADAD-SHUMA-USUR (c. 1186–1172).
Little is known about his reign. A
kudurru says that he gave land to his
son and crown-prince MARDUK-APLA-
IDDINA I. Building inscriptions mention work on the Ekur temple at
Nippur and the Egalmah temple in Isin.

Brinkman 1976: 253–9; 1993, in RlA 8 1/2: 52;
Boese 1982

Menachem

King of Israel, founder of the fifth
dynasty of Israelite kings (c. 752–742).
He was originally a military governor
of Tirzah and became king of Israel
after he took Samaria from the usurper Shallum, whom he killed. In II
Kgs. he is described as ruthless. He
became a vassal to the Assyrian king
TIGLATH-PILESER III and collected
substantial amounts of silver from
the citizens of Israel. He was succeeded by his son PEKAHIAH.

Mitchell 1993, in CAH III/2: 322–26b; Shea
1978

Menua

King of Urartu (c. 810–785/780), son
and successor of ISHPUINI, with whom
he was associated in rule. He went on
campaigns with his father and partici-
pated in important cult activities. After
his father's death, Menua continued
the policy of expansion and consolidation. He incorporated the area around
Luhiuni in the southern Transcaucasus
and began the conquest of Mannaean
territories, using mass deportations.
He thus helped to create the powerful
state that lasted until the late 7th
century. He undertook a remarkable
building programme, creating a strategically placed network of fortresses
and defences. He also built temples
dedicated to the chief god Haldi and
embarked on large-scale civic works
such as cisterns, granaries and, most
famously, a canal named after him,
which transported water over a distance of 75 km to the capital city,
Tushpa (modern Van). Many of these
constructions are identified as Menua's work by inscriptions.

Barnett 1982, in CAH III/1: 341–4; Salvini
1993, in RlA 8: 1/2: 63–4

Merneptah

Egyptian pharaoh of the 19th Dynasty, son and successor of RAMESSES
II (1224/1213–1204). His most famous campaign was fought against
the Libyans. In his celebration of that

war, the 'Israel Stele', he briefly mentions the Israelites in Palestine, the earliest attestation of the name. The friendship pact concluded with the Hittites was still in force and Merneptah sent grain to Anatolia when this country suffered a famine.

Kuhrt 1995: 206, 209, 386–7

Merodach-baladan (Babylonian Marduk-apla-iddina II)

Babylonian king, chief of the Chaldean tribe of Bit-Yakin, possibly grandson of ERIBA-MARDUK (721–710). He took up the fight against Assyrian domination and allied himself with Elam. His considerable acumen in uniting discordant tribal factions in Babylonia and his ability for tactical manoeuvring made him a formidable enemy of the Assyrian king SARGON II. Not surprisingly the Assyrian annals depict Merodach-baladan as the arch enemy. They also suggest that he failed the Babylonians. They accuse him of favouritism towards the tribal population to the detriment of the urban inhabitants of the old cities. The Babylonian sources, on the other hand, emphasise that he upheld the traditional qualities of a good Babylonian ruler; he maintained the privileges of the cult cities, kept the irrigation system in good order, endowed temples, and fought a valiant battle against the treacherous Assyrians. Both accounts are biased; nevertheless it appears that Merodach-baladan succeeded in uniting his country and during his reign the land prospered.

He first makes an appearance in the Assyrian annals in 732 when TIGLATH-PILESER III fought against MUKIN-ZERI and subdued the southern tribes. He is referred to as the 'King of the Sealand' who brought tribute to the Assyrian monarch. Having established himself as king of Babylon after the death of Tiglath-pileser's son SHALMANESER V in 722, he profited from internal upheaval in Assyria. An attempt by SARGON II to return Assyrian control of Babylonia failed at the Battle of Der (720). Only in 710 did Sargon's attention revert to Babylonia and thus began a protracted struggle which was to engage the Assyrian king in the south until 708. Sargon's tactic was to separate the Babylonian forces from their Elamite allies, and twice defeated Merodach-baladan's troops, once at Dur-Yakin, his southern capital. After the initial defeat, Sargon moved towards Babylon and Borsippa, which submitted, and Sargon formally ascended the Babylonian throne himself. Merodach-baladan asked for military assistance from Elam's king SHUTRUK-NAHHUNTE II who, preferring to remain neutral, refused. This forced Merodach-baladan to make another stand against Sargon but in 709 he was defeated again and his capital Dur-Yakin was sacked. However, after Sargon's death in 705 he rallied his supporters once more to challenge the new Assyrian king, SENNACHERIB, whom he confronted with two forces: one stationed at Cutha, the other at Kish. Sennacherib vanquished the allies at Cutha and descended on Babylon where he captured Merodach-baladan's wives and other members of the court and had them, together with substantial booty from the royal treasury, transported to Assyria. He installed BEL-IBNI on the throne, who was replaced in 700 by his own son ASHUR-NADIN-SHUMI. In the same year he mounted a final campaign against the southern tribes of Babylonia. Merodach-baladan fled to the marshes and escaped to the Elamite side where he presumably died within the next few years.

A portrait of this intrepid king survives on a kudurru.

Brinkman 1984: 46–60, 1991, in CAH III/2: 26–32

Mesanepada
Sumerian king of the First Dynasty of Ur, son of MES-KALAM-DUG. On some votive objects he bears the title 'King of Kish'. He also appears in the Sumerian King List as the father of A-ANEPADA

Sollberger and Kupper 1971: IB4a, b, c, IB5a

Mesha
King of Moab, son of Khemosh-yat (9th century). He was the ruler of a small state in Syria and is remembered because he set up a stele inscribed in Moabite. It records his fight against Israel under AHAB in order to regain territories that he regarded as belonging to Moab. He thus got possession of Ataroth and Nebo where he killed all inhabitants and plundered the temple treasure. He also refers to his building activities, which were made possible by prisoners of war and booty.

Smelik 1985: 33–5; Kuhrt 1995: 469–71; Niccacci 1994

Mesilim (= Mesalim)
Early Dynastic king of Kish (c. 2400). His name appears on several votive objects found at Lagash and Adab in which he uses the still enigmatic title 'King of Kish'. EANNATUM and EN-METENA recall Mesilim as arbiter in the boundary dispute between Lagash and Umma. This points to the possibility that he had wide-reaching influence and respect. The actual place of his residence remains as yet unknown.

Hallo and Simpson 1971: 46; Sollberger and Kupper 1971: IA3a, b, c; Cooper 1983; Edzard 1993, in RlA 8, 1/2: 14

Mes-kiag-nunna
Sumerian king, third(?) of the First Dynasty of Ur. His wife, whose name is not preserved, dedicated a calcite bowl for his life, in one of the earliest inscriptions written in Akkadian. According to the later Tummal texts he was the first to rebuild the temple of Enlil in Nippur.

Sollberger and Kupper 1971: IB6a; Edzard 1993, in RlA 8, 1/2: 93

Micah
Hebrew prophet, born at Moreshet-Gath near Lachish in Judah. He was a younger contemporary of ISAIAH and was active during the reigns of JO-THAM (740–735), AHAZ (c. 735–715) and HEZEKIAH (715–687). He spoke out against unjust rulers, religious corruption and oppressive land-owners, and predicted the fall of Israel and Judah, as well as the destruction of Jerusalem as a punishment. His description of the ideal king is thought

to have influenced the reform programme of Hezekiah.

Mitchell 1991, in CAH III/2: 328, 348; Allen
1978

Midas (= Mita)

King of Phrygia, known as Mita of
Mushki from Assyrian sources (8th
century). He attempted to draw local
rulers into an alliance against Assyria,
but in 709 he made overtures to his
governor in Cilicia, as described in a
letter from SARGON II.

We first hear of him in 718 connected with Kiakki of Shiriktu (Central
Anatolia) and he continued to support
various dynasts in that area. Assyrian
military attacks eventually prompted
Mita to send envoys to Sargon to sue
for peace and offer tribute.

The Greek sources that refer to a
king Midas report that he dedicated a
throne at Delphi, married a daughter
of Agamemnon, king of Kyme in
Aeolia, and committed suicide after a
devastating Cimmerian attack.

It has been suggested that the
skeleton discovered in the Great Tumulus at Gordium was that of Mita/
Midas. It belongs to the same period
as the rock inscriptions found at
Yazilikaya, though there is no epi-
graphic evidence in the tomb itself,
which was equipped with lavish funerary gifts in bronze and wooden
furniture.

Mellink 1991, in CAH III/2: 622–34; Starr
1990: 15–16; Hawkins 1994, in RlA 8/3.4:
271–3;

Mithridates I

Parthian king, brother of his predecessor Phraates I (171–139/38). Under
his rule the Parthian empire grew in
power and expanded westwards to
include, for a while, Mesopotamia.
Benefiting from the defeat of the
Seleucids against the Romans he first
consolidated his position in the east,
establishing Parthian control. Then he
moved against the satrap of Media,
who blocked the way to Mesopotamia. After prolonged fighting Mithridates was successful and he appointed
his own governor over Media. By July
141 he had conquered most of Mesopotamia and occupied Babylon and
Seleucia.

A cuneiform tablet from Uruk
reports that his authority was recognised there too. He adopted the
ancient Persian title 'king of kings'
and used the epithet 'philhellene' in an
attempt to enlist the support of the
local Greek population.

The Seleucid king Demetrios II
Nicator was also captured in 141,
but fighting continued for at least the
next three years because of the serious
attacks on Babylonia by the local ruler
of Elymais.

Colledge 1967: 28–30; Schippmann 1980:
23–6; Wiesehöfer 1996: 121, 133, 139

Muballit-sherua

Assyrian princess, daughter of ASHUR-
UBALLIT I. She was married to KAR-
AINDASH, son of the Babylonian king
BURNABURIASH II, in a dynastic mar-
riage.

Gadd 1975, in CAH II/2: 28; Kuhrt 1995: 352

Mudammiq
Assyrian temple official, a man of wealth and importance who belonged to a professional organisation and lived at Assur (*c.* 650–620). His important archive has been recovered there.

Fales and Rost 1991; Fales, in Waetzold and Hauptmann 1997

Mugallu
Syro-Hittite king of Melid during the reigns of ESARHADDON and ASHURBA-NIPAL (7th century). Having been on good term with the Assyrians he captured the city of Melid which had been under their control and held on to it in spite of attempts by Esarhaddon to win it back. During the time of Ashurbanipal he had become ruler of Tabal as well and went to Nineveh with his daughter as a present for the king, complete with dowry. Later on he conspired with the Lydian ruler DUGDAMME against the Assyrians, for which he was punished, according to an inscription in the Ishtar temple (*c.* 640).

Hawkins 1982, in CAH III/1: 428, 429, 432; 1995, in RlA 8: 406; Grayson 1991, in CAH III/2: 127–8, 145; Starr 1990: lvii, 4–14

Mukannishum
High functionary and official under king ZIMRI-LIM at Mari. He was minister for transport, trade and industry for some fourteen years. Seventy letters by and from him have survived in the palace archives.

Rouault 1977

Mukin-zeri *see* Nabu-mukin-zeri

Mulissu-kabtat
Assyrian prophetess, probably from Nineveh. It appears from the affectionate and intimate tone of her oracular report that she may have looked after ASHURBANIPAL when he was young.

Parpola 1997: li, 38–9

Mulissu-mukannishat-Ninua
Assyrian queen, wife of ASHURNASIRPAL II and subsequently also of SHALMANESER III, daughter of Ashur-nirka-dani, the chief cupbearer (*rab šaqe*).

Fadhil 1990

Murashu
Family of Babylonian businessmen, attested during the reign of ARTAXERXES I and DARIUS II (*c.* 465–405). Copious sources concerning its commercial activities are preserved in a voluminous archive discovered in Nippur. They concern agricultural contracting, leasing of land, and short-term lending.

Cardascia 1951; Stolper 1985; 1995, in RlA 8: 428

Mursili I
Hittite king of the Old Kingdom, grandson and successor of HATTUSILI I (*c.* 1620–1590). Building on his predecessor's expansion of the Hittite kingdom he made further efforts to enlarge his realm. He fought in northern Syria and destroyed the powerful

city of Aleppo. In a surprise sortie he marched southwards and raided Babylon in an unprecedented demonstration of Hittite mobility and military organisation. He also fought against the Hurrians and, like Hattusili I before him, dedicated the spoils of his victory to the national gods.

According to the edict of TELEPINU he was murdered by his sister HAR-APSILI and her husband HANTILI, 'his cup-bearer', who took over the throne as a result.

Kuhrt 1995: 243–5; Wilhelm 1995, in RlA 8: 434–5

Mursili II

Hittite king of the Empire period, son of SUPPILULIUMA I and successor and brother of ARNUWANDA II (1330–1295/ 1321–1295). Like his father he was a successful and vigorous king who managed to consolidate the empire and subdue insurrections. In his 'Ten Year Annals' he records his triumph against the western kingdom of Arzawa, which had sided with the Egyptians under ARNUWANDA I. He deported many inhabitants and drove the ruling family into exile. He also defeated Arzawa's ally, Ahiyawa. In the north he campaigned against the raiding Gasga people based in the Pontic mountains, but with ultimately limited success. In Syria he faced an uprising by a confederacy of several subject states which, combined with Assyrian pressure, made it necessary for the king to intervene personally. He installed a new viceroy in Carch-

emish, and concluded treaties with Aleppo, Amurru and Ugarit.

Houwink ten Cate 1967; 1970; Gurney 1990: 32–4; Klengel 1992:1 15–16; Kuhrt 1995: 254–8; Ünal 1995, in RlA 8: 435–40

Mursili III *see* Urhi-Teshup

Mushezib-Marduk

Chaldean tribal chief of Bit Dakkuri who ruled Babylonia from 693 to 689. After the capture of the Elamite puppet ruler NERGAL-USHEZIB by SENNA-CHERIB he managed to establish himself on the Babylonian throne to continue the bitter struggle against Assyrian domination. In 691 (or 690) he managed to persuade numerous groups hostile to the Assyrians, such as Elamites, Babylonians, Arameans and others, to join forces and challenge the Assyrian army. They fought at Halule near Samarra, and although Sennacherib claims that victory was his, the outcome may have been less than decisive since Mushezib-Marduk was able to rule Babylonia for another one or two years. In 689 Sennacherib launched his punitive expedition against Babylon, which was taken after a lengthy siege and, according to Sennacherib's inscription on the rock-face of Bavian, totally destroyed. Mushezib-Marduk was taken to exile in Assyria where he presumably died.

Brinkman 1991, in CAH III/2: 37–8; Grayson, in ibid.: 107–9

Mutakkil-Nusku

Little-known Assyrian king, eighty-fifth in the Assyrian King List. He was engaged in some internal conflict, since the enigmatic entry records that he carried away his brother, presumably NINURTA-TUKULTI-ASHUR, to Babylon and 'held the throne for his tablet', though only briefly (1133).

Grayson 1972: 146–7; Brinkman 1995, in RlA 8: 500

Mutallu (= Muwatalis)

1 Anatolian king of Gurgum, who submitted to SHALMANESER III in 858.
2 Anatolian king of Kummuh, son of TARKHULARA (c. 712–708). According to SARGON II he was said to have killed his father to seize the throne. He removed him and made Marqas a province.
3 King of Kummuh, initially on good terms with Assyria. After the defeat of Urartu he received the province of Melid from SARGON II in 713. In 708 Sargon denounced him for paying tribute to Urartu and sent his generals against Kummuh. Mutallu himself escaped but Kummuh (with Melid) became a province of Assyria.

Barnett 1982, in CAH III/1: 356; Hawkins, in ibid.: 420–3; 1995, in RlA 8: 502

Mutarris-Ashur

High-ranking Assyrian military commander and Chief Eunuch who served under SHAMSHI-ADAD V. He was sent to lead the king's second campaign against the Nairi land, in the region around lake Van.

Grayson, in Dietrich and Loretz 1995: 93–8

Mut-Ashkur

Assyrian king, son and successor of ISHME-DAGAN and grandson of the dynasty's founder, SHAMSHI-ADAD I (c. 1750). He is known from the Mari texts. His father arranged for him to marry the daughter of the Hurrian king Zaziya.

Brinkman 1995, in RlA 8: 500

Muwatalli (= Muwatalis) (II)

Hittite king of the empire period, son and successor of MURSILI II (c. 1295–1282/1271). He concluded a treaty with Wilusa, in west Anatolia, and maintained his hold on the Syrian provinces. His army clashed with the Egyptians under RAMESSES II near Qadesh. Though the Egyptian claimed victory, the Hittites were left in control of the Damascus area. In Anatolia he was forced to move the Hittite capital to Tarhuntassa, probably because Hattusa had been destroyed by the Gasga people. In an attempt to deal with these people he set up a new province in the north, ruled by his brother HATTUSILI III who was eventually able to retake Hattusa and possibly also rebuilt the great cult centre of the Hittite weather god at Nerik.

Gurney 1990: 35; Klengel 1992: 116–18; Kuhrt 1995: 258; Ünal 1995, in RlA 8: 524–7

N

Nabonassar (Babylonian Nabu-Nasir)

King of Babylon, successor of NABU-SHUMA-ISHKUN (747–734). For most of his reign he relied on the help of the powerful Assyrian king TIGLATH-PILESER III to subdue the troublesome Aramean and Chaldean tribes, some parts of whom were deported and resettled elsewhere. This brought a much greater stability to Babylonia than had been possible in previous years. In return the Assyrian monarch assumed the title 'king of Sumer and Akkad' and had freedom of movement throughout the Babylonian territories. There are some reports of local disturbances and revolts in various cities, notably Borsippa and Uruk. The king died in his palace after an illness and was succeeded by his son NABU-NADIN-ZERI.

Brinkman 1968: 226–34; 1991, in CAH III/2: 24

Nabonidus (Babylonian Nabu-na'id)

Babylonian king (555–539). He was not of royal blood but claimed descent from a scholar and counsellor, Nabu-balatsu-iqbi. His mother was ADDA-GUPPI, whose lengthy autobiographical inscription suggests that the family had close connections with NEBUCHADNEZ-ZAR II and NERIGLISSAR. It is possible that Nabonidus married one of Nebuchadnezzar's daughters. He had an important position and when Neriglissar died he seems to have arranged for the designated successor, Labashi-marduk, to be killed. His assumption of royal power found general acceptance and he seems to have enjoyed the support of the army. He had to march to Syria to re-establish Babylonian supremacy and brought back prisoners and booty which were used in building projects in all principal Babylonian cities. He established his daughter

EN-NIGALDI-NANNA as *entum* priestess at Ur and granted revenues to the temple of Eanna at Uruk.

He led further campaigns against cities in Syria and Palestine and engaged in skirmishes with the Arabs. According to the Babylonian Chronicle he then went to the oasis city of Teima where he was to stay for ten years, having gained control over several other oasis towns in the area. During his absence he delegated the running of the state to the crown-prince BEL-SHAR-USUR but the New Year's festival was not celebrated. A stele found in Harran justifies his desertion of Babylon by claiming that the citizens of Babylon, Borsippa, Nippur, Uruk, Ur and Larsa had rebelled against him. This may have been the result of a priest-led opposition to his preference for the cult of the moon god at Harran. The real reasons for his move to Teima may have been more complex; it has been suggested that he wanted to strengthen Babylonian control over the trade-routes through Arabia, especially the spice and incense trade and to extend the empire's power further westwards. The religious argument that accuses Nabonidus with irreverence towards Marduk is largely tendentious. At any rate, he returned in 543 or 542, apparently following the advice of his diviners, and resumed royal command. He celebrated the New Year festival and restored the statue of Sin to Harran.

However his absence may have precipitated the almost unimpeded advance of the Persians. In 539 CYRUS II marched down the Diyala river and fought a victorious battle at the Babylonian city of Opis which led to the surrender of Sippar. Nabonidus fled. Within days the Persians had entered Babylon which offered no resistance. Belshazzar may have been killed and Nabonidus surrendered. According to BEROSSUS his life was spared and he moved to Carmania, where he died.

Wiseman 1993, in CAH III/2: 243–51; Beaulieu 1989; Sack 1983; Röllig 1964; Rashid 1979; Berger 1973; Mayer 1998

Nabopolassar (Nabu-apla-usur)

Chaldean king of Babylon (626–605). He was the first ruler of the so-called Third Dynasty of the Sealand, the last Mesopotamian state to be ruled by a local dynasty.

He began his career as an official appointed by Assyria, but he soon made himself independent as king of the Sealand. According to the Babylonian Chronicle 'no king was recognised in Babylon' for one year after the death of KANDALANU. The control of Babylonia was contested in struggles between the Assyrian army under ASHUR-ETIL-ILANI and SIN-SHARRA-ISHKUN and Babylonian troops under Nabopolassar. The Babylonian Chronicle reports that Nabopolassar attacked Assyria in a series of campaigns, moving upstream along the rivers and defeating the Mannean allies of the Assyrians. Following the Median victory that resulted in the destruction of Tarbisu and Assur in 614, he made an alliance with the Median king CYAXARES. In spite of the serious threat to the Assyrian empire, Sin-sharra-ishkun began counter-attacks against Nabopolassar. Retaliation was swift. The Median and Babylonian troops attacked Nineveh in 612 and took the city after a three-month siege. This left Nabopolassar in control of Babylonia and increasingly large areas of Assyria. The Egyptians, who had already come to the aid of Sin-sharra-ishkun, marched into Palestine and Syria to safeguard their interests in the region, though Nabopolassar was checking their advance at Harran. In the following years he consolidated his northern frontier, aided by the crown-prince, his son NEBUCHADNEZZAR (II). The Babylonian presence in northern Syria was contested by the Egyptians, eventually forcing Nabopolassar to retreat. The decisive victory against the Egyptians was won at Carchemish by Nebuchadnezzar in 605 when Nabopolassar was dying in Babylon.

In Babylon, the capital of a newly independent state, he was responsible for initiating the comprehensive restoration and building work which his successor and son was to bring to a splendid conclusion

Oates 1993, in CAH III/2: ch. 25; Zawadzki 1988

Nabu-ahhe-eriba
Assyrian scholar, teacher and possible a close adviser of ASHURBANIPAL. Sixty of his letters and reports that he sent to the king were discovered at Nineveh.

Parpola 1970: 38–51; 1983: 64–83

Nabu-ahhe-iddin
Babylonian businessman, second generation of the EGIBI family (6th century). He had commercial dealings with NERIGLISSAR and served as royal judge under NABONIDUS, amassing a considerable fortune. The family's rise to prominence can be dated to his time.

Ungnad 1941–44; Krecher 1970; van Driel 1985–86

Nabu-apla-iddina
King of Babylon, son and successor of NABU-SHUMA-UKIN I. He began his reign in c. 870 and seems to have ruled for a considerable, if unspecified, time. He was a successful and capable ruler and maintained stability and peace with Assyria. In his final years he concluded a peace treaty with SHALMANESER III, who had succeeded ASHURNASIRPAL II to the Assyrian throne. He also managed to defeat the Suteans and halt their incursions into his territory. Babylonia experienced a cultural renaissance, inaugurating a period of lively literary activity. Various contemporary inscriptions commemorate the resettling of cult centres and the restoration of rites and offerings in the great temples of the land.

Brinkman 1968: 182–92

Nabu-apla-usur
see Nabopolassar

Nabu-bani-ahi
Babylonian scribe (6th century). He was a member of the prestigious EKUR-ZAKIR family and had an important

position at the Eanna temple in Uruk during the reigns of AMEL-MARDUK and NERIGLISSAR.

Sack 1977

Nabu-bel-shumati

Chaldean tribal chief and king of the Sealand in southern Mesopotamia; son of MERODACH-BALADAN.

During the rebellion of SHAMASH-SHUMA-UKIN against his brother, the Assyrian king ASHURBANIPAL, Nabu-bel-shumati sided with the former. In 651 he captured a regiment of auxiliaries that the Assyrian monarch had sent to him in the belief that he was on his side. He was closely allied with various Elamite rulers who occupied the throne in rapid succession. Like his father before him he was successful in undermining Assyrian efforts to establish superiority in the south and he was equally reviled by Assyrian chroniclers and letter writers as inherently evil and treacherous. The Sealand was eventually subdued by a force led by BEL-IBNI, and Nabu-bel-shumati fled to Elam. When Ashurbanipal demanded his extradition from the Elamite king, Khumban-khaltash, Nabu-bel-shumati committed suicide and only his corpse, packed in salt, was delivered to Nineveh.

Malbran-Labat 1975; Brinkman 1991, in CAH III/2: 56– 9; Grayson 1991, in CAH III/2: 151–2

Nabu-kudurru-usur
see **Nebuchadnezzar I**

Nabu-mukin-apli

First king of the so-called Dynasty of E, which ruled Babylonia from 979 to 732. Despite his relatively long reign (979–994), times were hard and the country suffered from frequent invasions by Aramean tribes, as later chronicles report. Several kudurrus refer to difficulties in the collection of taxes.

Brinkman 1968: 171–4

Nabu-mukin-zeri (Mukin-zeri)

Chief of the Bit-Amukani tribe, later king of Babylon (731–729). He deposed NABU-SHUMA-UKIN II, who had ruled only briefly after assassinating NABU-NADIN-ZERI. The disturbances connected with these violent rebellions were a matter of great concern to the Assyrians. The Synchronistic History and other sources confirm that TIGLATH-PILESER III pursued the Babylonian king, who mobilised various tribes in his defence. Although the Assyrian king did not actually capture Nabu-mukin-zeri he could cut off his support and with the backing of some Babylonian factions declared himself ruler over much of southern Babylonia (728–7).

Brinkman 1968: 235–40; 1984

Nabu-na'id *see* **Nabonidus**

Nabu-nadin-zeri (= Nadinu)

Babylonian king, son and successor of NABONASSAR (733–732). He was killed by NABU-SHUMA-UKIN II in a revolt.

Brinkman 1968: 234–5; 1975, in CAH II/2: 25

Nabu-nasir *see* Nabonassar

Nabu-sharra-usur

Assyrian high-ranking official under SHALMANESER IV; governor of Rimusus, and probably a eunuch.

Grayson, in Dietrich and Loretz 1995: 85–98

Nabu-shuma-ishkun

Babylonian king originating from Chaldea, the southern part of the country, successor of ERIBA-MARDUK (*c*. 760–748). According to contemporary records from Borsippa, the town experienced severe disturbances when local citizens had to defend themselves and their lands against violent attacks from other Babylonians. On occasions the situation was so serious that the customary processions of the gods' statues could not take place. This may point to a general period of unrest within the country during the king's reign.

Brinkman 1968: 224–6

Nabu-shumu-libur

Eleventh and last king of the Second Dynasty of Isin, successor of Marduk-zer-[x] (1034–1027). His name is preserved on a marble duck weight, on which he is called 'King of the World'. In reality, the political situation during his reign must have been very volatile, with increasing inva-sions by tribes in the western provinces. Apart from omens of ill fortunes preserved in the Religious Chronicle, nothing more concrete is known.

Brinkman 1968: 147–8

Nabu-shuma-ukin I

King of Babylon, successor and perhaps son of SHAMASH-MUDAMMIQ. Only the start of his reign can be dated (895). He was a contemporary of the Assyrian kings ADAD-NIRARI II and TUKULTI-NINURTA II. According to the Synchronistic History relations between the two countries were at first hostile, with the Assyrians de-spoiling Babylonian towns, but after an exchange of daughters in marriage the rulers established peace which was to last for more than eighty years. He re-established Babylonian independence and prosperity and his descendants held the throne for several generations.

Brinkman 1968: 180–2

Nabu-shuma-ukin II

King of Babylon who took the throne from NABU-NADIN-ZERI during a rebellion. He only ruled for one month (in 732), after which he was replaced by NABU-MUKIN-ZERI.

Brinkman 1968: 235; 1991, in CAH III/2: 25

Nabu-zer-kitti-lishir

Governor of the Sealand, son of MERODACH-BALADAN. During the reign of ESARHADDON he revoked his loyalty oath to Assyria, imposed by SENNACHERIB on the Chaldean tribes, and launched a revolt. He besieged the city of Ur but Esarhaddon sent troops which forced him to lift the siege. He escaped to Elam but was murdered there.

Grayson 1991, in CAH III/2: 39, 41, 45

Nabu-zuqup-kena

Scribe and astrologer who lived at Calah. He was the editor of the famous astrological omen series *En-uma Anu Enlil*, as well as other learned works, as colophons show. He was the father of ADAD-SHUMA-USUR, physician of SENNACHERIB, ESARHADDON and ASHURBANIPAL.

Hunger 1972

Nadab

King of Israel, son and successor of JEROBOAM I (910–909). He was assassinated during a campaign against the Philistines by BAASHA, who established a new dynasty in Israel.

Mitchell 1982, in CAH III/2: 462

Nahhunte-Utu

Elamite queen, wife of SHILHAK-INSHUSHINAK (1150–1120). She was probably the first wife of his brother KUTIR-NAHHUNTE and the mother or sister of HUTTELUSH-INSHUSHINAK and seven other royal children. She was no doubt a key personage in the dynasty of the Shutrukids. The habit of Elamite kings to claim descent from a sister's sibling makes it difficult to establish who was descended from

whom. She is mentioned in several of Shilshak-Inshushinak's building inscriptions with the epithet 'beloved wife', as well as on a door-hinge of temple of Simut and Manzat at Susa, dedicated by Hutteludush-Inshushinak.

Hinz 1972: 130–1, 34–5; Vallat 1985: 43–50

Nammahani

Last ruler of a dynasty founded by GUDEA of Lagash. He is known from year names and a few building inscriptions and was eventually defeated by URNAMMU.

Edzard 1997: 194–202

Naplanum

First king of Larsa, contemporary of IBBI-SIN, the last king of Ur III. He was a contemporary of IHBI-ERRA, king of Isin (*c.* 2025–2005). He bore an Amorite name and may have been an Amorite. Nothing else is known about him.

Gadd 1971, in CAH I/2: 628, 632, 659

Naqi'a-Zakutu

Assyrian queen-mother, married to SENNACHERIB while he was crown-prince, mother of ESARHADDON and grandmother of ASHURBANIPAL (7th century). She gained much authority after the death of ASHUR-NADIN-SHUMI, which placed her own son next in line to the throne. She had a special part of the palace for her own use and had great influence with Esarhaddon. She received reports and oracles concerning the king's health.

Her influence grew even more after Esarhaddon's death on campaign in 669. She made courtiers and others re-affirm their loyalty oaths to Ashurba-nipal.

Lewy 1952; Parpola and Watanabe 1988: n.8; Borger 1988; Grayson 1991, in CAH III/2: 138–9

Naram-Sin

1 Akkadian king, son of MANISHTUSU (2260–2223). Like his grandfather, SARGON OF AKKAD, he was one of the most illustrious Mesopotamian kings and ruled for thirty-seven years. Like Sargon he became the subject of several literary composi-tions, some glorifying his military prowess, others of a cautionary nature, linking the downfall of the dynasty to acts of hubris. In his inscriptions, which are less numer-ous than those of his grandfather, he introduced two innovations: first the title 'king of the four quarters', which suggests dominion over the whole world, and secondly the use of the determinative hitherto reserved for the writing of divine names. The epithets in the inscriptions of his courtiers likewise suggest that he introduced a form of divine kingship to Mesopotamia although later gen-erations, with the notable exception of the kings of Ur from the Third Dynasty, did not generally perpetu-ate the custom. Historically, little is known about the chronology and events of his reign, but evidence from monuments, foundation inscrip-tions, year names, and not least from later accounts, allow the reconstruc-tion of the major events.

Initially and repeatedly he had to face rebellions in different parts of his considerable empire, which en-tailed long-distance and arduous campaigns. His most famous stele, now in the Louvre, depicts the king ascending a steep mountain, while the text describes his victory over the Lullubi. He consolidated the northern frontiers, destroyed Ebla and laid the foundations of the palace at Nagar (Tell Braq). He then pushed north-west, to the timber-rich mountains of the Leba-non, the Amanus, the Taurus, and, according to later tradition, reached the Mediterranean coast. Relations with Elam were consolidated in a long treaty. In spite of extensive and arduous campaigns, his reign en-joyed a degree of stability and prosperity that became proverbial.

Gadd 1971, in CAH I/2: 440–3; Hallo and Simpson 1971: 60–8; Hirsch 1963; Sollberger and Kupper, 1971 IIA4a–r; Cooper 1980; 1983; 1983a; Farber 1983; Goodnick-Westenholz 1983; 1997; Glassner 1986; Gelb and Kienast 1990: 81–112, 226–75; Frayne 1993: 84–181; Hinz 1967; Amiet 1976; Tinney 1995

2 Old Assyrian ruler. According to the Assyrian King List the son of SAR-GON I, he was actually the son of IPIQ-ADAD I of Eshnunna, who had gained control over Assur (around 1900). He expanded the influence of Eshnunna well to the west into the area of the upper Habur. He was

succeeded by Erishum II, a member of the Puzur-Ashur Dynasty.

Gadd 1971, in CAH II/1: 1

3 Ruler of Eshnunna during the Old Babylonian period, son and successor of IPIQ-ADAD II. He was a contemporary of SHAMSHI-ADAD I of Assyria and YAHDUN-LIM of Mari. He was an ally of the latter and may have defeated the Assyrians. He ruled for nine years, was deified and called himself 'king of the world' in his extant inscriptions, which show that he enjoyed a degree of independence and hegemony, at least over the Diyala region.

Frayne 1990: 553–6; Yuhong 1994: 84–6

Nazi-bugash
Usurper of the throne of Babylon during the Kassite Dynasty (1333). According to the Synchronistic History he was removed from his position by the Assyrian king ASHUR-UBALLIT I and replaced by KURIGALZU II.

Brinkman 1976: 260–1

Nazi-Maruttash
Twenty-third king of the Kassite Dynasty of Babylon, son and successor of KURIGALZU II (1307–1282). The Synchronistic History reports conflict between Assyria and Babylonia, perhaps following further Babylonian incursions in Elamite lands, which resulted in the defeat of the Babylonian troops. The strained relationship was alleviated by a new border agreement between Nazi-Maruttash and ADAD-NIRARI I.

Brinkman 1976: 262–86

Nebuchadnezzar I (Babylonian Nabu-kudurru-usur)
Fourth king of the Second Dynasty of Isin, son and successor of NINURTA-NADIN-SHUMI, who reigned for twenty-two years (1126–1105). His decisive victory over the Elamites, who had been a powerful threat to Babylonia for generations, assured his place in Mesopotamian historical memory as one of the great rulers. He achieved a quasi legendary status comparable to that of SARGON OF AKKAD, a parallel which he consciously encouraged through the use of ancient royal epithets. The campaign against Elam, which was ruled by HUTTELUSH-INSHUSHINAK, culminated in the politically significant recovery of the cult statue of Marduk and another deity, taken to Elam during a raid at the end of the Kassite dynasty. Although in military terms the victory against Elam did not result in lasting peace, the recovery of the gods' statues improved the morale of the Babylonians and ensured the enduring popularity of Nebuchadnezzar. His relations with Assyria were tenuous, and according to the Synchronistic History he conducted several border raids. In Babylonia he restored sanctuaries throughout the land. It has been suggested that the elevation of Marduk to the position of supreme god of the Babylonian pantheon dates from his period. Later sources also

suggest that he made the city of Babylon the royal capital.

Brinkman 1968: 104–16; 1975, in CAH II/2: 454–7; Kuhrt 1995: 377–81

Nebuchadnezzar II (Babylonian Nabu-kudurru-usur)

King of Babylon, son and successor to NABOPOLASSAR, the founder of the Third Dynasty of the Sealand (605–562). He was one of the greatest and longest reigning monarchs of Mesopotamia. The sources for his reign are rich and varied; in addition to the Babylonian Chronicle and the later history of BEROSSUS, there are numerous, detailed building inscriptions, as well as administrative and economic texts.

During Nabopolassar's lifetime he was appointed crown-prince and both accompanied his father on military campaigns, e.g. at Harran, and was sole commander, e.g. at Zamua. The greatest success in these early years was the victory over the Egyptians at Carchemish in 605. This brought Syria and the Mediterranean coast under Babylonian control. Nabopolassar's death happened during this campaign and Nebuchadnezzar moved ahead of his army to Babylon to take up the kingship. He returned to Syria-Palestine soon afterwards, and the consolidation of Babylonian power in the region was his main task in the following years. The main antagonist was Egypt (ruled then by pharaoh NECHO II), though the various smaller states and tribal confederations such as Judah, Moab, Ammon, etc., were quick to exploit the conflict between the two foreign powers to further their own interests. But by 601 Nebuchadnezzar had won the upper hand and driven Egypt from Asia, although the situation in Syria still demanded his personal presence there for some time to come. Best known from the Biblical sources is the revolt of the Judean king JEHOIAKIN, who tried to enlist Egyptian support. Nebuchadnezzar besieged Jerusalem, which was captured in March 597 and Jehoiakin was taken into exile in Babylon. Another rebellion was instigated by ZEDEKIAH, whom Nebuchadnezzar had appointed as regent in Jerusalem, and this resulted in the second siege and destruction of the city in 587. He went on to conquer another intransigent city, Tyre, and may have established Babylonian sovereignty over Cilicia.

Having thus gained control over most areas that had been under either Assyrian or Egyptian control, he began the task for which he is most famous, the rebuilding of Babylon and of twelve other major Mesopotamian cities, an enormously ambitious and extremely costly undertaking. Not only were the city walls almost completely rebuilt, with large portions of the wall fashioned from kiln-baked bricks, but he built the famous Processional Street, lined with glazed bricks decorated with reliefs of the animals sacred to the chief god Marduk. It originally passed through the equally splendid and monumental Ishtar-Gate, which German archaeologists have reconstructed in the Berlin Museum. He added huge tracts to the palace begun by Nabopolassar, adorned with glazed bricks and roofed with cedars, and completed the sacred precinct of Babylon, the temple of Esagila and the ziggurat, Etemenanki. He also constructed law courts, administrative buildings and citadels, and built a stone bridge over the Euphrates. The immense labour force that such large-scale projects demanded consisted of prisoners of war, as well as corvée workers, including contingents of foreign specialist craftsmen. His building inscriptions show that he strove to immortalise himself as a pious ruler in the Babylonian tradition, a king of justice, dedicated to the service of the gods and the scribal arts, and who relied on his architectural works to establish a name that would be remembered forever.

Wiseman 1991, in CAH III/2: 229–40; 1956; 1985; Albright 1956; Koldewey 1914; Lambert, W.G. 1965; Malamat 1956; Sack 1982

Nebuchadnezzar III *see* Nidinti-Bel

Necho I
Egyptian pharaoh, first of the Twenty-sixth (Saïte) Dynasty (672–664). When ASHURBANIPAL had completed his invasion of Egypt in 667/6, he lists Necho as one of the local rulers and calls him 'King of Memphis and Saïs'; all were vassals of the Assyrian king. Many of these rulers plotted to support the deposed TAHARKA in a comeback but Ashurbanipal crushed this planned rebellion brutally and they were deported to Nineveh. Only Necho was spared, perhaps for his loyalty, although the Assyrian records

do not specify the reason. He was honoured and confirmed in office as king of Saïs by Ashurbanipal. His son PSAMMETICHUS I was to enjoy a similar good relationship with the Assyrian monarch.

James 1991, in CAH III/2: 700–1; Kuhrt 1995: 634–6

Necho II
Egyptian pharaoh of the Twenty-sixth Saïte Dynasty, son and successor of PSAMMETICHUS I (610–595). Like his father, in his last years he took an active role in providing a balance of power in western Asia with dramatic consequences for Judah. The Babylonian Chronicle reports that an Egyptian army supported the Assyrian attack on Harran under ASHUR-UBALLIT II which was forced to withdraw before the advance of NABOPO-LASSAR and his Babylonian troops. In the following year the Assyrians renewed their efforts, this time with success, and again with Egyptian help. It is possible that the biblical account (II Kgs. 23:29; II Chron. 35:20–4) of the ill-fated attempt by the Judean king JOSIAH to stop the march of the Egyptians may have occurred before the second Harran campaign. In the ensuing battle at Megiddo Josiah was killed. Necho deposed and deported his son and successor JEHOAHAZ II and appointed JEHOIAKIM as vassal-king in Jerusalem, which was forced to pay substantial tribute to Egypt.

For a few years Necho controlled large parts of Syria-Palestine, as far as Carchemish, partly the result of the collapse of Assyria in 609. The Egyptian presence there provoked the new major power, Babylonia. The Egyptian army was defeated by NEBUCHADNEZZAR in 605 in the battle of Carchemish. This was followed by a period of fighting between Egypt and Babylonia until 601, when a battle on Egypt's frontier ended indecisively, although it seems likely that Necho conceded control of the Levant to Nebuchadnezzar at this point.

An important achievement of Necho was the creation of an Egyptian navy. He began work to cut a canal from the Nile to the Red Sea and, according to Herodotus, sent a Phoenician expedition to circumnavigate Africa. Like his father he had contact with Greek cities from which he recruited mercenary soldiers.

James, T.G.H. 1991, in CAH III/2: 715–18, 720–72; Kuhrt 1995

Nehemiah
Jewish governor of Jerusalem (c. 445–433) under ARTAXERXES I, whose cup-bearer he was according to the Old Testament book that bears his name. His book describes his involvement in the building of the walls of Jerusalem, as well as the restoration of the temple.

Mitchell 1991, in CAH III/2: 438–9; Myers 1965

Nergal-apil-kumua
Assyrian high-ranking official under ASHURNASIRPAL II, governor of Calah,

and overseer of the palace, probably a eunuch.

Deller and Millard 1993

Nergal-erish
Assyrian high-ranking official, governor of Rasappa under ADAD-NIRARI III, probably a eunuch, whose name appears on various land grants inscribed on stone stelae. He seems to have been given control over most of the Jezireh.

Grayson, in Dietrich and Loretz 1995: 98; Grayson 1993; Galter 1990

Nergal-etir
Babylonian scholar and astronomer who sent a number of oracles and reports to the Assyrian court in the first third of the 7th century.

Hunger 1992: 135–58

Nergal-ushezib
Babylonian king who ruled briefly between 694 and 693. He was put on the throne by the anti-Assyrian Elamite faction, which had kidnapped the Assyrian appointed ruler, ASHUR-NADIN-SHUMI, son of SENNACHERIB. He managed to take Nippur but was defeated soon after in battle against Sennacherib and taken to Nineveh where he was executed.

Grayson 1991, in CAH III/2: 36–7; Grayson, in ibid.: 108

Neriglissar (Babylonian Nergal-sharra-usur, biblical Nergal-sharezer = Nergal-sharra-usur)

Babylonian king, son of Bel-shum-ishkun, a governor of the Puqudu tribe, husband of the daughter of NEBUCHADNEZZAR II, KASHSHAIA, who was the sister of his predecessor AMEL-MARDUK (559–556). He began his career as an official under Nebuchadnezzar and was also a wealthy businessman. According to BEROSSUS he led a conspiracy against Amel-Marduk, who was then king of Babylon, whom he deposed in 560. The Babylonian Chronicle records a successful military campaign to Cilicia to safeguard Babylonian holdings in the area of Piriddu. He died soon after his return. His chosen heir was his son Labashi-marduk, who was killed by NABONIDUS.

Wiseman 1993, in CAH III/2: 241–3; Albright 1956; Sack 1978

Nidinti-Bel (= Nebuchadnezzar III)

Babylonian rebel leader who revolted against DARIUS I in 522, soon after the latter's accession to the Persian throne, taking the name Nebuchadnezzar (III). He claimed to be a son of NABONIDUS and was accepted as king by the Babylonians. Half a year later he was defeated in battle by Darius and executed.

Cuyler-Young 1988, in CAH IV: 58; Kuhrt, in ibid.: 129

Nidnusha

Viceroy of Der (21st century). In a fragmentary inscription he calls him-self 'a just judge, who oppresses no one, who sets free the oppressed man and woman'.

Frayne 1990: 676

Nin-banda

Early Dynastic Sumerian queen, wife of MESANEPADA. She is known from the inscription on her seal.

Sollberger and Kupper 1971: IB4b

Ninurta-apil-Ekur

Assyrian king, son of ILI-HADDA, off-spring of ERIBA-ADAD I (1192–1180). The Assyrian King List states that during the reign of his predecessor, a son of TUKULTI-NINURTA I, he went into exile to Babylon and tried to seize the throne. According to the Synchro-nistic History he fought against the Babylonian king ADAD-SHUMA-USUR. An unusual number of palace decrees survive from his reign, regulating the behaviour of women in the royal harem. This suggests that there were problems in the palace following the take-over of power while members of the previous incumbent's family were still at the court.

Grayson 1972: 139–11

Ninurta-kudurri-usur I

Second king of the short-lived Bazi Dynasty, successor of EULMASH-SHAKIN-ZUMI (988–986).

Brinkman 1968: 162–3

Ninurta-kudurri-usur II

Second king of the Dynasty of E, son and successor of its founder, NABU-MUKIN-APLI. He ruled for some eight months in 944.

Brinkman 1968: 175

Ninurta-nadin-shumi

Third ruler of the Second Dynasty of Isin (1132–1127). He succeeded ITTI-MARDUK-BALATU, though it is not clear whether there was any family relationship between them. He was followed by his son, NEBUCHADNEZZAR I, who in turn passed on the monarchy to his son and grandson. According to a fragmentary Assyrian chronicle the Babylonian king made incursions northwards into Assyrian territory as far as Arbail. His Assyrian contemporary was ASHUR-RESHA-ISHI I.

Brinkman 1968: 100–1

Ninurta-tukulti-Ashur

Assyrian king, eighty-fourth in the Assyrian King List, son of ASHUR-DAN I (1133). An important archive concerning food distribution and ritual offerings in the royal palace has survived from his time, as well as fragments of Babylonian letters sent to Assyria which report meetings between the Assyrian and Babylonian kings at the border. The historical implications of these are unclear. According to the Assyrian King List he was deported to Babylon by his brother MUTAKKIL-NUSKU.

Grayson 1972: 143–6; Brinkman 1968: 102ff.; 1975, in CAH II/2: 452

Niqmadu II

King of Ugarit during the Amarna period. He acceded to the throne before the campaign of SUPPILULIUMA I (c. 1360/1335). As a result Ugarit became a vassal of the Hittites, as a long treaty recovered in Ugarit specifies. Although the terms were favourable for the local dynasty and did not include obligations to send troops in support of the Hittites, the yearly tribute demanded by Suppiluliuma was very substantial. During the time of the Syrian rebellion PIYASHILI of Carchemish sought his assistance but he seems to have remained neutral. He ruled until the early years of MURSILI II. Relations with Egypt were apparently good; an alabaster vessel inscribed with Niqmadu's name was recovered in Egypt.

Klengel 1992: 131–4; Kuhrt 1995: 306–9

Niqmadu (of Qadesh)

King of Qadesh, successor and son of AITAGAMA, whom he killed. He began his reign in the ninth year of MURSILI II. Eventually he was taken prisoner by the Hittites and brought before the Great King (Mursili II) who was in Syria at the time. His further fate is unknown.

Klengel 1992: 159–60

Niqmepa

1 King of Yamhad, son of YARIM-LIM II, father of IRKABTUM and YARIM-LIM III (18th century).

Klengel 1992: 62

2 King of Mukish, son of IDRIMI,

contemporary and subject of the Hurri-Mitanni king SHAUSHTATAR (15th century).

Klengel 1992: 89

3 King of Ugarit, son of NIQMADU, brother and successor of Arhalba, who only ruled for two years before the Hittite king MURSILI II installed Niqmepa as king of Ugarit (c. 1339/ 1329). His reign is one of the longest (some fifty years) and well documented. He had to accept a new treaty with Mursili which confirmed Ugarit's vassal status but reduced its territory in favour of Carchemish. He was put under obligation to appear regularly before the Great King (Mursili) and support him in case of war or rebellion. Niqmadu remained a faithful vassal of the Hittites, although trading relations with Egypt were also maintained. He had good relations with other Syrian principalities such as Amurru, and married his son AMMISHTAMRU II to AHAT-MILKI, daughter of BEN-TESHINA.

Klengel 1992: 135–9; Kuhrt 1995: 309–10

Nishi-inishu

Babylonian princess, daughter of SIN-KASHID, king of Uruk (c. 1900). She was installed as a *nin-dingir* priestess of the god Lugalbanda at Uruk. Her father built for her the *gipar*, the house of such priestesses.

Frayne 1990: 455

Nuptaya

Wealthy Babylonian woman, daughter of IDDIN-MARDUK, married to ITTI-MARDUK-BALATU, a member of the EGIBI family (6th century). He made a will, leaving her all his considerable fortune.

Wunsch 1995/6: 37–41

Nur-Adad

King of Larsa (1865–1850). His inscriptions emphasise building activity in Ur, Eridu and Larsa made necessary after the calamitous change in the course of the Euphrates. It was the king's responsibility to take countermeasures and reroute the river, resettle the temporarily displaced populace and rebuild the damaged civic structures and temples. Much of these works were continued and completed by his son and successor SIN-IDDINAM.

Edzard 1957: 142–5

Nur-ahum

Governor of Eshnunna during the period of the First Dynasty of Isin, successor and possibly son of SHU-ILIYA. He had difficulties with Elam and Subartu and had to ally himself with the powerful Isin king ISHBI-ERRA. He is mentioned in a Sumerian letter to IBBI-SIN. Bricks with his standard inscriptions were discovered at Ur.

Frayne 1990: 485–8; 1997: 438; Yuhong 1994: 7–11

Nur-ili

Little-known Assyrian king in the 15th century. According to the Assyrian King List he was the son of ENLIL-NASIR I and ruled for twelve years.

Grayson 1972: 37

Nur-Mer

Ruler (*šakkanakku*) of Mari during the period of the Gutian hegemony (*c.* 2153–2148). He is mentioned in dynastic lists and on a building inscription.

Durand 1985: 151, 155

O

Omri

King of Israel, founder of a new dynasty (885–874). He was the commander of the armed forces under ELAH. When the latter was assassinated by ZIMRI, his troops declared Omri king while he was campaigning against the Philistines. He returned to besiege Zimri at Tirzah and forced him to commit suicide. This did not make him an uncontested ruler, as according to I and II Kings, there was a rival party that supported Tibni, another contender. The rivalry came to an end with Tibni's death six years later. The biblical account in Kings has little to say about Omri, who was apparently an able ruler, other than to accuse him of idolatry. His name appears also in the inscription by MESHA of Moab, who reports that Omri had taken over substantial parts of the Moabite lands. He also left an impression on the Assyrians, who were to refer to Israel as the 'house of Omri' for long after his death. He moved the capital from Tirzah to Samaria, perhaps because of its strategic position. His building work shows the influence of Phoenician architectural methods, especially in the use of ashlar masonry. When he died he is reported to have been buried there, although neither his nor his descendants' graves have yet been found.

Mitchell 1982, in CAH III/1: 465–9

Osorkon II

Egyptian pharaoh of the Twenty-second Dynasty (c. 874–850). According to I Kings he was on good terms with AHAB, king of Israel, whom he may have supported, together with the other Syrian kings, in their battle against SHALMANESER III at Qarqar (853). According to the latter's Black Obelisk, a country called Musri sent tribute of rhinoceros, elephants, monkeys and an antelope to Assyria, but the identification of Musri with Egypt at that time is uncertain.

Edwards 1982, in CAH III/1: 553–62

Osorkon IV (= biblical So, Assyrian Shilkanni)

Egyptian pharaoh of the Twenty-second Dynasty (c. 730–715), whose capital was at Saïs in the Delta. He received messengers from the Judean king HOSHEA, who was trying to gain support for his anti-Assyrian policy, much to the annoyance of SHALMA-NESER V. In c. 720 he had sent his commander-in-chief to assist the king of Gaza against SARGON II, although he could do nothing to stop the Assyrians from taking the city. Four years later Sargon acknowledges that he had received a gift of twelve fine horses from Osorkon. This is the last we hear of this king.

Edwards 1982, in CAH III/1: 575–6

P

Panammu I

Aramaic king of Sam'al, son of *QRL*, (first half of the 8th century). He left a statue of the storm god with an account of his reign written in Aramaic.

Hawkins 1982: CAH III/1: 408; Donner and Röllig 1962–8: no. 215; II, 226

Panammu II

Aramaic king of Sam'al, grandson of PANAMMU I (*c.* 733/2). According to an inscription by his son, Bar-Rakib, he barely survived the blood-feud that killed his predecessor Bar-sur. He escaped to Assyria for some time and eventually took over the kingship.

Hawkins 1982, in CAH III/1: 408; Donner and Röllig 1962–8: no. 215; II, 226

Parrattarna

Hurrian king of Mitanni (late 15th century). In the 'autobiography' of IDRIMI he appears as the king who granted Idrimi permission to regain his ancestral territory of Aleppo, albeit as a vassal of Mitanni.

Kuhrt 1995: 291

Parysatis

1 Persian queen, daughter of Andia, half-sister and wife of DARIUS II. She is mentioned in Greek as well as Babylonian sources. In the former she is portrayed as a ruthless schemer, not shrinking from poisoning rivals. The Babylonian archives of the MURASHU family document her considerable private wealth.

Brosius 1996: 65–9, 110, 123, 127–8

2 Persian princess, daughter of AR-TAXERXES III. She became one of the wives of ALEXANDER THE GREAT.

Brosius 1996: 30, 77

Pekah

King of Israel (740–732). He seized the throne after killing PEKAHIAH, son of MENACHEM. According to II Kings and II Chronicles, he instigated an anti-

Assyrian policy and attacked AHAZ of Judah in Jerusalem, who alerted TIGLATH-PILESER III, then campaigning in Syria, to the situation. In 732 the Assyrians invaded Israel. Pekah was killed by HOSHEA, son of Elah.

Mitchell 1993, in CAH III/2: 326–35

Pekahiah
Ruler of Samaria, son of MENACHEM, king of Israel, whom he succeeded (742–740). He was assassinated by PEKAH.

Mitchell 1993, in CAH III/2: 326

Perdiccas
Macedonian general and military leader (*chiliarch*) under ALEXANDER THE GREAT. Together with Craterus and Antipater he formed a triumvirate to control the empire after Alexander's death; this was short-lived because of mutual distrust. His main quarrel was with PTOLEMY (I), whom he attacked in 321. He was killed in a conspiracy at his own headquarters when the campaign ran into difficulties near Memphis.

Will 1984, in CAH VII/1: 25–36

Phraates II
Parthian king, son and successor of MITHRIDATES I (139/8–128). He inherited the throne at a young age and his mother acted as regent. During his reign the Seleucids made the last attempt to win back Mesopotamia and the eastern provinces under ANTIOCHUS VII. They were initially successful and Phraates retreated. He then launched a counter-attack, which

resulted in the defeat and death of Antiochus. Phraates died soon afterwards in a campaign against nomadic tribes who threatened the original homeland of the Parthians.

Schippmann 1980: 27–9

Pisiri
Syro-Hittite king of Carchemish (738–717), a contemporary of TIGLATH-PILESER III and SARGON II, mentioned in the Assyrian annals. He is thought to have paid tribute to the former, though a gap in the text that lists the subdued rulers makes this uncertain. Sargon suspected him of plotting with Mita of Mushki (MIDAS), and had him deported to Assyria. Some sculptures with defaced hieroglyphic Luwian inscriptions are thought to date from his reign.

Hawkins 1982, in CAH III/1: 412, 418

Pit(k)hana
Anatolian king of Kussara, mentioned in the Assyrian texts from the first level of Kültepe, the trading colony near the city of Kanesh, which Pithana captured. He appears as a contemporary (and vassal?) of the Assyrian king ERISHUM (c. 1814).

Larsen 1976; Kuhrt 1995: I, 226–9

Piyashili (Assyrian Sharri-Kushuh)
Hittite prince, son of SUPPILULIUMA I, who made him king of the Syrian dependency of Carchemish (c. 1498–1313). He ruled this city during the last years of Suppiluliuma, the brief reign of ARNUWANDA II, and

the first nine years of MURSILI II, while he acted as military commander of the Hittite army stationed in Syria. He was the founder of a dynastic line of Hittites based in Carchemish that was to rule for five generations. His contemporaries were SHATTIWAZA of Mitanni and NIQMADU II of Ugarit, with whom he concluded treaties. He witnessed the expansion of Assyria and withstood several revolts against Hittite domination of Syria. He died during a stay in the Hurrian town of Kummani during the festival of the goddess Hebat.

Klengel 1992: 120–2

Protothyes *see* Bartatua

Psammetichus I
Egyptian pharaoh, second of the Twenty-sixth (Saïte) Dynasty, son and successor of NECHO I (672–664). He succeeded in uniting Egypt again after the Assyrian domination. According to Herodotus, he was made ruler of the Delta district of Saïs by ASHURBANIPAL after the latter's invasion of Egypt in 664/3. He effectively eliminated other Delta rulers, perhaps aided by a contingent of foreign troops sent by GYGES of Lydia. Then he went to Upper Egypt to preside over the adoption of his daughter Nitocris by Amenirdis II, chosen successor to the influential post known as the 'God's Wife of Amun' at Thebes. By this adoption he secured the support of the powerful Theban priesthood and effectively took control of southern Upper Egypt. In the so-called 'Adoption Stele' he claims to

have united again the two crowns of Upper and Lower Egypt. He seems to have pursued a policy of neutrality towards Syria-Palestine and his relationship with Assyria remained friendly. Ashurbanipal did not interfere in Egyptian affairs and seems to have regarded Psammetichus, who from an Assyrian point of view was a puppet ruler, as a potential ally against the Babylonians. The Babylonian Chronicle mentions that an Egyptian army supported the Assyrians in their pursuit of NABOPOLASSAR.

James 1991, in CAH III/2: 707–14

Psammetichus III
Egyptian pharaoh, last of the Twenty-sixth Dynasty, son and successor of AMASIS. He had occupied the throne for only a few months when the Persian king CAMBYSES II invaded Egypt in 525. According to Herodotus the Egyptians, supported by a contingent of Greek and Carian mercenaries, unsuccessfully challenged the Persians at Pelusium and withdrew to Memphis which was taken soon afterwards. Cambyses originally spared Psammetichus' life, but when he discovered that he had began to plot against him, he had him killed and Cambyses was declared King of Upper and Lower Egypt.

James 1991, in CAH III/2: 720

Ptolemy I
Founder of the Ptolomaic Dynasty in Egypt, son of Lagus, a Macedonian, one of the generals and *diadochi* of ALEXANDER THE GREAT (304–285).

After Alexander's death he became satrap of Egypt and consolidated his hold on the province throughout the ensuing wars over the succession to Alexander's empire. In 312 he invaded Palestine with the help of SELEUCUS I, then a fugitive from Babylon, and beat Demetrius, the son of ANTIGONUS, at Gaza. In 311, after the murder of the surviving son of Alexander, the combatants made peace and he became the undisputed ruler of Egypt. He tried to extend his territories further and invaded Cyprus and various Greek towns, all of which were lost in a counter-offensive. His main antagonist in the dispute over Syria-Palestine was Antigonus. When Antigonus was killed in 301 Palestine was assigned to Seleucus, which led to a conflict between the two dynasties which was to last for generations.

Ptolemy had a reputation as a man of letters, and was credited with the foundation of the library of Alexandria. He also wrote a history of Alexander's campaigns.

Turner 1984, in CAH VII/1: 119–33

Ptolemy II Philadelphus

King of Egypt, second of the Ptolomaic (or Lagid) Dynasty, son and successor of PTOLEMY I (285–246). He was first a co-regent with his father and then he ruled alone from 283. He continued the wars against the Seleucids and in Syria-Palestine, his antagonist being ANTIOCHUS II. Having sustained defeats on the Anatolian shore, he made peace and married his daughter Berenice to Antiochus.

Turner 1984, in CAH VII/1: 133–59; Heinen, in ibid.: 413–20

Ptolemy III Euergetes

King of Egypt, son of PTOLEMY II and Arsinoë, the latter's sister (246–221). When his sister Berenice and her husband ANTIOCHUS II were murdered by his former wife Laodice, he marched into Seleucid territories to avenge their deaths. He made further conquests in Anatolia and thus substantially extended Ptolomaic territories. He eventually lost the eastern provinces and northern Syria to SELEUCUS II but retained naval control over the Aegean.

Turner 1984, in CAH VII/1: 158–60; Heinen, in ibid.: 420–1

Ptolemy IV Philopater

Egyptian king of the Ptolemaic dynasty, son and successor of PTOLEMY III (221–145). According to the Greek historian Polybius his reign marked the beginning of the decline of the Ptolemaic empire. He fought without success against ANTIOCHUS III over Syria and was forced to sign a peace treaty with him. He later embarked on a re-conquest, the Fourth Syrian War, and won a victory at Raphia in 217. The province was lost again in the fifth war, to remain a Seleucid possession until the Roman conquest of the area.

Heinen 1984, in: CAH VII/1: 435–40

Pu-abi

Sumerian queen whose name appears
on a seal found in the Royal Graves at
Ur dating from the Early Dynastic III
period, *c.* mid-3rd millennium). The
splendid head-dress with golden leaf
pendants, now in the British Museum,
may have belonged to her.

Sollberger and Kupper 1971: IB1a

Puduhepa

Hittite queen, wife of HATTUSILI III,
daughter of a Hurrian priest, Pentip-
sarri. Before her marriage she served
as a priestess of the goddess Hebat at
Kummani in Kizzuwatna. Numerous
letters and documents written by and
to her have survived. She seems to
have taken an active part in diplomatic and religious matters. She promoted a synchretism between Hurrian
and Hatti deities and introduced a
number of Hurrian magic rituals.

Otten 1975

Pulu *see* Tiglath-pileser III

Pushu-kenu

Assyrian merchant and businessman,
active in the copper trade with Anatolia. His name and those of his sons
and daughters frequently appear on
tablets found in the trading colony of
Kültepe. He was a contemporary of
the kings IKUNUM and Sharrum-ken
(around 1910).

Garelli 1963: 35, 111f.; Larsen 1976, 1982

Puzur-Ashur

Assyrian merchant and entrepreneur
who conducted trade in copper from
his base in Assur (19th century). He
employed various agents to represent
his interests in Cappadocia, the main
point of supply for the metal.

Drecksen 1996: 131–9

Puzur-Ashur III

Assyrian king of the 16th century.
According to the Assyrian King List he
was the son and successor of ASHUR-
NIRARI I and ruled for twenty-four
years. He is also the first Assyrian king
to appear in the Synchronistic History,
where he is described as a contemporary of BURNABURIASH of Babylon.
A few of his building inscriptions were
found at Assur.

Grayson 1972: 34–6

Puzur-Eshtar

Governor (*šakkanakku*) of Mari, contemporary of AMAR-SIN. Two of his
votive statues have survived.

Spycket 1981: 240–5; Durand 1985: 151;
Frayne 1997: 445–7

Puzur-Inshushinak *see* Kutik-Inshushinak

Puzur-Marduk

Military commander of Ur at the time
of IBBI-SIN who complains in a letter
that his incompetence or treachery
resulted in the loss of the city during

the Amorite invasion (late 20th century).

Gadd 1971, in CAH I/2: 615

Puzur-Numushda (= Puzur-Shulgi) Governor of Kuzallu in the Ur III period. He lived through the time when the Ur III empire was breaking up. Various letters show that as a ruler of a provincial city he had to ingratiate himself with more powerful contemporaries. He used the name composed with the royal name SHULGI at the time when the latter still commanded his loyalty, but when his city was taken by the usurper ISHBI-ERRA he sent a desperate message to IBBI-SIN for support.

Gadd 1971, in CAH I/2: 614

R

Rakhianu (biblical Rezin) of Damascus

Aramean king who fought a long-running war against Assyrian control of Syria, forming alliances, one of which was defeated by TIGLATH-PILESER III in 733. According to II Kings and Isaiah, Rezin, together with PEKAH of Israel, attacked AHAZ of Judah when he refused to join them in revolting against Assyria, but was captured and executed.

Hawkins 1982, in CAH III/1: 413–14

Ramesses II

Egyptian pharaoh, third ruler of the New Kingdom Nineteenth Dynasty, son of Sety I (1304–1237). He was the most prominent and longest reigning king of the later New Kingdom. His most famous engagement was the battle of Kadesh (in his fifth year) against the Hittites. Egyptian records, most notably on the pylons of the Amun temple at Karnak, mark this as a triumph but since the boundaries between the two countries hardly changed it must have been less than decisive. In 1256 Ramesses concluded a peace treaty with HATTUSILI III, whose daughter became one of his many wives who between them were to bear him nearly eighty sons. After the peace agreement with the Hittites Ramesses consolidated his interest in Palestine and built a strong line of defences all along his borders.

Kuhrt 1995: 204–9, 328

Ramesses III

Egyptian pharaoh of the Nineteenth Dynasty (1184–1150). He was an energetic and long-reigning ruler who built numerous monuments in Egypt. His greatest achievement was to protect Egypt from the turmoil and chaos that had engulfed Anatolia, Syria and the Levant. He left a written and pictorial account of this on the walls of Medinet-Habu, the funerary temple he founded in western Thebes. He reports that in his eighth year he fought an important battle in the delta against the so-called 'sea-people', who are described as having come from the north, and partly by ship: an unstoppable host who had destroyed the Hittite empire and swept everything before them. Only Ramesses, so he claims, could check their advance and annihilate them utterly. Such language is ideological hyperbole and his victory was perhaps less great than stated, and the enemy not so formidable. However, although many of the Egyptian holdings in the Levant were lost, Egypt did continue to enjoy prosperity.

Kuhrt 1995: 386–93

Rashil
Babylonian scribe and scholar, who sent numerous reports and oracles to the Assyrian court (*c.* 679–665).

Hunger 1992: 218–28

Rehoboam
King of the united kingdom of Israel and Judah, then only of Judah, son of SOLOMON and his wife Namaah (931–913). He succeeded his father on the throne of the united kingdoms in Jerusalem, but soon moved his residence to Shechem, in an attempt to secure the support of the northern tribes. Rehoboam, however, refused to grant their petition to relieve their tax and labour burdens. This sparked off the rift that developed into a rebellion by the northern tribes, who elected JEROBOAM as their leader and later king. Rehoboam tried to persecute him and planned a campaign against the North, but was persuaded to desist from the latter plan by the prophet Shemaiah. Thus the northern kingdom of Israel came into existence, leaving

Judah with a considerably smaller territory, as other subject states also broke away. In Rehoboam's fifth year the Egyptian pharaoh SHOSHENQ invaded Palestine, both Judah and Israel, capturing the major cities and plundering the country. In I Kgs. 14:2 Rehoboam is criticised for introducing pagan cult practices, although he was said to have repented before his death. According to II Chron. 12:16 he was buried in Jerusalem.

Mitchell 1982, in CAH III/1: 453–61

Remanni-Adad
Assyrian high-ranking official under ASHURBANIPAL (671–660). His titles include 'chariot driver of the king' and 'prefect of the horses of the New Palace'. He must have been very wealthy as indicated by numerous purchases of land, property and slaves, documented in his private archive.

Fales and Postgate 1992: 239–87

Rim-Sin
King of Larsa, son of KUDUR-MABUK, brother and successor of WARAD-SIN, he enjoyed the longest recorded rule in ancient history – sixty years, from 1822 to 1763.

His reign concludes the period of transition from the fall of Ur III to the rise of Babylon under HAMMURABI (*c.* 2000–1792), characterised by the rivalry of the cities Larsa and Isin for the control of Mesopotamia and by the emergence of smaller independent kingdoms in the north, which successfully challenged attempts of centralisation by Isin and Larsa kings.

In the early part of his reign, when Isin was already in decline, we hear only that Rim-Sin rebuilt temples and dedicated statues to the gods. In his thirteenth year he defeated a coalition of hostile cities, led by the king of Uruk, Irdanene. The high point of his career – eleven subsequent years were named after this event – was the capture of Isin in 1796. It gave him control over the entire area south of Babylon. With the growing importance of Babylon, and the rivalry between Amorite sheikhdoms in the north, as documented by letters in Mari archives, peace was precarious but Rim-Sin remained a powerful ruler. When Rim-Sin hesitated to join a Babylonian alliance against Elam, Hammurabi turned against Larsa. He first laid siege to the fortified town of Mashkan-shapir, took it, and, supported by troops sent by ZIMRI-LIM of Mari, attacked Larsa in 1764. The city, defended by substantial forces, held out for six months, after which Rim-Sin and his sons were taken to Babylon, where Rim-Sin presumably died. Hammurabi destroyed the fortifications but spared the city.

Rim-Sin's status in Mesopotamian history has recently been re-evaluated, especially with regard to his administrative and legal reforms. These allowed greater control by the state and laid the basis for efficient centralisation and reorganisation of private, temple and crown land, which had previously been thought of as characteristic for the Old Babylonian period.

Gadd 1971, in CAH I/2: 641–3; van de Mieroop 1993

Rimush

King of Akkad, son and successor of SARGON OF AKKAD (c. 2284–2275). According to his inscriptions, he faced widespread revolts which he successfully suppressed. He also records a victorious campaign against Elam and Barakhshe. A number of his votive offerings have been found in excavated temples in several Mesopotamian cities.

Sollberger and Kupper 1971: IIA2a–e; Gadd 1971, in CAH I/2: 434–7; Hirsch 1963; Foster 1985; Gelb and Kienast 1990: 66–74, 191–219

Rusa I

King of Urartu, son and successor of SARDURI II (735–714). He fought in the northern region of Lake Sevan where he claims to have defeated twenty-three kings. Other inscriptions refer to his promotion of the cult of Teshub, the Hurrian weather god.

Like all Urartian kings, he built fortresses, especially in the Lake Sevan area. In his dealings with Assyria, as recorded in Assyrian annals, Rusa gained the support of Urzana, ruler Ardini, the capital of the border province of Musasir. He then used diplomacy to make further allies in an anti-Assyrian coalition, most notably with Mita of Mushki (MIDAS) and AMBARIS of Tabal. He also had Aza, who had been installed as king of

Mannai by SARGON II, assassinated and replaced him with his brother Ullusunu. This last act provoked Sargon to action. In 714, as described in detail in his report known as the 'Letter to the god Assur', he left Assyria with a large force which prompted several local rulers to submit. Sargon made a surprise attack on the Urartian camp; Rusa escaped but Sargon continued his march, laid waste to the Urartian provinces and sacked the city of Musasir. Meanwhile the Cimmerians had begun their invasion. When Rusa marched to meet them in battle in 714 his army was beaten, nine of his governors were killed, and although he himself escaped, he fell into a depression and committed suicide. Sargon claims that the reason for this was his destruction of Musasir.

Barnett 1982, in CAH III/1: 351–5

Rusa II

King of Urartu, son and successor of ARGISHTI II (680–640). He was a contemporary of ESARHADDON and ASHURBANIPAL. During his long reign Urartu regained much of its former wealth and influence, which is thought to have been due to the king's efforts in improving the infrastructure of the country, building new towns and fortresses. He also built fortifications near Lake Urmia, as well as in Transcaucasia, and moved the royal residence from Tushpa to Toprakkale near Van.

According to Assyrian annals, he undertook campaigns in Anatolia against the Phrygians and Neo-Hittite principalities, making common cause with DUGDAMME, leader of the Cimmerians. In *c.* 640 he made overtures to Assyria, but Ashurbanipal was unmoved. He had the envoys' tongues torn out and flayed them alive. Rusa's son and co-regent during his last years, SARDURI III, submitted to Ashurbanipal four years later.

Barnett 1982, in CAH III/1: 358–63

Rusa III

King of Urartu, called son of Ermina, probably the brother of RUSA II (*c.* 610–590). Not much is known from his reign; his name occurs on a huge granary at Armavir and a series of bronze shields from the temple of Haldi found at Toprakkale.

Barnett 1982, in CAH III/1: 363

S

Sabium

Third king of the First Dynasty of Babylon, son of SUMU-LA-IL (1844–1831). He began his career as governor of Sippar. His year names record the building of walls, temples and canals.

Edzard 1957: 151

Sammu-ramat *see* Semiramis

Samsi (= Shamshi)

Arab queen who fought against the Assyrian king TIGLATH-PILESER III in 732, as an ally of RAKHIANU of Damascus. Her forces were defeated and she fled the battlefield. Some time later she travelled to Assyria to bring tribute to Tiglath-pileser. He allowed her to continue to reign, albeit with an Assyrian official at her side. She later sent tribute to SARGON II as well.

Grayson 1991, in CAH III/2: 79

Samsu-ditana

Last king of the First Dynasty of Babylon, son and successor of AMMI-SADUQA (1625–1595). According to a later Babylonian chronicle he lost his kingdom and probably his life when the Hittite king MURSILI I attacked and destroyed Babylon.

Gadd 1973, in CAH II/1: 225– 6; Kuhrt 1995: 230

Samsu-iluna

King of Babylon in the Old Babylonian period, son and successor of HAMMUR-ABI OF BABYLON (1749–1712). His ninth year (1741) is called 'year of the Kassite army', which signals the first sign of pressure exercised by a people who subsequently ruled Babylonia for several centuries. There were several rebellions such as a general revolt of 'enemy lands' under the leadership of Isin, then ruled by Rim-sin II. By the end of his thirty-eight-year reign Samsu-iluna had lost control of the south, where ILUMA-ILUM had founded the 'Sealand Dynasty'.

Edzard, in Bottéro *et al.* 1965–7 (vol. 1): 202; Cassin, in Bottéro *et al.* 1965–7 (vol. 2): 12; Frayne 1990: 372–403

Sangara

King of Carchemish (*c.* 670–848). He first appears in the Assyrian documents as paying tribute to ASHURNA-SIRPAL II in 882. In 857 he paid tribute again, this time to SHALMANE-SER III, who had just completed his conquest of the Syro-Hittite states.

Grayson 1982, in CAH III/1: 256; Hawkins, in ibid.: 389, 391

Sarduri I

King of Urartu, son of a certain Lutipri (844–832), a contemporary of SHALMANESER III and SHAMSHI-ADAD V. In 844 when the Assyrians, under the command of field marshal DAIIAN-ASHUR campaigned against Urartu, Sarduri fought them near the river Arsanias. The Assyrians claimed victory, although in subsequent years Daiian-Ashur repeated his attacks.

Sarduri was the first Urartian king to have his deeds recorded in Assyrian cuneiform writing, examples of which have survived on rock-cut monuments in Tushpa and other sites.

Barnett 1982, in CAH III/1: 337–8

Sarduri II

King of Urartu, son of Argishti I (764–734). His extensive annals, carved in rock niches in Van, as well as inscriptions on stelae, provide information about his campaigns.

He consolidated gains made by his father in the west by subduing the king of Melid and marched further into northern Syria. He was active in the Transcaucasian area where he defeated local rulers. He also clashed with the Assyrians (under ASHUR-NIRARI V) in the district of Arme. A rock inscription on Lake Cildir, on the pass to Georgia, marks the most northerly point reached by an Urartian king. He also organised an alliance against Assyria with Arpad, Melid and Gurgum. In a battle with TIGLATH-PILESER III in 742 he had to flee when the Assyrian king captured his camp, leaving his bed and his seal to fall into the hands of Tiglath-pileser's, who, eight years later, invaded Urartu without, as he claims, any opposition. Checked in his military ambitions, Sarduri seems to have contented himself with building a fortress at Cavustepe called Sarduri-hinili. He was buried next to his father in a rock tomb at Van.

Barnett 1982, in CAH III/1: 348–51

Sarduri III (Assyrian Ishtar-duri)

King of Urartu, son of RUSA II (640–610), defeated by the Cimmerians and Elamites, he sent an envoy to ASHURBANIPAL to offer submission, as depicted on a palace relief from Nineveh. His seal was found on a granary door and a tablet at Karmir-Blur. Otherwise nothing is known about this king.

Barnett 1982, in CAH III/1: 363

Sargon I (Assyrian Sharru-kenu)

Old Assyrian ruler, son of IKUNUM (20th century). He completed the restoration of the fortification wall of Assur. His beautifully engraved seal shows the king being introduced to the god Ashur by the moon god Sin.

Lewy 1971, in CAH I/2: 710–11, 767–8

Sargon II

Assyrian king, successor of SHALMA-NESER V (721–705). One of the great Assyrian warrior kings, he completed the programme of conquests begun by TIGLATH-PILESER III. His accession to the throne was probably irregular; his throne-name *sharru-kenu* means 'legitimate king', and he never refers to his parentage in any of his inscriptions. He may have been a usurper or a younger son of Tiglath-pileser. One text, known as the Assur Charter, reports that the gods had chosen Sargon to avenge the 'unlawful' imposition of taxes on the holy city, which his predecessor Shalmaneser was said to have ordered. At any rate, since the inhabitants of Assur and Harran were later granted tax exemption, they may have supported Sargon in his bid for power.

The instability that preceded his accession triggered a series of rebellions in Assyria's vassal states. In Syria-Palestine YAUBIDI of Hamath began a large-scale revolt. Sargon defeated his coalition in 720 at Qarqar, then marched south along the Palestinian coast, reconquered Gaza, and stationed a garrison at the Egyptian border. Pharaoh OSORKON IV sent tribute.

In Babylonia MERODACH-BALADAN II had seized the throne after Shalmaneser V's death. The Assyrian army was beaten by the Elamite allies of Babylonia, and Sargon had to wait ten

years before he could make good these losses.

In Anatolia his enemies were the Phrygians (known then as Mushki) and the Urartians. Their rulers, MIDAS (= Mita of Mushki) and RUSA I of Urartu, incited smaller states in the buffer zone between their territories and Assyria to rebel against Sargon, who reacted with a series of military campaigns. Mita sued for peace in 709.

His eighth campaign (714) is vividly described in his annals. Initially intended to secure the Mannaean provinces, it led to a confrontation with Urartu. After an arduous march through mountainous terrain, Sargon defeated the Urartian camp in a surprise attack. Following the advice of his diviners, he stormed the city of Musasir on the eve of a lunar eclipse, which can be dated to 24 October 714. The town was sacked and the temple looted, an event commemorated on palace reliefs at Khorsabad, now in the British Museum.

In Babylonia Sargon enforced Assyrian control between 710 and 708, taking over the throne and forcing Merodach-baladan into exile. During his stay in Babylon he received tribute from numerous countries, including Dilmun in the Persian Gulf and Cyprus.

This success was followed by the official inauguration of his new capital Dur-Sharrukin (Khorsabad). The ruins, excavated in the nineteenth century, revealed remains of a huge palace, appointed with costly fittings, the walls covered in carved reliefs depicting his campaigns. He reports that he created a large park planted with exotic trees, and built shrines for the major deities.

Further trouble in the northern province of Tabal forced Sargon to march into battle again. He met his death on the way, under unknown circumstances.

Brinkman 1983; 1991, in CAH III/2: 86–102; Kuhrt 1995: 497–8; Tadmor 1958; Lanfranchi and Parpola 1990; Thomas 1993; Oded 1979

Sargon of Akkad

King and founder of the Akkadian Dynasty (2340–2284). According to later Mesopotamian tradition he was one of the most important rulers, the first to consolidate the political and administrative unity of the country. He became the subject of legendary narratives describing his rise to power from humble birth and his campaigns to distant places. He also features in historical omen texts from the Old Babylonian period as an exemplary, successful, king.

Apart from these secondary and historically unreliable records, there are inscribed votive objects and royal inscriptions, though most of these are known only from much later-date copies. He seems to have promoted the use of Akkadian in official inscriptions.

The chronology of his rise to power and the sequence of his conquests thereafter are difficult to establish. Sargon (hardly his original name, as it means 'rightful king'), held office at the court of Ur-zababa of Kish, and at some point took over the rulership of Kish. He always called himself first 'king of Akkad', after the city he

apparently founded. He records that he defeated LUGALZAGESI of Uruk, and then subdued one Sumerian ruler after the other. He seems to have made attempts to reorganise administrative structures and made various moves, not of a military nature, to consolidate control over the Sumerian cities. He appointed his daughter ENHEDUANNA to the influential position of *entum* priestess at Ur. He extended mercantile interests, sometimes by military means, to secure the safety of supply routes.

In his fifty-six-year reign he laid the foundations for a powerful empire that made a lasting impact on most areas of the Near East.

Gadd 1971, in CAH I/2: 417–34; Kuhrt 1995: 44–50; Hirsch 1963; Glassner 1986, 1988; Goodnick-Westenholz 1983; 1997; Gelb and Kienast 1990: 62–6, 157–90; Sollberger and Kupper 1971: IIA1a–d; Frayne 1993: 7–39; Liverani 1993: 25–40

Saul

First king of Israel according to Samuel I and I and II Chronicles (c. 11th century). The biblical accounts contain folk tale and legendary elements but are thought to be historically plausible. It seems that he was one of several contenders for political leadership among the Israel tribes, made legitimate by the prophet Samuel. Saul initiated administrative and military institutions, particularly a centralised command structure and a standing army. His court may have been at Gibeah, which is perhaps to be identified with Tell el-Ful. He subdued the enemies of Israel and built the foundations for its subsequent development into a monarchical state.

He is said to have been killed by the people of the Canaanite city of Berooth.

Eissfeldt 1973, in CAH II/2: 570–80; Kuhrt 1995: 443–7

Seleucus I Nicator

Macedonian general, chief of cavalry, one of ALEXANDER THE GREAT's *diadochi* (305–272) who distinguished himself in the Indian campaign. After Alexander's death, he was made *chiliarch* to the regent PERDICCAS and may have been involved in the latter's murder in 321. At the second partition of Alexander's empire he became satrap of Babylonia. In 316 he was dislodged by ANTIGONUS and fled to Egypt, whose ruler, PTOLEMY I, he supported against the other Macedonian chiefs. Ptolemy's victory in Gaza in 313 made it possible for him to return to Babylon and recover his satrapy. He managed to gain control over the eastern province of Persis, Susiana and Media. In Babylon, a new dating system was introduced to inaugurate the era of the Seleucids, which began on 3 April 311. Antigonus made further raids into Babylonia, which according to a Babylonian chronicle brought terrible suffering to the country. Seleucus finally defeated Antigonus at Ipsus in 301 and incorporated the satrapy of Syria and half of Anatolia into his realm, which then had almost the same extent as that won by Alexander.

He made efforts to create an effective system to administer this world empire and founded a number of cities, such as the Syrian Apamea, named after his Persian wife APAMA. The new capital became Seleucia-on-the-Tigris.

He continued to fight other *diadochi* in the west. When he attempted to occupy Macedon, he died in September 281, stabbed by a son of Ptolemy.

Sherwin-White and Kuhrt 1993: *passim*; Sherwin-White, in Kuhrt and Sherwin-White 1987: 14–22 and *passim*

Seleucus II

Seleucid king, son and successor of ANTIOCHUS II (246–226). The murder of his father, his Ptolomaic wife, Berenice, and her child, was avenged by PTOLEMY III in a series of invasions known as the Third Syrian War, in which Ptolemy annexed the eastern provinces. Seleucus held on to northern Syria and the western Iranian provinces, where he campaigned against the Parthians. He was defeated at Ancyra by his younger brother Antiochus Hierax, and had to leave him in possession of Anatolia. He is said to have been killed by a fall from his horse.

Sherwin-White and Kuhrt 1993: *passim*

Seleucus III Soter

Seleucid king, successor of SELEUCUS II (227–223). He tried to regain Anatolia from Attalus of Pergamum, but was murdered on campaign by conspirators in his army.

Meister 1984, in CAH VII/1: 430–4

Semiramis (Assyrian Sammu-ramat)

Assyrian queen, daughter-in-law of SHALMANESER III, wife of SHAMSHI-ADAD V and mother of ADAD-NIRARI III. According to a recently discovered stele she accompanied the king on a military campaign, an event otherwise unheard of in Assyrian history. Her name is sometimes included in dedication texts and she also had her own monument, complete with titles, in the famous row of stelae at Assur. Her influence and standing within the empire has been compared to that of other powerful officials such as SHAM-SHU-ILU.

She became the subject of later legendary tales and is mentioned by Herodotus as the builder of embankments in Babylon.

Schramm 1972; Grayson 1982, in CAH III/1 274–5; 1996: 204–5, 226

Sennacherib (Assyrian Sin-ahhe-eriba)

Assyrian king, son and successor of SARGON II (704–681). Sources for his reign are abundant, including the royal inscriptions, letters, astronomical reports, the Babylonian Chronicles, as well as the biblical account, some of which represent conflicting views of the same events. The chronology of his reign is still unclear. He is an important figure in the Babylonian tradition since much of his military efforts were concentrated on this area.

After the sudden death of his father, MERODACH-BALADAN, who had been forced to flee from Babylon by Sargon, returned from his Elamite exile and mustered an army augmented by Aramean, Chaldean and Elamite troops. Sennacherib took Cutha and defeated the Babylonian and allied forces. He proceeded to Babylon, and from there marched down to the marshes, where Merodach-baladan was in hiding. He punished the rebellious cities and appointed a puppet ruler, BEL-IBNI, as king of Babylon. In 700 he took up his campaign against the southern tribe of Bit-Yakin, who were allied to Merodach-baladan. The latter fled to the Elamite side of the gulf coast, where he later died in exile. Sennacherib installed his eldest son ASHUR-NADIN-SHUMI on the Babylonian throne, after deposing Bel-ibni, and then launched a punitive expedition against bases of fugitive Bit Yakin rebels ensconced in Elam. For this purpose he brought Phoenician-built ships to the Tigris and attacked from the sea. While he was celebrating his victory won at the river Ulay, he heard that the Elamites had invaded northern Babylonia, captured Sippar, and had kidnapped the Assyrian prince regent. In his place on the Babylonian throne they had installed NERGAL-USHEZIB, who took Nippur in 693. The latter was defeated and taken to Nineveh. Sennacherib, furious at the abduction of his son, attacked Elam and fought a major, if inconclusive, battle against a Babylonian–Elamite coalition in 691. MUSHEZIB-MARDUK, son of Merodach-baladan, claimed the Babylonian throne, which he retained for the next two years. In 690 Sennacherib began the siege of Babylon. The city held out for fifteen months. He sacked the temples and took the statues of gods away. According to Babylonian sources, he devastated the city.

The Assyrian royal annals describe his campaigns against Judah, also mentioned in II Kgs. 18; though the two accounts are as yet difficult to reconcile and to date. It is likely that Sennacherib made several attempts to force king HEZEKIAH to pay tribute. The sack of the Judean fortresses, Lachish and Azekah, depicted on the palace reliefs from Nineveh, must have occurred at the time.

He undertook major building operation in Nineveh, which became the royal capital from then on. His inscriptions stress that he took personal interest in all aspects of building; reliefs show him inspecting the transport of a colossal bull statue and the construction of aqueducts. The death of the crown-prince seems to have been a tragedy that overshadowed his later life. The attack on Babylon, the 'sacred' city, was seen as sacrilegious by various pro-Babylonian factions in Assyria.

In 681 Sennacherib died a violent death. The Babylonian Chronicle, the Bible, and various other later sources, all claim that he was killed by his own son. Some scholars now suggest that ARDA-MULISSU may have been responsible.

Parpola 1980; Brinkman 1983; Parpola and Watanabe 1988; Galter 1984; Grayson 1991, in CAH III/2: 103–22; Mayer 1995; Na'aman 1974

Shabako

Egyptian pharaoh of the Twenty-fifth (Nubian) Dynasty (*c.* 716–702), he extended his territory to include Lower Egypt and probably moved his residence to Thebes. Egypt began to feel the effects of the south-western campaign of the Assyrian kings. Shabako was careful not to antagonise the Assyrians, unlike one of his predecessors, OSORKON IV, who had put himself out for an ally and was defeated by SARGON II. When Yamani of Ashdod rebelled against Sargon, Shabako did not grant him asylum but delivered him to the Assyrians instead. This was favourably received at Nineveh. At least two seal impressions with the figure of Shabako were found there, which may suggest that diplomatic relations existed between Egypt and Assyria at the time.

James 1991, in CAH III/2: 689–93

Shadditu

Assyrian princess, daughter of SENNACHERIB, sister of ESARHADDON. One of her land purchases is recorded on a surviving business document.

Fales and Postgate 1992: 200–1

Shagaragti-Shuriash

King of the Kassite Dynasty of Babylon, successor and perhaps son of KUDUR-ENLIL (1245–1233). There are no records about the political events of his reign, but the numerous economic tablets issued during his time seem to fit an age beset with various economic and social difficulties, such as high indebtedness and the recourse to self-enslavement in lieu of repayments.

Brinkman 1976: 287–312; Cassin, in Bottéro *et al.* 1965–7 (vol. 2): 31f.

Shahurunuwa

Hittite king of Carchemish, son of PIYASHILI. His rule lasted throughout the length of the reign of MUWATALLI II (*c.* 1313–1333). He may have taken part in the Battle of Kadesh, where the Hittite forces defeated the Egyptian army (*c.* 1275). He faced Assyrian attacks during the reign of ADAD-NIRARI I.

Klengel 1992: 123–4

Shallim-ahhe

Assyrian king in the Old Assyrian period, son and successor of Puzur-Ashur I (late 20th century). A building inscription was discovered at Assur, commemorating restorations of the Assur temple. He is also mentioned in the letters found at the Assyrian trading post *karum* Kanesh in Cappadocia.

Larsen 1976: 56–7; Grayson 1987: 14

Shallurtum

Daughter of SUMU-LA-IL, king of Babylon. She was married to SIN-KASHID of Uruk and is known from seal inscriptions.

Frayne 1990: 463

Shalmaneser (Assyrian Shulmanu-ashared) I

Assyrian king, son and successor of ADAD-NIRARI I (1274–1245). He left numerous inscriptions, including accounts of his military deed, inscribed on alabaster tablets.

In his first year he successfully confronted a new enemy in the north-east, called Uaratru (later known as Urartu), and destroyed Arinna. He consolidated Assyrian control over Mitanni (Assyrian Hanilgabat) and defeated its king SHATTUARA II, who had challenged Assyrian suzereinty. Other rebellions, such as that of the Qutu, were also suppressed.

Under Shalmaneser the royal inscriptions take on a new tenor, developing the theme of the holy war under the guidance of the god Assur who leads the Assyrian king to victory. The texts elaborate on the punishments meted out to defectors and disloyal subject nations. Other documents record building projects, particularly the rebuilding of the Assur temple at Assur and the Ishtar temple at Nineveh.

Grayson 1972: 79–100; 1987: 180–230; Cassin, in Bottéro *et al.* 1965–7 (vol. 2): 81–3

Shalmaneser II

Little-known Assyrian king, son and successor of SHAMSHI-ADAD IV (1030–1019).

Grayson 1976: 68–70; Grayson 1991: 124

Shalmaneser III

Assyrian king, son and successor of ASHURNASIRPAL II (858–824). Sources for his reign are abundant; no king left more royal inscriptions and annals than Shalmaneser III. He also instigated the custom of summarising his campaigns in order of his regnal years.

He had the formidable task of maintaining the empire of his father in the face of growing unrest. He seems to have been able to turn internal dissent among his rivals to his own advantage, and could bide his time to wait for the opportune moment to make a decisive move. He expanded Assyrian influence, albeit at the cost of almost incessant military activity.

From the start he faced problems in the west. Some states in northern Syria and southern Anatolia formed a coalition under the leadership of Bit-Adini. After several attempts Shalmaneser defeated them, and Bit-Adini became a province of the empire. In 853 there was another serious conflict with Arab, Egyptian and Phoenician troops, as well as a contingent of soldiers in the pay of AHAB of Israel, according to biblical sources. This alliance was led by the kings HADAD-EZER (or in Assyrian Adad-idri) of Damascus and IRHULENI of Hamath. Shalmaneser met and fought them at Qarqar on the Orontes river, described on a stone stele discovered at Kurkh. Shalmaneser claimed victory, having put '25,000 men to the sword'. The fact is that the battle was not as decisive as he claims since he had to face the same coalition again within the next three years. Eventually, after his repeated onslaughts, as well as internal strife amongst allied states, the coalition dissolved. In 841 Shalmaneser collected tribute from the southern states, as the Black Obelisk records. King JEHU of Israel is shown bowing to the might of the Assyrian monarch.

When his Babylonian ally, MARDUK-ZAKIR-SHUMI, was in danger from a rebellion led by his brother, Marduk-bel-usate, Shalmaneser came to his aid and quelled the disturbance. He then made a tour of Babylonia's major temples, plundering Chaldean and Aramaic tribes on the way.

Other important campaigns were directed against the north, partly to secure the supply of timber from the Amanus, and partly to maintain Assyrian influence in Anatolia, where the kingdom of Urartu around Lake Van had become increasingly powerful. He records the destruction of settlements and the collection of tribute, particularly horses. The last campaigns of his reign were commanded by his general, DAIIAN-ASHUR, while Shalmaneser remained at his capital Kalhu (Nimrud). A rebellion broke out shortly before his death, according to the Eponym Chronicle.

Shalmaneser's building works were numerous; in Nimrud he erected the ziggurat, completed the Ninurta and Anu temple and constructed a huge fortress, dubbed Fort Shalmaneser by the excavators. In Assur he reconstructed the walls and gates of the city, and restored the Anu and Adad twin temple.

Grayson 1982, in CAH III/1: 259–81; 1996: 5–179; Kuhrt 1995: 487–90; Russell 1984; Dalley and Postgate 1984

Shalmaneser IV

Assyrian king, son and successor of ADAD-NIRARI III (782–773). There are few records from his reign, and it is clear that his commander-in-chief, SHAMSHU-ILU, played a major role in the events of his time. One stone stele records a campaign that he led against Damascus.

Grayson 1996: 239–44

Shalmaneser V

Assyrian king, son and successor of TIGLATH-PILESER III (729–722). He was also known as Ululaya, a nickname derived from the name of the month in which he was born, Ululu. Almost nothing is known of his short reign, except the sack of Samaria, which is reported in the Bible, as well as in the Babylonian Chronicle. The date of this is difficult to ascertain; some scholars suggest 722. His successor SARGON II later deported the inhabitants.

Shalmaneser V also occupied the Babylonian throne and there is some evidence in Aramaic sources of tensions in the south. According to a later Assyrian document, he imposed taxes on traditionally free cities such as Assur, which sparked a rebellion that cost him his life.

Brinkman 1991, in CAH III/2: 85–6

Shamash-eriba

Babylonian rebel leader who led an unsuccessful revolt against Persian rule during the reign of XERXES in 484.

Briant 1992

Shamash-mudammiq

Fourth king of the Dynasty of E, successor of MAR-BITI-AHHE-IDDINA (late 10th/early 9th century). According to Assyrian sources Babylonia was overrun by ADAD-NIRARI II, who annexed substantial parts to his empire.

Brinkman 1968: 177–80

Shamash-shuma-ukin

Assyrian king of Babylon, eldest son of ESARHADDON and his Babylonian first wife ESHARRA-HAMAT, designated crown-prince (667–648). After Esharra-hamat's death in c. 673, Esarhaddon decreed that one of his younger sons, ASHURBANIPAL, should take on the throne of Assyria while Shamash-shuma-ukin, who was already in Babylonia, where he served his father as an administrator, was to be king of Babylon. When Esarhaddon died in 669, Ashurbanipal acceded to the Assyrian throne, but he only installed his brother as king of Babylon a full year later in 668 and made him dependent monarch, forced to swear an oath of allegiance. For the first sixteen years their relations were generally peaceful but resentment against such unequal position, as well as Shamash-shuma-ukin's strong pro-Babylonian sentiments, are thought to have contributed to his resentment and a growing alienation between the brothers. When Ashurbanipal delayed to come to Babylonia's defence, after invasions by the Elamites and raids by nomadic tribes, and continued to be slow at returning cult statues and cult furniture previously taken from

Babylonian temples by SENNACHERIB, and generally continued to treat his older brother much like vassal king and nominal ruler, the latter sought for allies against Ashurbanipal. He won the support of Elam, Arabian tribes who had begun to establish themselves in Syria, and other rulers of western Asia. When Ashurbanipal heard of the plot against him, he first used diplomacy to sway the Babylonian support to his side. The first outbreak of warfare occurred in 652. Shamash-shuma-ukin had the support of northern and central Babylonia, the Chaldean and Aramean tribal areas, while the Assyrians counted on the allegiance of the non-tribal urban south, who resented the Chaldean hegemony. The outcome of the battles varied, with Assyrian successes being matched by Babylonian gains for the first two years. After the mutiny within the camp of the Elamites in 651 and the defeat of NABU-BEL-SHUMATI, son of MERODACH-BALADAN, the Assyrian side became dominant. Ashurbanipal's troops set siege to a number of cities, such as Borsippa, Cutha, Sippar and also Babylon, which was finally taken after two years, with epidemics and famine raging in the city. Shamash-shuma-ukin's fate is unknown; he was thought to have died in his palace when the city was set on fire.

Brinkman 1991, in CAH III/2: 47–57; Grayson 1991, in CAH III/2: 147–51

Shamshi-Adad I

Old Assyrian king, successor of Erishum II, but not of royal blood himself (1813–1781). His father was an Amorite chief, ILU(A)-KABKABI. According to one tradition he led an Assyrian army to Babylonia. On his return he seized the city of Ekallatum and after the death of NARAM-SIN of Akkad he usurped the throne of Assur. Shamshi-Adad was the first Assyrian king to use the title šar kiššatim, 'King of the Universe'. It appears that he controlled a large territory, stretching east to Lake Urmia and south to Babylon, where he made treaties with HAMMURABI, and west to the Mediterranean. Correspondence preserved in the Mari archives is an important source for his reign, since Shamshi-Adad had installed his son YASMAH-ADDU as governor of Mari. According to these letters the king was kept informed about the economy and administration of his realm. They document his diplomatic activities, marriage alliances on his own behalf and that of his sons, treaties and military expeditions. He appointed another son, ISHME-DAGAN, as governor of Ekallatum, who was to succeed him on the throne.

Kupper 1973, in CAH II/1: 1–10; Grayson 1987: 47–76; Yuhong 1994; Kuhrt 1995: 88

Shamshi-Adad III

King of Assyria, son of Ishme-dagan II. In one of his few extant inscriptions he reports to have restored the dilapidated tops of the ziggurats (probably of the Anu-Adad temple at Assur), originally built by SHAMSHI-ADAD I.

Grayson 1972: 32–3

Shamshi-Adad IV

Assyrian king, son of TIGLATH-PILESER I (1053–1050). According to the Assyrian King List, he came from Babylonia and deposed ERIBA-ADAD II. Only fragmentary building inscriptions survive.

Grayson 1976: 64–6; Grayson 1991: 117–21

Shamshi-Adad V

Assyrian king, son and successor of SHALMANESER III (823–811). At the start of his reign a rebellion broke out, contesting his succession. He fought for four years to establish himself on the throne and seems to have had to rely on help from his Babylonian ally, king MARDUK-ZAKIR-SHUMI, who had been assisted in similar circumstances by SHALMANESER III. He led military campaigns against the north, but it was his expedition against Babylonia that was seen as the most significant event of his reign. The reasons for this invasion are never made clear, possibly it had something to do with problems following the succession of Marduk-zakir-shumi. Shamshi-Adad destroyed several important cities such as Dur-Papsukkal and Der, amassing substantial booty. He claims to have captured MARDUK-BALASSU-IQBI and his entourage, and to have them taken to Nineveh where they were flayed. This brutal campaign had a traumatic impact on Babylonia, which remained without a king for twelve years.

Grayson 1996: 180–99; 1982, in CAH III/1: 269ff.; Parpola and Watanabe 1988: 4–7; Kuhrt 1995: 490–1

Shamshi-ilu

Assyrian military commander (*turtānu*) under ADAD-NIRARI III and SHALMANESER IV (late 9th–early 8th century). He probably came from a noble lineage of the Bit-Adini tribe, appointed governors when SHALMANESER III annexed their territory as an Assyrian province. Shamshi-ilu may have been educated at the Assyrian court and later rose to high office in the army. His residence was in Til Barsip. His name appears in many public monuments, such as a colossal stone lion, with an account of his victorious campaigns against ARGISHTI I of Urartu, and on stone stelae recording land transfers and border agreements with Syro-Hittite kings. He was one of the leaders, if not the prime mover, in the Damascus campaign of 796.

Grayson 1996: 203, 231–6, 239–40; 1982, in CAH III/I: 273–9; Hawkins 1982, in CAH III/1: 404–5; Donbaz 1990; Lemaire and Durand 1984; Kuhrt 1995: 492–3

Shar-kali-sharri

Akkadian king, son of NARAM-SIN (*c.* 2223–2198), last of the Sargonic dynasty. Some of the year names of his reign survive, but few royal inscriptions.

He constructed the Enlil temple at Nippur, a project that was begun by his father. Judging from the frequency with which this task is mentioned, he seems to have regarded it as particularly important. He also built temples at Babylon.

Towards the end of his twenty-five-year reign he had to defend his empire from foreign incursions, particularly

from the east (Elam) and the north-
west (Amorites). He also fought repeatedly against the Gutians. When he
died, the former empire that his father
and grandfather had assembled was
reduced to a small state, the result not
only of invasions but the drive for
independence in Mesopotamia itself.

Gadd 1971, in CAH I/2: 454–6; Sollberger and
Kupper 1971: IIA5 a–f; Hirsch 1963; Gelb and
Kienast 1990: 113–19, 276–82; Frayne 1993:
182–208

Sharriya

Governor of Eshnunna during the Old
Babylonian period, successor of IPIQ-
ADAD I.

Frayne 1990: 531; Yuhong 1994: 36–7

Sharri-Kushuh *see* Piyashili

Sharrish-takal

Governor and oracular priest of Akkad under NARAM-SIN. He dedicated a
statue to an unknown deity at Susa for
the life of his master, perhaps on the
occasion of the treaty between
Naram-Sin and HITA of Elam. A seal
of his was found at Tello.

Hinz 1971, in CAH I/2: 652

Sharru-kenu *see* Sargon I

Shasa

Wife of the Sumerian king of Larsa,
URUINIMGINA (2378–2371). Like BAR-
ANAMTARA, the wife of LUGALANDA,
she held a prominent position in the
temple. It appears that her statue

received regular barley offerings, perhaps indicative of cultic deification.

Gadd 1971, in CAH I/2: 120; Selz 1992

Shattiwaza (previously read Kurtiwaza or Mattiwaza)

Hurrian king of Mitanni, son of
TUSHRATTA (*c.* 1340). He narrowly
escaped with his life after the palace
intrigue that killed his father. He fled
to Anatolia, asking for protection
from SUPPILULIUMA I, the Hittite
king, who imposed a treaty on Shattiwaza, married him to one of his
daughters, and installed him as governor under Hittite rule, thus ending the
independence of Mitanni.

Kuhrt 1995: 292–3; Wilhelm 1989: 37–8

Shattuara I

Ruler of Mitanni, son and successor of
SHATTIWAZA (*c.* 1290). He came into
conflict with ADAD-NIRARI, who had
him deported to Assyria, although he
was later allowed to return. A further
rebellion against Assyrian suzerainty
resulted in his death and the destruction of Taide, his capital.

Wilhelm 1989: 39

Shattuara II

Hurrian ruler of Mitanni, son of
Wasashatta (*c.* 1240), who fought
the Assyrian king SHALMANESER I.

Wilhelm 1989: 40

Shaushgamuwa

King of Amurru, son of BENTESHINA,
during the reign of his Hittite overlord

TUDHALIYA IV to whom he was bound by a treaty (*c.* mid-13th century) forbidding him to trade with Assyria, then at war with Hatti. Otherwise he is mainly known because of the role he played in the complicated affair of the royal divorce at Ugarit. His sister was married to AMMISHTAMRU II of Ugarit, who divorced her and sent her back to her family, apparently under order of the Hittite king. At some point the Ugaritic king demanded his repudiated wife back and Shaushgamuwa handed her over.

Klengel 1992: 142, 172–4; Kuhrt 1995: 310–13; Kühne 1973

Shaushtatar

Hurrian king of Mitanni, son of Parsatatar (*c.* 1430/1420), a major figure in Mitanni history, though most information about his reign comes from a later document, the vassal treaty between SHATTIWAZA and the Hittite king SUPPILULIUMA I. He substantially extended the borders of the Mitanni kingdom, controlled Nuzi and Alalakh, Kizzuwatna in Cilicia, Ugarit, and conquered the city of Assur.

Kuhrt 1995: 293; Wilhelm 1989: 27–9

Shennam

King of Urshum, an important trading city in north-east Syria, who was on good terms with ZIMRI-LIM of Mari (18th century).

Klengel 1992: 76

Shibtu

Queen of Mari, wife of ZIMRI-LIM, daughter of YARIM-LIM I of Aleppo (18th century). As documented in the Mari letters, she had wide-ranging administrative and political responsibilities, especially during her husband's frequent absences from the capital, when she acted as the quasi-official head of state and main royal representative in the cult. Her letters furthermore reveal private concerns and her interest in the well-being of her family.

Batto 1974: 8–21; Dossin 1948, 1967

Shilkhakha *see* Silhaha

Shilhak-Inshushinak

King of Elam, brother and successor of KUDUR-NAHHUNTE (1150–1120). His reign is well documented; sources include not only several lengthy royal inscriptions, but king lists and other documents, mainly concerning building projects (such as temple of Inshushinak). He maintained control over the territories conquered by his father, SHUTRUK-NAHHUNTE I, and extended his forays into the Zagros, the Assyrian heartland, and possibly into the Iranian interior. His relations with Babylonia are not very clear, he may have imposed excessive tribute, which sparked rebellion. He made punitive expeditions against the north-eastern parts of Babylonia, around Nuzi and the Diyala region, and occupied several Assyrian towns. However, there is little evidence that he retained direct political control over Babylonia.

Hinz 1972: 128–33; Carter and Stolper 1984: 41–2

Shilwa-Teshup

Prince of Arrapha, eldest son of king ITHI-TESHUP (second half of the 15th century), well known from the Nuzi archives as an entrepreneur. He had at least two wives, Shasuri and Nashmu-naia, who had been his concubine.

Cassin, in Garelli 1974: 376–8

Shirikti-Shuqamuna

Third king of the Bazi tribe who ruled over Babylonia. He was the successor and probably son of NINURTA-KUDURRI-USUR I and ruled for only three months in 986.

Brinkman 1968: 164

Shoshenq I (biblical Shishak)

Egyptian pharaoh, founder of the Twenty-second Dynasty (945–924), a Lybian by birth though educated in Egypt. His capital and that of his successors was Tanis in the Nile Delta. He established a strong rule in Egypt, having gained control over the powerful priesthood of Thebes. He undertook a campaign to Palestine, which was weakened by the break-up of SOLOMON's kingdom. I Kgs. 11 and II Chron. 12 record that he invaded in REHOBOAM's fifth year, destroying cities and plundering the temple in Jerusalem, as well as gathering booty from the northern kingdom of Israel. It seems to have been a raid; he did not reimpose Egyptian control over Palestine. His relations with the kings of Tyre and Byblos remained friendly. He died rather suddenly, and was most likely buried in Tanis.

Edwards 1982, in CAH III/1: 539–49; Kitchen 1986: 292–302, 432–47

Shu-Dagan

Ruler (*šakkanakku*) of Mari during the Old Akkadian period (*c.* 2205–2200). According to the dynastic list, he was the son of IDIDISH.

Durand 1985: 152

Shu-ilishu

Second king of the Dynasty of Isin, successor of ISHBI-ERRA (1984–1955). He built the so-called Dublalmah, a monumental gate-building in Ur.

Edzard 1957: 70–1

Shu-iliya

King of Eshnunna, son of ITURYA (late 21st/early 20th century). During his reign Eshnunna become largely independent. Shu-iliya adopted the title 'king' (*lugal*) and was deified. He was on good terms with ISHBI-ERRA of Isin.

Yuhong 1994: 2–5; Frayne 1997: 433–7

Shulaya

Babylonian businessman, son of Zera-ukun, representative of the first generation of the EGIBI family, during the reign of NEBUCHADNEZZAR II (6th century).

Ungnad 1941–44; Krecher 1970

Shulgi

Sumerian king, second ruler in the Third Dynasty of Ur (Ur III) (2094–2047), he consolidated the empire founded by URNAMMU.

Sources for the first twenty years of his reign are sparse and record mainly the restoration and dedication of temples. Thereafter a wealth of data, year names and royal inscriptions, report campaigns against the inhabitants of the mountainous regions of the eastern and north-eastern border to secure the long-distance trade routes vital to the Ur III economy. They also defended his territory against the influx of foreign peoples, such as the Hurrians. In the east Shulgi extended his influence over the Susiana.

He restructured the legal and administrative systems to achieve a tightly centralised bureaucracy and public control over production and distribution, as documented by substantial numbers of administrative texts, found at the capital and various provincial centres.

He extended state control over the large temple estates, making them accountable and taxable. Shulgi's statues received regular offerings in special chapels; deification during his lifetime, an event unprecedented in Mesopotamian history, may have been an attempt to justify such measures.

Literary compositions, so-called 'royal hymns' are preserved on later copies. They praise the king in an elaborate style, presenting him as an exemplary king, youthful, vigorous, a good soldier and father to his people, even knowledgeable in the scribal arts.

He may have died a violent death, possibly together with his consorts GEME-NINLILA and SHULGI-SHIMTI.

Gadd 1971, in CAH I/2: 600–7; Klein 1981, 1981; Kramer 1983; Michalowski 1977; Frayne 1997: 91–234

Shulgi-shimti

Wife and queen (*nin*) of king SHULGI of the Ur III dynasty. Her economic activities are documented in the Drehem archives and show her influence at court.

Michalowski 1977; Steinkeller 1981

Shunashshura

Hurrian king of Kizzuwatna (*c.* 1400). He signed a peace treaty with the Hittites (probably TUDHALIYA II) which granted Kizzuwatna considerable independence.

Wilhelm 1989: 29

Shursa-Damu (= Shurshi)

King of Emar, mentioned in the Ebla archive texts (*c.* 2500).

Pettinato 1986: 141

Shu-Sin

Sumerian king, fourth of the Third Dynasty of Ur, successor and, officially, 'son' of AMAR-SIN, but probably, like the latter, a son of SHULGI (2037–2027).

Accounts of his military exploits come from later copies of inscribed trophies, stelae and statues, dedicated to the gods of the country. He tried, with some success, to consolidate his hold over the eastern and north-eastern provinces, partly through force of arms, partly by entrusting capable governors and commissioners (*sukkalmah*) to keep order. An infiltration of the Amorite tribes from the west was initially held off by military engagements, but in an attempt to safeguard his territory he ordered the building of a 170-mile wall.

Shu-Sin, like Shulgi, figures as the subject of erotic poems of a later date.

Hinz 1971, in CAH I/2: 608–11; Leick 1994: 111–29; Frayne 1997: 285–360

Shutruk-Nahhunte I

Elamite king, probably the founder of a new dynasty known as the Shutrukids (1185–1155), he left numerous inscriptions and is often mentioned in Babylonian literature. He consolidated his rule over Elam by touring the country, collecting inscribed stelae on the way. He seems to have had a passion for such monuments, which he set up at Susa, complete with a record of their acquisition.

He launched a carefully prepared attack against Babylonia, conquered Sippar and imposed heavy tribute on defeated towns and villages. Then he took Kish and Babylon, drove out the last Kassite king, ZABABA-SHUM-IDDINA, and replaced him with his own son, KUDUR-NAHHUNTE. He returned with much booty and tribute, including some of the most illustrious Babylonian monuments, stelae by MANISHTUSU and NARAM-SIN of Akkad, as well as the large stone inscribed with the laws of HAMMUR-ABI. They were discovered at Susa by French archaeologists some 3,000 years later.

Hinz 1972: 121–7; Carter and Stolper 1984: 35–6, 39–40

Shutruk-Nahhunte II
(= Shutur-Nahhunte)

Elamite king, sister-son and successor of HUMBAN-NIKASH I (717–699). His name was originally Shutur-Nahhunte but in a conscious attempt to emulate his famous predecessor, he changed it to Shutruk-Nahhunte, thereby linking the new Elamite kingdom to the lineage of the Shutrukids.

The sources for his reign are his own inscriptions, as well as Assyrian and Babylonian records. He reports that he led successful campaigns to enlarge his territory, endowed temples, and set up stelae for the gods.

According to Assyrian sources, the Babylonian king MERODACH-BALADAN, his former ally, sent rich presents to Shutruk-Nahhunte, asking him for asylum, which the threat of reprisals by SARGON II deterred him from granting. However, in 703, after SENNACHERIB had succeeded Sargon, Shutruk-Nahhunte and Merodach-Baladan set out together with a force of Elamite troops. After initial success they were defeated. Merodach-baladan fled to his tribal allies in the marshes and Shutruk-Nahhunte went back to Elam, where he was taken prisoner by his younger brother HAL-LUSHU-INSHUSHINAK, who then usurped the Elamite throne.

Hinz 1972: 140–7: Carter and Stolper 1984: 45–6, 50

Shuttarna II

Hurrian king of Mitanni (early 14th century). According to the Amarna correspondence he married one of his daughters to AMENOPHIS III of Egypt and also lent him the statue of the goddess Shaushga/Ishtar of Nineveh which was believed to have healing powers.

Klengel 1992: 97; Kuhrt 1995: 294–5; Wilhelm 1989: 30

Shu-turul

Akkadian king, son of DUDU (2168–2154), last known ruler of the Akkadian (or Sargonic) empire; some of his votive inscriptions survive.

Sollberger and Kupper 1971: IIA8a–b; Gelb and Kienast 1990: 122; Frayne 1993: 214–17

Sidqulanasi

Citizen of Carchemish at the time of king APLAHANDA (18th century), a rich and influential businessman, known from the Mari archive. He corresponded with ZIMRI-LIM, and was the agent in charge of supplying the court with wine, timber and grain from Carchemish.

Klengel 1992: 71

Silhaha (= Shilkhakha)

Elamite king, son of EPARTI, second in the dynasty of the 'Kings of Anshan and Susa'. He is thought to have introduced the title *sukkalmah* ('Grand regent') that was to denote independence from Mesopotamia. Later tradition regarded him as the founder of the dynasty.

Hinz 1972: 92–3; 1971, in CAH I/2: 640, 662

Silli-Sin

Ruler of Eshnunna in the Old Babylonian period (19th century). A few year names have survived and his name also appears on servant seals and similar objects.

Frayne 1990: 587–9

Simbar-Shipak

First ruler of the Second Sealand Dynasty (1026–1009). He seems to have originated from the Sealand, though it is not certain whether his Kassite name points to a Kassite background. The New Babylonian Chronicle reports that he carried out repairs on temples that had been damaged during the Aramean and Sutean invasions (towards the end of the Second Dynasty of Isin). He reinstalled priests in Sippar and returned a throne for the god Marduk to the temple at Nippur. Contemporary sources suggest that he controlled roughly the same area as the kings of the Second Isin Dynasty and that he was regarded as a legitimate king in Babylonia. He died a violent death, probably in a palace revolt.

Brinkman 1968: 150–5; Frame 1995: 71–4

Simut-wartash

Elamite king, son of ATTAHUSHU, brother of SIRUKTUH I (*c.* 1770–1768) and named as his co-regent.

Hinz 1972: 95; Carter and Stolper 1984: 29

Sin-ahhe-eriba *see* Sennacherib

Sin-balassu-iqbi

Babylonian official, governor of Ur (665–650). His repair works are recorded in a monumental building inscription.

Brinkman 1969: 330, 336–42

Sin-gamil

King of Uruk in the Old Babylonian period, son and successor of SIN-IRIBAM (early 19th century). Three extant building inscriptions refer to temple building.

Frayne 1990: 466

Sin-iddinam

King of Larsa, son and successor of NUR-ADAD (1849–1843). According to his inscriptions he carried out restoration and irrigation works and asserted Larsa's control over Nippur, Ur and Lagash. According to a later omen the king was killed by a piece of masonry which fell from the roof of the Shamash temple.

Edzard 1957; 145–9; Frayne 1990: 157–87

Sin-iribam

King of Uruk in the Old Babylonian period, successor of SIN-KASHID (*c.* 1898), only known from year names.

Frayne 1990: 465

Sin-kashid

Old Babylonian king who ruled in Uruk, probably at the time of NUR-ADAD of Larsa (19th century). He called himself 'king of the Amnanu', tribes then beginning to settle in Babylon. He never mentions his father and may have started a new dynasty. He left numerous building inscriptions, and is particularly remembered for his building activities in Uruk where, among others, he enlarged and restored sanctuaries the Eanna.

Edzard 1957: 154–5; Frayne 1990: 440–64

Sin-leqqe-unninni

Babylonian master scribe and incantation priest in the Kassite period (mid-2nd millennium). According to Mesopotamian scribal tradition he was the author or editor of the eleven-tablet version of the *Epic of Gilgamesh*. Several much later scribes claim him as their 'ancestor'.

Dalley 1989: 47f.

Sin-magir

King of Isin, successor of UR-DUKUGA (1827–1817), known from a few inscribed seals and from a clay cone in which his 'concubine' Nuttuptum writes that she had built a store-house 'for the life' of Sin-magir.

Sollberger and Kupper 1971: 181–2; Frayne 1990: 97–101

Sin-muballit

Fifth king of the First Dynasty of Babylon, son of APIL-SIN, (1812–1793), father of HAMMURABI OF BABYLON. Most of the year names refer to the building of walls, fortifications and canals. He formed an alliance with Isin, Uruk and other cities against Larsa, but was defeated by Larsa's king, RIM-SIN.

Edzard 1957: 152–3; Frayne 1990: 331

Sinqisha-amur

Assyrian prophetess from Arbela. She seems to have had a long career, spanning over thirty-one years. Some of the oracles she sent to ESARHADDON are noteworthy for their doctrinal content.

Hunger 1992: iv

Sin-sharra-ishkun

Assyrian king, son of ASHURBANIPAL, brother and successor of ASHUR-ETIL-ILANI (623–612). The sources for this penultimate Assyrian king are difficult to interpret, and reconstructions such as the one below, speculative and hypothetical.

He was older than his brother, who succeeded to the Assyrian throne after Ashurbanipal's death in 627. After a prolonged power struggle he took over the kingship in 623. In his first years he was on campaigns in Babylonia to contest the growing influence

of the NABOPOLASSAR. He had the support of Sippar, Uruk and Nippur, cities with pro-Assyrian sympathies, and formed alliances with the Mannaeans and the Egyptians against the Babylonians, who had allied themselves with the Medes. Their incursions into the Assyrian heartland, and the sack of Assur in 614, prompted him to launch a counter-attack in 613. In the following year the Medes and Babylonians attacked the capital Nineveh and took it after a three-month siege. The end of Sin-sharra-ishkun is uncertain; in one tradition he is said to have perished in the palace fire, according to another source he lived to plead for his life.

Oates 1991, in CAH III/2: 175–80

Sin-shumu-lishir

Assyrian courtier under ASHURBANI-PAL, a eunuch. He was instrumental in placing the king's surviving younger son ASHUR-ETIL-ILANI on the throne, when Ashurbanipal died in 627. He seems to have used his private guards to protect the prince and imposed a treaty on three individuals to guarantee their loyalty to the young king.

Oates 1991, in CAH III/2: 172–3

Siruktuh I

Elamite king, son of SILHAHA, brother of ATTAHUSHU (c. 1800–1772), contemporary of HAMMURABI OF BABYLON. He appointed his mother as regent of Susa. According to the Mari tablets he was an ally of Eshnunna against the expanding power of Hammurabi of Babylon. It is likely that he was killed in the siege of Razama which Hammurabi managed to break. He was succeeded by his brother SIMUT-WARTASH.

Hinz 1972: 94–5; Carter and Stolper 1984: 28–9, 31, 37

Siwe-palar-huhpak

Elamite ruler, sister-son of SIRUKTUH I. He was appointed regent of Susa after the death of his aunt who had held the office before him. He succeeded his uncle SIMUT-WARTASH to the throne of Elam in *c*. 1768. He may have played a part in the coalition against HAMMURABI OF BABYLON formed by ZIMRI-LIM of Mari, the queen of Gutium, the king of Malgium and the Subarians, which Hammurabi defeated in 1764. This was the end of Elamite independence and henceforth the regent only called himself governor of Elam, rather than *sukkalmah*. Later Elamite tradition regards Siwe-palar-huhpak as one of the great rulers of the country, and he may have established greater political control in the Iranian highlands.

Hinz 1972: 995–7; Carter and Stolper 1984: 26, 29, 37, 80

Smardis *see* Bardiya

Solomon

King of Israel, son and successor of DAVID (*c*. 9th century).

According to the books of Samuel and Chronicles, the only sources for his reign, he inherited a relatively stable and prosperous kingdom from his father and is said to have taken a primary interest in the cult, particularly the building of a temple in the capital Jerusalem. But he was also encouraging Israel's economic development and trading possibilities, partly by forging alliances with experienced Phoenician entrepreneurs. He strengthened the bureaucratic institutions such as the tax system and state labour workings. The subjugation of Israel's dependent states proved difficult to maintain, and by Solomon's death the Syrian states of Zobah and Damascus had become independent. The subsequent increase in pressure on the remaining vassal states may have contributed to the collapse of the Davidic monarchy after Solomon's demise.

Eissfeldt 1975, in CAH II/2: 587–605; Kuhrt 1995: 453–7

Sosandros

Greek citizen of Uruk, son of Diodor. He appears as a witness in a sale transaction dated to 162, during the Seleucid era.

Funck 1984: 82f.

Sumu-abum

First ruler of the First Dynasty of Babylon (1894–1881), then a small state in middle Babylonia. His year names record the building of city walls and fortifications, as well as battles against other Babylonian cities.

Edzard 1957: 122–4; Frayne 1990: 324

Sumu-il (Sumu-El)

King of Larsa (1894–1866), who continued the expansion of Larsa's influence that begun under GUNGU-NUM. Year names tell of armed clashes in northern Babylonia. He built new canals and barrages, which not only ensured the water supply of his region, but deprived the rival city of Isin of water. At the end of his reign, according to an inscription by a later ruler, SIN-IDDINAM, Larsa was threatened by an invasion which only divine intervention could save. Sumu-il is the first ruler of Larsa whose name was written with the sign for 'god'.

Edzard 1957: 108–10; van Dijk 1965; Frayne 1990: 130–7

Sumu'epuh

Amorite king of Yamhad when YAH-DUN-LIM and YASMAH-ADDU ruled in Mari (c. 1809–1780). He initiated a dynasty that was to rule from Halab (Aleppo) for 200 years. He fought against SHAMSHI-ADAD I, captured one of his fortresses and relations continued to be tense after Shamshi-Adad had gained control over Mari.

Dossin 1970: 17–44; Charpin and Durand 1983: 117–21; Klengel 1992: 51–4

Sumu-la-Il

Second king of the First Dynasty of Babylon (1880–1845). During much of his long reign he fought against other cities, notably Kish, which he destroyed, and nomadic tribes who formed changing alliances with various cities. Like his predecessor SUMU-ABUM, Sumu-la-Il strengthened his defences, building walls and fortified strongholds.

Edzard 1957: 124–6; Frayne 1990: 325–6

Sumuyamam

King of Mari, brother of YAHDUN-LIM, who ascended the throne after the latter's violent death (c. 1795). He was soon deposed by SHAMSHI-ADAD I, who installed his son YASMAH-ADDU as governor of Mari.

Dossin 1970: 17–44; Charpin and Durand 1983: 117–21; Yuhong 1994: 108–10

Suppiluliuma I

Hittite king of the empire period, son and successor of TUDHALIYA III, (1370–1330/1344–1322). He conquered important provinces in Syria and incorporated Kizzuwatna, a mainly Hurrian territory, into his domain. He fought, at first unsuccessfully, against TUSHRATTA of Mitanni but eventually penetrated into Mitanni and sacked its capital Washshukanni. The Mitannian crown-prince SHATTIWAZA took refuge in Hattusa and was later installed on his native throne as a Hittite vassal. He attacked Syrian states, especially Amurru, Aleppo and Alalakh. Having established control over Mitanni and much of Syria, he sought to establish good relations with Egypt. According to a Hittite document, the widow of Tutankhamen sought to marry a son of Suppiluliuma, who was murdered on the way. Another more successful dynastic alliance was concluded with Babylonia; he married a daughter of the Babylonian king. At the end of his reign the country suffered a severe plague brought back by Hittite soldiers, to which several members of the royal family succumbed.

Kuhrt 1995: 252–4; Houwink ten Cate 1970; Gurney 1990: 26–32; Klengel 1992: 108–12; Moran 1992: 114–16

Suppiluliuma II

Hittite king of the empire period, son and successor of TUDHALIYA IV

(1210–1205). Official records only record a sea-battle near Cyprus and building at the rock shrine of Yazilikaya. However, the capital Hattusa was destroyed, never to be used as a Hittite city again. The length of his reign and the identity of the people who sacked Hattusa remain obscure.

Kuhrt 1995: 265

T

Taharka

Egyptian pharaoh of the Twenty-fifth Dynasty, successor of Shebiktu (690–664). Most records from his reign concern building projects in Nubia. He took an active interest in the affairs of Syria-Palestine, partly by continuing commercial exchanges, and partly by pursuing an aggressive policy towards obstreperous rulers. This brought him into conflict with the Assyrians, who were campaigning in Syria and the Levant. ESARHAD-DON, particularly, who had succeeded his father SENNACHERIB, was anxious to minimise the danger posed by Taharka's activities. According to the Babylonian Chronicle, the first campaign by Esarhaddon against Egypt ended in an Assyrian defeat. But three years later he was back, this time striking in a lightning attack. Moving from Palestine southwards, he destroyed one Egyptian garrison after the other, entered Egypt, and captured and sacked Memphis. Among his prisoners were members of Taharka's family who were taken to Assyria. Taharka escaped, either to Thebes or to Nubia, and soon began to make trouble again, stirring up a revolt against the Assyrian authorities. Esarhaddon left Assyria to deal with the matter, but died on the way. He was succeeded by ASHURBANIPAL, who promptly led a second and successful invasion to Egypt. He defeated Taharka's army, who fled to Thebes, and when this was also taken by Ashurbanipal, he retired to Napata (in Nubia), where he died in 664. He was buried in Nuri, near Gebel Barkal.

James 1991, in CAH III/2: 695–701; Grayson, in ibid.: 110–11, 143–4

Tahir-Dashinu

Eblaite princess who married a king of Byblos (c. 2500). Documents from the great Ebla archive record the provisions for her retinue which escorted her to Byblos.

Pettinato 1986: 129

Talmi-Teshup (Luwian Ura-Tarhunzas)

Hittite king of Carchemish, son and successor of INI-TESHUP; he ruled during the reign of the Hittite kings SUPPILULIUMA I and ARNUWANDA II (14th century), and was regarded by the former as a partner of equal status, according to a surviving treaty. He maintained good relations with AM-MURAPI of Ugarit, and personally mediated in his divorce from the Hittite princes Ehli-Nikkal.

Klengel 1992: 127, 148; Hawkins, 1976–80, in RlA V: 433–4

Tammaritu I

Elamite ruler of Hidali, appointed by ASHURBANIPAL after his victory over TEPTI-HUMBAN-INSHUSHINAK (653).

Hinz 1972: 156; Carter and Stolper 1984: 50–1

Tan-ruhuratir

Elamite king of the Shimashki dynasty, son of Indattu I (c. 1945–1925). He was married to MEKUBI, daughter of the Babylonian king of Eshnunna BILALAMA. He left inscriptions that record building within the sacred precinct of Susa.

Hinz 1971, in CAH I/2: 660; 1972: 85; Carter and Stolper 1984: 21,148

Tarkhulara

Syro-Hittite king of Gurgum (c. 743–711). He had joined the anti-Assyrian alliance against TIGLATH-PILESER III on the side of Urartu and Melid. When the Assyrian king asserted his sovereignty and made Gur-gum and Melid vassal-states, Tarkhulara was allowed to stay on the throne. He was murdered by his son MUTALLU, probably in 721/11.

Hawkins 1982, in CAH III/1: 412, 420

Tashmetum-sharrat

Neo-Assyrian queen, wife of SENNA-CHERIB. According to a building inscription, discovered on stone lion-sphinxes at Kuyunjik, part of the palace complex was built for her, 'a palace of loveliness, delight, and joy built . . . that she may have her fill of well-being'.

Galter et al. 1986

Tehip-tilla

Wealthy land-owner and palace official at the court of Nuzi. He left an extensive archive recording his business transactions.

Wilhelm 1989: 46–7

Teispes

Persian king of Anshan, ancestor of the Achaemenid kings (c. 650–620). Apart from genealogical references, he is known from an inscribed seal found in Persepolis.

Miroschedji 1985: 287

Telepinu

Hittite king of the Old Kingdom period (c. 1525). Circumstances of his reign are obscure but he is best remembered for the so-called Edict of Telepinu, an important historical document that laid down rules for legitimate and peaceful succession to the Hittite throne, an attempt to bring to stop the murderous palace intrigues that habitually disrupted the transfer of power during the Old Kingdom.

Kuhrt 1995: 244–50

Telepinu of Aleppo

Hittite prince, son of SUPPILULIUMA I, ruler of Halab (Aleppo) (14th century). He was trained to be a priest of the weather god and probably maintained this function while he was ruler. He was a contemporary of PIYASHILI of Carchemish and continued to reign under the Hittite kings ARNUWANDA II and MURSILI II.

Klengel 1992: 128–9

Tempt-agun

Elamite prince, son of KUTIR-NAHHUNTE, appointed to be Prince of Susa (*c.* 1698–1690). He left an inscription declaring that he built a temple for the life and benefit of his family, including his 'gracious mother', Welkisha.

Hinz 1972: 98

Tepti-Humban-Inshushinak
(Assyrian Teumman)

Elamite king, successor of URTAKI (*c.* 664–663). His Elamite inscriptions are mutilated beyond comprehension and present knowledge about this reign comes mainly from Assyrian records.

He first seized power at Susa and persuaded Urtaki to join him in an invasion of the East Tigris area while ASHURBANIPAL was in Egypt, perhaps to support SHAMAS-SHUMA-UKIN. They caused some damage but were driven back by the Assyrians.

He usurped the throne after a revolt, and the royal family and other nobles, headed by Shilshak-Inshushinak II, fled to Assyria. While Ashurbanipal was occupied in Syria-Palestine and Anatolia, he felt free to consolidate his power. In 653 he prepared for an invasion of the east Tigris region, held by Assyria. Ashurbanipal countered, and faced with formidable fighting force of Assyria, he withdrew to his stronghold in the mountains. The decisive battle was fought on the banks of the river Ulay. Temti-Humban-In-shushinak was killed when he attempted to flee, as depicted on a palace relief from Nineveh. Another relief shows his severed head suspended from a tree in the garden where ASHURBANIPAL sits relaxing with his wife.

Hinz 1972: 152–6; Grayson 1991, in CAH III/2: 148–9; Carter and Stolper 1984: 49–50; Bryce 1988

Tette

King of Nuhashe (in north-western Syria) and vassal of SUPPILULIUMA I, king of the Hittites, who made a treaty with him (14th century). This ended in the early years of the reign of MURSILI II. The annals of this king mention that Tette rebelled against the Hittites, and was at some point aided by the Egyptians. The revolt was suppressed and Tette lost his throne to his brother.

Bryce 1988; Klengel 1992: 154–5

Tiglath-pileser I (Assyrian Tukulti-apil-eshara)

Assyrian king, son and successor of ASHUR-RESHA-ISHI I (1114–1076). He instigated an important change in the format of the royal inscriptions, now referred to as 'annals', which was to be followed for the remainder of the Assyrian empire. The accounts of the king's military exploits were ordered chronologically and the texts contain numerous references to the ideological underpinnings of Assyrian kingship as the institution sanctioned by the great gods.

Tiglath-pileser, having reorganised his chariots and troops, first turned northwards, where new peoples had settled in the areas previously controlled by the Hittites, who had disappeared as a political force in the 13th century. He pursued his northern campaigns for some years, penetrating deep into Anatolia, destroying towns and imposing tribute. He crossed Lake Van and defeated the army of the Nairi people, gathering substantial booty. Other regions, like Melid, submitted without battle.

When he had subdued the north Tiglath-pileser turned westwards, towards Lebanon and reached the Mediterranean Sea.

A persistent problem were the various Aramean tribes based in Syria, who raided local communities, destroyed crops, and evaded direct military confrontations.

In his thirtieth year he marched against Babylonia, where NEBUCHAD-NEZZAR I had made incursions against Assyrian territory and had captured Ekallate. It took considerable effort to defeat him, and in retaliation Tiglath-pileser penetrated deep into Babylonia and conquered important cities such as Dur-Kurigalzu, Sippar of Anunnitum, Babylon and Opis, and burned the palace of MARDUK-NADIN-AHHE.

Tiglath-pileser was also remembered for furthering the development of cuneiform law and literature. It was during his reign that the Middle Assyrian Laws and the Court Edicts were compiled, and a library was set up in Assur. Like his predecessors he was responsible for building public monuments and temples throughout the land. He also took an interest in planting parks and gardens, which he stocked with foreign and native trees and plants.

He epitomised the ideal Assyrian king; the annals depict him as the tireless commander of a mighty army, devotee of the great gods, executing their command to spread the power of Assyria, chief architect and builder, and maintainer of law and social order. After a reign of thirty-nine years he died and was succeeded by his son ASHARED-APIL-EKUR.

Grayson 1976: 1–45; Grayson 1991: 5–84; Kuhrt 1995: 358–61

Tiglath-pileser II

Assyrian king, son and successor of ASHUR-RESHA-ISHI II (966–935).

Grayson 1976: 73–4; Grayson 1991: 129–30

Tiglath-pileser III (Babylonian Pul(u))

Assyrian king (744–727). According to the Assyrian King List he was a son of ASHUR-NIRARI V, though it is more likely that he was not of royal lineage, and took the throne as a usurper during a rebellion in Kalhu (Nimrud). After a period of political dissent, weak leadership and a gradual but persistent shrinking of the borders, Tiglath-pileser's reign marks a period of regeneration, vigorous expansion and new conquests which restored Assyria to the status of a major international empire. He was an indefatigable campaigner who marched out with his armies every year but one. He made the army into a faster moving and better disciplined body, streamlined the administration and initiated the systematic deportation of peoples, which resulted in massive shifts of population.

In his first year he made his presence felt in Babylonia; having subdued the troublesome Aramean tribes, he toured the ancient cult cities.

He then turned his attention to Anatolia, where Urartu had become a formidable power. When the Urartian king, SARDURI III, offered military assistance to Assyria's disloyal vassal, MATI'ILU of Arpad, Tiglath-pileser used this as an opportunity to engage in hostilities. He moved against Arpad in 743, and when he was attacked by a major Urartian force he successfully defended himself, forcing Sarduri to flee. Arpad was taken after a prolonged siege in 740. News of this victory prompted a number of Syrian states to offer tribute.

The following year he marched against Ullubu, in the Armenian Taurus, which became an Assyrian province, where he built fortresses and resettled deportees. In 738 he faced a Syrian coalition, this time headed by Azriyan. He conquered numerous cities and forced other districts, including remoter areas such as Tabal and Arabia, to pay him tribute.

In 735 he launched a direct attack against Urartu and set siege to the capital Tushpa without succeeding in taking it. However, the invasion, complete with the sacking of many fortified cities, was effective in demonstrating the power of the Assyrian army. There was to be no more war with Urartu, and Tiglath-pileser could consolidate his northern frontier.

He directed his attention towards the borders with Egypt and marched south-west, along the Phoenician coast, capturing Gaza in 734; Hamath, Damascus and Tyre paid tribute. The following year saw another rebellion, organised by RAKHIANU of Damascus. Tiglath-pileser defeated him in 733 but besieged Damascus without success. Rakhianu assembled a force consisting of various auxiliary troops, including an Arab contingent under the leadership of the queen SAMSI, but was defeated.

These successes in Syria allowed the Assyrian king to concentrate on the east. He stabilised his borders along the Zagros mountains and the Diyala river and forced the Mannaean ruler to pay him tribute.

In 732 there were problems in Babylon when NABONASSAR died and a rebellion broke out, headed by MUKIN-ZERI. Tiglath-pileser only interfered with an armed force when his attempts to influence the population of Babylon against the usurper failed to dislodge him. In 729 he marched south, captured Mukin-zeri in his provincial capital Shapiya, and then entered Babylon in triumph to have himself declared rightful king of Babylon, assuming the throne-name Pulu. He was anxious to maintain the traditional roles of the king of Babylon by leading the processions of the New Year Festival and honouring the Babylonian gods.

His royal inscriptions speak primarily about his military campaigns, although they also refer to his building projects at Nimrud.

Grayson 1975: 248–9; Kuhrt 1995: 496–7; Brinkman 1993, in CAH III/2: 32–40; Mitchell 1993, in CAH III/2: 322–38

Tirigan

King of Akkad, last of the Gutian Dynasty (late 22nd century). He was defeated by the Uruk king UTUHEGAL, as described in the latter's Victory Monument. According to this inscription Tirigan had only been on the throne for forty days before the battle against the king of Uruk. He fled and sought refuge in a town called Dubrum, whose inhabitants handed him over to Utuhegal.

Gadd 1971, in CAH I/2: 462; Römer 1985

Tisha-Lim

Queen of Emar, wife of Rusi-Lim, mentioned in the Ebla archive as having concluded a treaty with Ebla.

Pettinato 1986: 141; Archi 1990; Dietrich and Loretz 1993

Tish-atal

Hurrian king, contemporary of SHU-SIN of Ur (*c.* 1970). According to an inscription he ruled over Eshnunna.

Wilhelm 1989: 11; Whiting 1976

Tud(t)anapshum

Entum priestess of the god Enlil during the reign of NARAM-SIN of Akkad. She may well have been his daughter since it was a custom that such elevated positions were filled with princesses. No other such priestesses serving this particular god are known.

Michalowski 1981: 173–6; Gelb and Kienast 1990: 105–6

Tudhaliya I

Hittite king of the early empire period (1430–1410 or 1420–1400). He stands at the beginning of a new dynastic line that was to make the Hittite realm an international power on a par with Egypt and Mitanni. Tudhaliya expanded his frontiers eastwards to incorporate Isuwa, a copper producing district beyond the Euphrates in Anatolia. In the west he made alliances with Ahhiyawa and Arzawa.

Kuhrt 1995: 250–1

Tudhaliya III

Hittite king of the Empire period (1380–1370/1355–1344), son and successor of ARNUWANDA I, father of SUPPILULIUMA I. According to the so-called Deeds of Suppiluliuma, Tudhaliya resided in Samuha from which he imported the cult of the Black Goddess.

Kuhrt 1995: 252

Tudhaliya IV

Hittite king of the Empire period, son and successor of HATTUSILI III (*c.* 1245–1215/1239–1209). He made great efforts to reconstruct the old capital, Hattusa, which had been destroyed during the reign of MUWATALLI II. He was also at pains to revitalise the religious cult at Yazilikaya, near the old capital, where his image, protected by the god Sarruma, is carved into the rock-face. Recently discovered texts show that he may have shared power with his cousin KURUNTA, who ruled the province of Tarhuntassa.

Klengel 1991; Kuhrt 1995: 264–5

Tukin-khatta-migrisha

Sumerian princess, daughter of IBBI-SIN. He married her to the *ensi* of Zabshali in Elam, in an attempt to establish greater control over the eastern provinces.

Gadd 1971, in CAH I/2: 611

Tukulti-apil-eshara *see* Tiglath-pileser I

Tukulti-Ninurta I

Assyrian king, son and successor of SHALMANESER I (1244–1208). There is an unprecedented number of documents pertaining to his reign, partly a result of the importation of Babylonian tablet collections and scribes.

He was one of the great expansionist rulers of the Middle Assyrian period. Building on the achievements of his predecessors he made Assyria a formidable military and economic power. However, his efforts to pacify the ever-increasing borders of the state were constantly subverted by the guerrilla tactics of the local populations and the fluctuating movements of pastoralist tribes, such as the Guti, who evaded direct confrontations with the Assyrian armies. One of the tactics employed by the Assyrians to counter such problems was the deportation and resettlement of substantial numbers of subject peoples.

He defeated a confederation of the Nairi kings in the north, but his most controversial victory was over Babylonia. In his eleventh year he defeated the Kassite king Kashtiliash V, taking him and a number of his subjects to Assyria. Tukulti-Ninurta himself assumed the Babylonian royal titles and began Assyrian rule over Babylonia that was to last some thirty-two years. One of the results of this annexion was a strong Babylonian influence in the Assyrian capital. He relocated the royal palace, complete with sanctuaries, from Assur to a new foundation, called Kar-Tukulti-Ninurta, some 3 miles outside the city. He also built a new temple for Ishtar at Assur and rebuilt other sanctuaries in the capital. Such grand and costly building works and perhaps the ambivalent attitude towards the Babylonian conquest may have caused dissatisfaction and unrest. According to the Chronicle P, Assyrian officers, possibly led by one of his sons, rebelled against the king;

he was locked in a room in Kar-Tukulti-Ninurta and killed.

Grayson 1972: 101–34; Cassin, in Bottéro *et al.* 1965–7 (vol. 3): 83–9; Kuhrt 1995: 355–8

She conducted numerous business deals, buying land and slaves.

Kupper 1973, in CAH II/1: 23–4; Starr 1937–9: 242ff.

Tukulti-Ninurta II

Assyrian king, son and successor of ADAD-NIRARI II, (890–884). His annals report an important campaign to Anatolia, the lands of Nairi, which had lapsed in its tribute obligations. Tukulti-Ninurta destroyed numerous cities, deported inhabitants and took valuable booty. He then re-installed the local ruler Amme-Baal, after he made him swear an oath of loyalty.

In another account, rich in descriptive and topographical detail, he is said to have moved westwards across the Tigris to region of Samarra, where he fought against the Idu nomads. His march then became a triumphal display of Assyrian power; he entered Babylonian territory, visited Dur-Kurigalzu and Sippar, and then continued his tour to impress local rulers, collecting tribute and costly gifts.

He used the revenue to build strongholds in the various districts, make new arable land, and to re-populate the countryside. He also undertook building works on the palace at Assur and restored the city walls.

Grayson 1976: 97–113; 1982, in CAH III/1: 251–3; 1991: 163–88; Kuhrt 1995: 482–3

Tulpunnaya

Wealthy woman who lived at the Governor's Palace in Nuzi (14th century?).

Turam-dagan

Ruler (*šakkanakku*) of Mari during the Ur III period (*c.* 2071–2051), son of APIL-KIN, brother of ILI-ISHAR, known from dynastic lists and inscribed seals.

Durand 1985: 150, 151

Turam-ili

Wealthy merchant, active during the reigns of SHU-SIN and IBBI-SIN (*c.* 2035–2026). He belonged to a group of entrepreneurs who pooled their resources to finance trading expeditions.

van de Mieroop 1986

Tushratta

Hurrian king of Mitanni, son of Shattarna II and a minor when he was put on the throne by his brother Artshumara (mid-14th century). According to the Amarna correspondence he sent one of his daughters to Egypt to become a secondary wife of the pharaoh AMENOPHIS III. He also sent letters to his son (AMENOPHIS IV), as well as Tiye, the wife of Amenophis III. He also lent the pharaoh the healing statue of Shaushga/Ishtar of Nineveh.

He was murdered in a palace intrigue, and his son SHATTIWAZA was forced to take refuge with the Hittite king SUPPILULIUMA I.

Klengel 1992: 97, 111; Kuhrt 1995: 293–4; Wilhelm 1989: 30–7; Moran 1992: 41–99

Tutammu

King of Unqi (Pattin) (*c.* 738), known from the inscriptions of TIGLATH-PILESER III, to whom he was bound by a loyalty-oath. When he revolted against the Assyrian king, together with nineteen districts of Hamath, Tiglath-pileser seized his kingdom, and had him and his courtiers deported to Assyria, where he was probably executed as an oath-breaker.

Hawkins 1982, in CAH III/1: 410–11

Tuthmosis I

Egyptian pharaoh of the Eighteenth Dynasty (*c.* 1504–1491). He was the first Egyptian ruler to embark on large-scale military campaigns abroad, especially in the Levant. He even penetrated into Syria to confront the new power of Mitanni and erected a stele on the bank on the Euphrates.

Hayes 1973, in CAH II/1: 313ff.; Klengel 1992: 90; Weinstein 1981

Tuthmosis III

Egyptian pharaoh of the Eighteenth Dynasty (1479–1425), grandson of TUTHMOSIS I, son of Hatshepsut. Like his ancestor he led numerous campaigns against various states in the Levant and Syria, particularly against Mitanni. He won the battle at Megiddo, where he faced a coalition of 330 local chiefs and leaders. In his thirty-third year he reached the plain of Homs in Syria and crossed the Euphrates by boat, erecting a stele.

Hayes 1973, in CAH II/1: 316ff.; Klengel 1992: 91–5; Kuhrt 1995: 193

Tuthmosis IV

Egyptian pharaoh of the Eighteenth Dynasty, son of AMENOPHIS II (*c.* 1397–1387). According to the Amarna letters, the king fought a successful campaign in the Levant. He received one of the daughters of the Mitanni king ARTATAMA I for a wife.

Klengel 1992: 97

Tuttash-shar-libbish (= Tuta-shar-libbish)

Wife of the Akkadian king SHAR-KALI-SHARRI. Her name and epithet, '*narāmat* LUGAL' (beloved of the king), are preserved on two seals which belonged to court officials of the time.

Gelb and Kienast 1990: 44; Michalowski 1981: 176

U

Ulmi-Teshup
Anatolian king of Tarhuntassa, vassal of the Hittite king (possibly HATTU-SILI III), whose treaty with Ulmi-Teshup is preserved.

Gurney 1993: 13–28

Umakishtar *see* Cyaxares

Umman-menanu *see* Humban-numena

Ummannigash *see* Humban-nikash I

Untash-napirisha (read formerly as Untash-Humban)
Elamite king, son and successor of HUMBAN-NUMENA (1275–1240). Sources for his reign exist in Akkadian and Elamite, mainly preserved on votive objects.

He built on the peace and stability initiated during his father's reign. He built the great royal ceremonial and religious centre, called after himself Al-Untash-Napirisha (present-day Choga Zanbil) with its unusual and splendid ziggurat. He also constructed a canal with its own tidal basin, which is still in a good state of preservation today.

His only known campaign was a surprise raid into Mesopotamia, where he attacked and despoiled Eshnunna. This happened probably during the reign of the Kassite king KASHTILIASH IV. It is possible that Untash-napirisha and his wife Napir-isa were buried in the funerary vaults of Choga Zanbil. He had no son and was succeeded by his nephew Unpa-tar-napirisha.

Ghirshman 1966–70; Hinz 1972: 113–19; Carter and Stolper 1984: 33, 37–9, 160, 166, 217

Urad-Ea
Assyrian scribe and priest under ESAR-HADDON, chief chanter (*galamahu*) of the Assyrian king, as well as chanter of the moon god at Harran, and writer of several astrological reports and letters to the king.

Parpola 1970: 212–15; 1983: 259–62

Urad-Gula

Assyrian scribe, deputy chief physician of ESARHADDON and exorcist (*āšipu*) under ASHURBANIPAL, son of ADAD-SHUMA-USUR. Six of his professional letters on exorcism survive. He was unusual in combining two areas of professional competence.

Parpola 1970: 168–73; 1983: 215–18

Urad-Nana

Assyrian scribe, chief physician (*rab ase*) at the court of ESARHADDON (and perhaps ASHURBANIPAL). He wrote several important letters on the state of health of the royal family; one of which lists the children of the king.

Parpola 1970: 188–99; 1983: 229–55; 1993: 226–35

Ura-Tarhunzas *see* Talmi-Teshup

Ur-Baba (or Ur-Ba'u)

Ruler (*ensi*) of Lagash; he was either a contemporary of the last Akkadian king Shu-durul or he reigned during the troubled time between the reign of SHAR-KALI-SHARRI and Shu-durul. During his lifetime and that of his successor and son-in-law, GUDEA, Lagash enjoyed a fair amount of prosperity and independence, as his various inscriptions on votive offerings testify. His daughter, bearing the official name Enannepada, was appointed as high priestess of Nanna at Ur.

Sollberger and Kupper 1971: IIC2a–d; Gadd 1971, in CAH I/2: 458–89; Edzard 1997: 15–25

Urballu *see* Warpalas

Urdamane (Egyptian Tantamani)

Egyptian pharaoh, last of the Kushite (Twenty-fifth) Dynasty, successor (and probably a nephew) of TAHARKA (664–656). In a stele which he set up to record the contents of a dream and what happened after that, he claims that he made a triumphant entry into Egypt, captured Memphis and that the Delta rulers voluntarily submitted to him. Nowhere does he mention the new conquerors of Egypt, the Assyrians. The cuneiform sources tell a different story. Urdamane is said to have indeed occupied Memphis and Heliopolis, but only until he was dislodged by ASHURBANIPAL, who set out from Nineveh to reclaim his Egyptian territories as soon as heard about Urdamane's take-over. He fled before the Assyrian advance, first to Thebes, and, when the city fell to Ashurbanipal, to Nubia. He never left Nubia and although his rulership continued to be formally acknowledged in Thebes he no longer exercised the role of pharaoh. This was the end of the Kushite Dynasty.

James 1991, in CAH III/2: 701–3; Grayson, in ibid.: 143–4

Urdu-Nanna *see* Ir-Nanna

Ur-gar

Ruler (*ensi*) of Lagash, son-in-law of UR-BABA, successor of UR-NINGIRSU. He left some inscribed votive objects

Sollberger and Kupper 1971: IIC6a–b

Urhilina *see* Irhuleni

Urhi-Teshup (= Mursili III)

Hittite king of the empire period, brother and successor of MUWATALLI (1282–1275/1271–1264). Little is known of his brief reign, except that he attempted to reduce the territories and power of his uncle, who ruled in the northern province Hakpissa, which had been set up by Muwatalis. The so-called 'Apology of Hattusili III' records the seven-year strife between the two Hittite rulers which Hattusili III won. Urhi-Teshup was taken prisoner and exiled to the Syrian province of Nuhassi.

Kuhrt 1995: 258–63; Otten 1981

Urikki

Anatolian ruler of Que. He sent tribute and owed allegiance to TIGLATH-PILESER III (*c.* 730). He also appears as having some status under SARGON II, as mentioned in a letter which the Assyrian king sent to his representative in Que.

Postgate 1973

Urlumma

Early Dynastic Sumerian king of Umma (*c.* 2400). He attacked neighbouring Lagash under its king ENANNATUM I and was defeated by the latter's son ENMETENA.

Cooper 1983

Ur-Mama

Ruler of Lagash, descendent of GUDEA. He is only known from a year name and inscribed votive offerings.

Edzard 1997: 192–3

Urnammu

King of Ur, founder of the Third Dynasty of Ur (2113–2096). He first ruled as governor of Ur, probably with the approval of UTUHEGAL, the king of Uruk, and was in control of the country after the expulsion of the Gutians. After the defeat of the ruler of Lagash, Urnammu took on the title of 'king of Sumer and Akkad', which expressed his sovereignty over the whole country. The year names reveal renewed trade activity, as do the various administrative texts from this period. He commissioned the excavation of canals to benefit agriculture and trade alike, but he remains best known for his impressive buildings, especially the ziggurats, at Ur as well as Uruk, a city that maintained close political and cultural ties with the capital throughout the Ur III period. Urnammu is also the subject of a various royal hymns, a literary genre that became very popular with the Ur III kings, in which the ruler is exhorted for his physical perfection and prowess, his military success, cultural and artistic distinction, and his close ties with the gods and legendary heroes of the First Dynasty of Uruk. One such poem refers to the end of Urnammu, apparently he was killed in battle, and describes his entry to the Underworld.

Gadd 1971, in CAH I/2: 597–600; Kuhrt 1995: 58–9; Hallo 1966; Sollberger 1954–6: 154–6; Klein 1981, 1981b; Kramer 1967; Frayne 1997: 9–90; Civil 1985

Ur-Nanshe

1 Early Dynastic Sumerian king of Lagash, succeeded by his son AKUR-GAL (c. 2550). He was not of royal birth himself, neither his father nor grandfather are called 'king' (*lugal*), and he claims to have been 'selected by divination to be the husband of [the goddess] Nanshe'. He left several votive inscriptions which commemorate mainly building activities, the digging of canals, etc. One outstanding artefact, a limestone plaque with a low relief, shows the king twice, once carrying a basket for the ritual inauguration of a temple, and again seated, raising a cup. In both instances he is in company of his children, his wife and three courtiers, all identified by Sumerian logograms. Several of his inscriptions mention ships from Dilmun, a reference to the growing importance of long-distance trade.

Sollberger and Kupper 1971: IC3a–f; Gadd 1971, in CAH I/2: 116–17; Cooper 1986: 22–31

2 Singer at the court of Mari during the Early Dynastic period, perhaps a eunuch musician because of his unusual dress and hairstyle in which he is represented on a statue (now at the Aleppo museum).

Postgate 1992: 126

Ur-Ninurta

Sixth king of the Isin Dynasty, but not the son of LIPIT-ESHTAR, thus outside the direct dynastic line (1923–1896). During his reign and those of his successors, Isin lost control of the country to Larsa. It was a period of unrest and renewed internal warfare. There were also economic problems, partly due to failures to maintain irrigation programmes. According to a year formula, Ur-Ninurta died a violent death, either in battle or in a palace revolt.

Edzard 1957: 103–4

Ur-Ningirsu

Sumerian ruler (*ensi*) of Lagash, son of GUDEA (22nd century). Like his father, he commissioned several statues and images of himself. His inscriptions refer mainly to buildings and the digging of canals.

Sollberger and Kupper 1971: IIC4a–f

Urtak(i)

Elamite king, successor and brother of HUMBAN-HALTASH II (674–663). He is only known from Assyrian sources; apparently he was on good terms with ESARHADDON, but changed tactics when ASHURBANIPAL was king. His cousin TEPTI-HUMBAN-INSHUSHINAK ousted Shilhak-Inshushinak II as ruler of Susa, and together with Urtaki launched an attack against Babylonia. Ashurbanipal reacted with bitterness to this treachery, recalling that he had sent him grain when there was a famine in Elam. When Urtaki heard that the Assyrian king was making ready to attack him, he turned back to Elam, where he died a sudden death.

Hinz 1972: 152–3; Carter and Stolper 1984: 49–50

Uruinimgina (previously read as Uru-KA-gina)

Early Dynastic Sumerian king of Lagash (*c.* 2378–2371), best known for his series of social and fiscal reforms, detailed in a long inscription. He took special measures against the increasing indebtedness of the populace and the excesses of taxation. He was defeated by LUGALZAGESI.

Gadd 1971, in CAH I/2: 140–2; Cooper 1983; 1986: 70–83; Steible and Behrens 1982: Ukg1

Ur-Utu

Kalu priest at Sippar, owner of an important archive.

Lerberghe and Voet 1991

Ush (also read as Gish)

Early Dynastic Sumerian governor of Umma who fought against EANNATUM of Lagash in the perennial dispute between the two cities. He was probably defeated by Eannatum.

Cooper 1983; Gadd 1971, in CAH I/2: 119

Utuhegal

Sumerian king of Uruk, famous for his expulsion of the Gutians. The vivid account of Utuhegal's victory over the 'Gutian hordes' under their king TIRIGAN is preserved on a tablet, which may have been copied from an original victory stele. Like some of his Akkadian predecessors he became part of traditional lore which found its way into the divination books. According to one of these omens he died by drowning while he inspected the building of a dam.

Gadd 1926; 1971, in CAH I/2: 461–2; Thureau-Dangin 1913: 98f.; Sollberger and Kupper 1971: IIK3a; Römer 1985

Uzziah

King of Judah, son and successor of AMAZIAH (767–740), with whom he probably shared a co-regency for the first few years. His long reign was relatively peaceful as he secured Judah's borders against the Philistines, Arabs and Ammonites. According to II Chron. 27: 21 he was struck with leprosy and his son JOTHAM was appointed co-regent for his last years.

Mitchell 1993, in CAH III/2: 327–9

Warad-Sin

King of Larsa, son of KUDUR-MABUK (1890–1878). He was installed as ruler of Larsa after his father had driven out the incumbent, SILLI-ADAD. He left more royal inscriptions than any other Larsa king. He was at pains to conduct himself like a traditional Mesopotamian ruler and seems to have spent much time, effort and wealth on religious buildings. Most of his inscriptions and year names refer to the reconstruction of temples at Ur, Zabalam and Larsa. He also presided over the installation of the *entum* priestess at Ur. Another important project was the rebuilding of the wall of Ur. He was succeeded by his son RIM-SIN.

Frayne 1990: 202–65; Stol 1976: 1–31; Sigrist 1985

Warassa

Governor of Eshnunna, successor of SHARRIYA, brother of BELAKUM, only known from a seal inscription (*c*. late 20th century).

Frayne 1990: 532–3

Warpal(aw)as (Assyrian Urballu)

Neo-Hittite king of Tuwana (= Tukhana, modern Nigde) (*c*. 738–710), mentioned in a letter that SARGON II sent to the governor of Que, concerning his ally Mita of Mushki (MIDAS), in which he urges him to deal with the remaining independent Anatolian principalities once and for all. However, Urballu managed to stay on the throne, no doubt because of skilful diplomacy in his dealings with neighbours and the Assyrians. He left some monuments inscribed in Luwian hieroglyphics.

Hawkins 1982, in CAH III/1: 413, 421; Postgate 1973: 28

Wassurme

Neo-Hittite king of Tabal (modern Cilicia), son of Tuwatis (738–*c*. 730). He left several hieroglyphic inscriptions, some put up on sculptures by his servants, and one monument of his own, which contains an account of his war against seven kings, in which he was allied to WARPALAWAS of Tuwana. He was a contemporary of TIGLATH-PILESER III, to whom he failed to pay tribute, whereupon the Assyrian king gave instructions to have him replaced by 'a son of a nobody', who was henceforth responsible for the expected payments to Assyria.

Hawkins 1982, in CAH III/1: 402, 413, 414, 417

Wullu

Private citizen and entrepreneur from Nuzi (*c.* 1400). His business transactions are documented in an archive that refers to the family's commercial activities over five generations.

Grosz 1988

X

Xerxes

Achaemenid king, son and successor of DARIUS I (486–465). He began his reign by having to suppress a rebellion in Egypt and another in Babylon. He then divided the large province of Babylonia into two administrative districts and tried to control his wide-spread dominions more effectively by redrawing boundaries. However, his reign marks a turning-point in Achaemenid history. The period of expansion was definitely over.

For most of his reign he was engaged in the west in an ultimately doomed attempt to subdue the mainland Greeks into accepting a Persian hegemony. After initial successes he lost the important naval battle at Salamis (480) and the land battle at Plataea in the following year. Revolts by the Ionian cities and the Greek islands supported by the newly founded Delian league, which was sponsored by Athens, followed these defeats. The final victory for the Greeks at the Eurymedon river in 466 resulted in the subsequent loss of the Achaemenid holdings in the west.

Xerxes was more successful in subduing the second Babylonian revolt, which broke out in 479, although it is now thought that he did not punish Babylon by the destruction of her temples.

Xerxes was murdered, together with the crown-prince Darius, in a palace coup which brought ARTA-XERXES to the Persian throne.

Kuhrt 1995: 670–1; Cuyler-Young 1988, in CAH IV: 71–8; Briant 1992; 1996: *passim*

Y

Yaggid-Lim

King of Mari, father of YAHDUN-LIM (late 19th century). We know little else about him other than that he concluded a treaty with the ruler of Terqa, ILU-KABKABI, and later came into conflict with him.

Kupper 1957; 1976–80, in RlA 5: 238; Yuhong 1994: 66–70

Yahdun-Lim

King of Mari, son of YAGGID-LIM (late 19th century). His official inscriptions record building activities in Mari, as well as large-scale irrigation projects but otherwise we know little about political events because the rich sources discovered in the archives of Mari date from the period beginning with the governorship of YASMAH-ADDU. However, it seems that Yahdun-Lim laid the foundations of Mari's prosperity and internal security by a series of military campaigns, mainly against neighbouring west Semitic tribes and petty kingdoms, which ensured relatively unencumbered passage for traders. He was killed by ILU-KABKABI, the father of SHAMSHI-ADAD I. He was briefly succeeded by SUMUYAMAM, his son, until the latter was replaced by an Assyrian governor, YASMAH-ADDU, son of Shamshi-Adad I.

Kupper 1973, in CAH II/1: 10–11; Charpin and Durand 1985, 239ff.; Kupper 1976–80, in RlA 5: 239–40; Klengel 1992: 49–52; Charpin, in Charpin and Durand 1994: 117–200; Yuhong 1994: 93–107

Yaqarum

First king of Ugarit according to an Ugaritic king list. A seal-legend identifies him as the son of NIQMADU.

Klengel 1992: 39

Yarim-Lim I

King of Yamhad during the Old Babylonian period, son of SUMU'-EPUH, (c. 1781–1765). According to the Mari letters he was one of the principal political players of his time, together with RIM-SIN of Larsa, IBAL-PI-EL of Eshnunna and AMUTPI'EL of Qatna. He benefited economically from international trade routes that crossed his territory. He granted ZIMRI-LIM of Mari asylum when the Assyrians had taken control of the city and married him to his daughter SHIBTU. Relations with Mari continued on a cordial basis, and the two rulers made journeys to various important towns, most notably Ugarit. He was also allied with HAMMURABI OF BABYLON and rulers of smaller states in Syria. On the other hand relations with Assyria and Eshnunna were hostile and led to protracted warfare.

Kupper 1973, in CAH II/1: 20–1; Dossin 1939; 1952b; Smith 1957; Wiseman 1976–80, in RlA 5: 261; Klengel 1992: 54–8

Yarim-Lim II
King of Yamhad, son of ABBA'EL, father of NIQMEPA (18th century).

Klengel 1992: 62

Yarim-Lim III
King of Yamhad, son of NIQMEPA, brother of IRKABTUM (18th century).

Klengel 1992: 63

Yariris
Syro-Hittite king of Carchemish, (c. first half of the 8th century). He left some finely carved and inscribed statues, in which he flaunts his international connections and claims that he could speak many foreign languages, as well as being literate in

different scripts. He was probably a contemporary of the Assyrian commander SHAMSHI-ILU.

Hawkins 1982, in CAH III/1: 496; 1974: no. 250

Yasmah-Addu
Governor of Mari, son of SHAMSHI-ADAD I, king of Assyria (early 18th century). Due to the extensive correspondence preserved in the archives of Mari, our picture of Yasmah-Addu is unusually vivid. In his own letters, as well as in those from his father and his brother, ISHME-DAGAN, installed as governor of Ekallatum, he comes across as indecisive. He father accuses him of indolence and too great a fondness of women, horses and fast chariots. After Shamshi-Adad's death, the exiled prince ZIMRI-LIM did not have too much trouble regaining his throne.

Dossin 1939; 1952; Kupper 1948; 1953; 1976–80, in: RlA 5: 269; Charpin and Durand 1985; Yuhong 1994

Yatar'ami
King of Carchemish, son of APLA-HANDA. He ruled for about two years beginning with year 9/10 of ZIMRI-LIM of Mari (c. 1765/6) and was replaced by his brother Yahdul-Lim, whose reign is poorly documented.

Klengel 1992: 73

Yirkab-Damu see Irkab-Damu

Z

Zababa-shum-iddina

Penultimate king of the Kassite dynasty of Babylon, he ruled for only one year (1158). He is not attested in contemporary records but a later Babylonian epic text refers to his forceful removal from the throne.

Brinkman 1976: 321–2

Zabaya

King of Larsa. Next to nothing is known about him. He was thought of as an ancestral figure of the Larsa dynasty. There are some building inscriptions that suggest he did indeed rule Larsa (c. 1941–1933).

Weisberg 1989

Zakur

King of Hamath (c. 796). He left a stele inscribed in Aramaic which was discovered in Afis. In this text he describes how he acquired the province of Luash. BEN-HADAD of Damascus had incited other local rulers against him and they besieged him in Hazrak, the capital of Luash. He states that he was saved by divine intervention, but it may more likely have been the Assyrian army.

Hawkins 1982, in CAH III/1: 403–4

Zakutu *see* Naqi'a-Zakutu

Zarriqum

Governor of Ashur during the Ur III period. His inscribed limestone slab, found in the ruins of the Ishtar temples at Assur, records his building projects and that he was a 'servant' of king AMAR-SIN of Ur.

Grayson 1972: 3

Zechariah

King of Israel, son and successor of JEROBOAM II (753–752). He only ruled for six months before he was assassinated by an otherwise unknown man called Shallum ben-Jabesh. With Zechariah the dynasty founded by JEHU came to an end.

Mitchell 1982, in CAH III/1: 508

Zedekiah (= Mattaniah)

Last king of Judah, son of JOSIAH, uncle of JEHOIAKIN (597–587). He was appointed to kingship by NEBU-CHADNEZZAR II to replace Jehoiakin, who had been deported to Babylon after the capture of the city by the Babylonians. His Jewish name, Mattaniah, was changed to Zedekiah. According to the books of Jeremiah and Kings, Zedekiah persisted in the anti-Babylonian machinations that had cost his predecessors their independence. His rebellious activities led to a further siege, which resulted in the destruction of Jerusalem in 587. As a punishment for his treachery towards Nebuchadnezzar his sons were executed before his eyes. Then he was blinded and taken prisoner to Babylon, where he died.

Mitchell 1991, in CAH III/2: 401–7

Zidanta I

Hittite king of the Old Kingdom (c. 1560–1550), successor of HANTILI I. Little is known of his reign except that he had killed the designated heir to the throne, Piseni, and was in turn murdered by his own son AMMUNA.

Kuhrt 1995: 245

Zimri

King of Israel, who succeeded ELAH whom he assassinated, together with all his descendants (885). He did not remain long on the throne because he killed himself in his palace by burning it down when OMRI, the commander-in-chief of the army, besieged him at Tirzah.

Mitchell 1982, in CAH III/1: 465

Zimri-Lim

King of Mari in the Old Babylonian period (c. 1775–1761). In the official tradition he was regarded as son of YAHDUN-LIM, but on a seal inscription as the son of a certain Hadni-[Adad]. When SHAMSHI-ADAD I appointed his son YASMAH-ADDU governor of Mari, Zimri-Lim, then a child, went into exile, probably to YARIM-LIM II, king of Yamhad, whose daughter SHIBTU he later married. After Shamshi-Adad's death he was able to gain control of Mari and acceded to the kingship.

Although there is a vast number of records, letters and other written material from his reign, preserved in the palace archives, the political situation of the time is very difficult to reconstruct. Zimri-Lim's kingdom was poised between the powers of Babylonia, Syria and Eshnunna, as well as threatened by nomadic groups. His letters reveal that he maintained wide-ranging intelligence networks and engaged in shifting diplomatic and military alliances with neighbouring rulers. He remained on good terms with Syria and Yamhad, and also with the Babylon under HAMMURABI, until the latter incorporated Mari into his domain and destroyed the city. Before this final event, Zimri-Lim profited mainly from the newly intensified international trade that passed through his territory. Another source of wealth was the textile manufacturing business. Thus he was able to complete a palace that became famous throughout the Near East of his time, a huge complex comprising some 6 acres. He is also unusual among potentates of the ancient world in deputising considerable political and administrative responsibilities to his wife, SHIBTU, and other female members of his family and entourage.

Kupper 1973, in CAH II/1: 10–16; Gates 1984;

Charpin and Durand 1985: 293–343; Batto 1974

Zuzu

Elamite King of Akshak who was defeated by EANNATUM, as the latter records in his inscriptions.

Sollberger and Kupper 1971: IC5b

Glossary

Achaemenids Persian dynasty named after the founder ACHAEMENES, which ruled after the defeat of the *Medes in the middle of the 6th century until the conquest of ALEXANDER THE GREAT (331). Their empire extended from the Iranian heartland, east into India, included all *Mesopotamia and most of Anatolia, Syro-Palestine and Egypt. Their greatest rulers were CYRUS II, CAMBYSES II and DARIUS I.

Akkad(e) (also read **Agade**)

1 As yet undiscovered city in northern Babylonia, said to have been founded by SARGON OF AKKAD, which became the capital of the Akkadian empire in the last third of the 3rd millennium.
2 The region around the city, north of *Sumer. From the time of the *Ur III the term 'Sumer and Akkad' denoted all of Babylonia.
3 The period when Mesopotamia was ruled by the dynasty founded by SARGON (*c.* 2340–2159).

Akkadian Linguistic term for various Semitic dialects spoken in Mesopotamia over a period of 2,000 years (such as Old Akkadian, *Babylonian, *Assyrian). The name derives from the region *Akkad and was used by Babylonian scribes of the *Ur III period to differentiate it from *Sumerian.

Aleppo City in Syria, sited on an important trade route between the Orontes and the Euphrates, which linked the Mediterranean and Anatolia to the Syrian hinterland and further east.

Amarna correspondence The term in reference to western Asia refers to the modern name (Tell el-Amarna) of Akhetaten, the city founded by AMENOPHIS IV (AKHNATON) where an important archive was discovered that also included documents from the reign of AMENOPHIS III. The archive contained letters, written in Babylonian on clay tablets, sent by various rulers from the Near East to the pharaoh. The time span covered by the archive is sometimes called the Amarna period (*c.* 1403–1306).

Ammon Kingdom in the Transjordan region, east of Palestine, south of the Yabok river. Like *Moab and *Edom often depicted as hostile to Israel in biblical sources.

Amorites Term for Semitic-speaking tribes, derived from the Akkadian *amurru*, also used for the language and area. Towards the end of the 3rd millennium they settled in increasing numbers in northern and middle Babylonia. The influx of Amorite tribes contributed to the downfall of the *Ur III dynasty. Some tribes became assimilated and formed chiefdoms and kingdoms in Mesopotamia and Syria in the 2nd millennium (e.g. *Mari, *Yamhad, Tuttul), others retained a nomadic or semi-nomadic existence as *pastoralists.

annals Yearly reports, primarily concerning military expeditions and building works, composed on behalf of Assyrian kings; apparently introduced by ADAD-NIRARI I (beginning of the 13th century).

Anshan City on the Iranian plateau (modern Tall-i Malyan), capital of *Elam, on the important trade route that linked Mesopotamia with the mineral-rich areas in Afghanistan.

Arabs Semitic-speaking, tribally organised people, subsisting on semi-nomadic and nomadic *pastoralism and trade, first mentioned in the 1st millennium in Assyrian records.

Arameans A group of peoples speaking a western Semitic language (Aramaic). Originally tribal *pastoralists, they emerged in the middle of the 2nd millennium to form states in Syria and northern Mesopotamia. In the 1st millennium Aramaic became the most widely spoken and understood language in western Asia. Written Aramaic first appeared around 800, in different types of alphabetic scripts.

Assur City in *Assyria (modern Qalat Sherqat), on the Tigris. It was the capital until 883 when ASHURNASIRPAL II moved the seat of government to *Kalhu, but it remained a ritually important place, seat of the eponymous god Assur, and served as the burial site for Assyrian monarchs.

Assyria The heartland of Assyria lies in the Jezireh region of present-day Iraq and Syria, bordered by the rivers Tigris and the Euphrates and their tributaries. The land was suited to rain-fed agriculture and herding. Major trade routes into

Anatolia and the Iranian plateau via the Zagros range, as well as southwards to Babylonia and west to the Mediterranean, went across the country and these contributed towards the development of thriving economies.

Assyrian East-Semitic dialect of *Akkadian spoken in Assyria. In accordance with the different historical periods one distinguishes between Old, Middle, and Neo-Assyrian.

Assyrian King List A chronologically ordered sequence of 112 Assyrian rulers from the beginning of the 2nd millennium to ASHUR-UBALLIT II (609). Several copies exist from the 1st millennium. It generally lists the name of the king, his father's name, and the length of his reign, with occasional remarks about particularly noteworthy events.

Babylon City on the Euphrates (south of modern Baghdad), which became capital of the kingdom established by HAMMURABI in the 18th century, and then again under NEBUCHADNEZZAR II and his descendants in the 1st millennium. It has been excavated by German archaeologists, revealing remains of a Neo-Babylonian city; older levels are not accessible due to high ground-water level at the site.

Babylonia From the *Kassite period onwards the term denoted all of southern Mesopotamia, in distinction to the northern kingdom, Assyria. *Babylon was its capital.

Babylonian Dialect of *Akkadian spoken in Mesopotamia since the beginning of the 2nd millennium. There are certain differences between Old, Middle and Neo-Babylonian.

Babylonian Chronicle There were several chronicles written in Babylon from the middle of the 2nd millennium onwards. Chronicle P (Grayson 1975: No. 22) records the dealings of the *Kassite Dynasty with their *Assyrian and *Elamite neighbours, another (Grayson 1975: No.1) deals with the period between 744 to 688 and dates from around 500/499. They depict events from a Babylonian point of view and thus often contradict and/or supplement other sources, like the Assyrian annals and royal inscriptions.

Bit-Adini Small Aramean state in Syria with the capital at Til Barsip (modern Tall Ahmar), in the first 3rd of the 1st millennium. It was intermittently independent from Assyrian domination.

Bit-Agusi Small Aramean state in Syria, in the first third of the 1st millennium.

It was eventually incorporated into the Neo-Assyrian empire. The capital was Arpad, modern Tell Rifa'at.

Bit-Yakin   Chaldean tribe in southern Babylonia (*Sealand) during the first half of the 1st millennium.

building inscriptions   The building of civic structures such as canals, dykes, city walls and quays, as well as palaces and temples, was the responsibility of kings and governors. In 3rd millennium Mesopotamia tablets or cone-shaped objects which listed the name of the person responsible for the construction or restoration, its purpose, and usually a date, were placed within the building. This custom was also adopted by other near-eastern civilisations. Building inscriptions are sometimes the only evidence for a person's existence. Those from the 1st millennium, especially from the Neo-Babylonian and Neo-Assyrian periods, are sometimes several hundred lines long, giving accounts of the large-scale building schemes of the time.

Canaanites   Semitic people who lived in the area known as Canaan, the Levantine coastal area, in the mid-2nd millennium. The Canaanites subsisted on agriculture and trade and built substantial cities along the coast. They were politically and culturally influenced by the Egyptians.

Carchemish   City on the Syrian upper Euphrates (modern Jerablus), with a long history of habitation, profiting from the trade between Anatolia and Syria and beyond, dominated by the *Hittites from the mid-2nd millennium until its conquest by the Assyrians (8th century).

Chaldeans   Semitic tribal peoples in southern Mesopotamia. The name comes from the Babylonian term for their region *māt kaldu*. The main tribes were the Bit-Yakin, Bit Amukani and Bit Dakkuri. They were very wealthy, and probably derived a lucrative income from the maritime Gulf trade that passed through their territory. They formed a dynasty that ruled Babylonia from 625 to 539. The term Chaldean was from then on also used to denote Babylonia, until well into the Roman period.

Cimmerians   Group of nomadic tribal peoples who invaded Anatolia in the first quarter of the 1st millennium. They were feared for their intrepid mounted warriors who raided the country and proved severely disruptive for the *Phrygians, *Urartians and other Anatolian smaller states.

cuneiform   A system of writing in which a cut reed stylus is pressed into soft clay to leave a wedge-like imprint (Latin *cuneus*), invented in Mesopotamia around 3000. Different versions of cuneiform writing were used to write various Near-

Eastern languages: Sumerian, Akkadian, Eblaite, Elamite, Ugaritic, Hittite and Hurrian. It was superseded by alphabetic scripts after the mid-1st century.

Damascus Oasis city in Syria, since at least the beginning of the 2nd millennium. Its situation on trade routes ensured its economic importance throughout the ages. It was conquered by the *Arameans in the last quarter of the 2nd millennium and then by the *Assyrians in the 8th century.

Diadochi Greek term meaning 'successor', denoting the Macedonian generals who amongst themselves divided ALEXANDER THE GREAT's empire after his death. They include Antigonus and Demetrius, Antipater and Cassander, SELEUCUS (I), PTOLEMY (I), Eumenes and Lysimachus. The wars they fought over the succession are known as the War of the Diadochi (c. 323–281).

Early Dynastic period Archaeological term referring to levels of Mesopotamian sites during the 3rd millennium until the *Akkadian period. There are three subdivisions; historical records are mainly from Early Dynastic III A (mid-3rd millennium).

Ebla City in the Orontes valley in Syria (modern Tell Mardikh), which was occupied by Semitic people in the mid-3rd millennium when it was the capital of a wealthy and powerful kingdom. The archives found at Ebla give details of the wide trade connections and the rich agricultural potential of the area. The city was destroyed in c. 2250, probably by an *Akkadian ruler. It was inhabited again in the *Old Babylonian period and finally destroyed in c. 1600. The texts were written in a Semitic language, now simply called Eblaite.

Ecbatana City in Iran (modern Hamadan), capital of the *Medes in the early 1st millennium, and thereafter the summer residence for the *Achaemenid and *Parthian kings.

Edomites Semitic tribes inhabiting Edom, the semi-desert south of the Dead Sea. Like the *Ammonites and *Moabites they are frequently mentioned in the Bible.

Elam Region east of southern Mesopotamia, in south-west Iran; it had strong cultural links with Mesopotamia from prehistoric times. Its inhabitants spoke a language that is not connected with any other known language (Elamite), which they wrote in *cuneiform. In the 3rd millennium Elam was conquered by the kings of *Akkad. During the last quarter of the 2nd millennium it became a powerful state under kings like UNTASH-NAPIRISHA and KIDEN-HUTRAN. From then Elam was closely involved in the history of Babylonia and Assyria until the 6th century.

---

en   Sumerian official title. The precise meaning is difficult to establish, and no doubt shifted from place to place and time to time, but at least in some cases it seems to have connotations with a high position in the temple hierarchy.

ensi   Sumerian title, which means something like 'governor' of a city. This could be used for the appointment issued by an overall ruler, as for instance in Elam during the Akkadian domination, or to refer to an independent ruler, such as GUDEA of Lagash.

entum   Babylonian term derived from the Sumerian word *en. It denotes a high priestly office held by a woman, often a member of the ruling dynasty. This tradition was established from at least the *Akkad period when SARGON OF AKKAD appointed his daughter ENHEDUANNA to serve the moon god at Ur. The practice lapsed after the *Old Babylonian period and was revived by NEBUCHADNEZZAR II. *Entus* lived in the *Gipar, within the precinct of the temple, at least in the *Ur III period and in the 6th century.

eponym (Assyrian *limmu*)   Assyrian official selected each year to give his name (eponym) to the current year. This constituted a dating system that was in use from the *Middle Assyrian period.

Eshnunna   Mesopotamian city in the east Tigris area (modern Tell Asmar). Before and during the *Old Babylonian period it was the capital of Warum, an independent kingdom, vying for supremacy with other states until its conquest by HAMMURABI OF BABYLON.

Gasga   Name for a people who in the 13th century appeared in Anatolia and fought against the *Hittites under MUWATALIS II, forcing them to temporarily move the capital.

Gaza   Town in southern Palestine, an important strategic link between Egypt and the Levant from the mid-2nd millennium and hence a strongly fortified garrison. In the 1st millennium it came intermittently under Assyrian control and was later taken by ALEXANDER THE GREAT.

Gipar   A Sumerian term for the part of a temple inhabited by high functionaries such as the *en or *entum.

Gordion   Town in central Anatolia near modern Polatli, in the mid-2nd millennium occupied by the *Hittites, from the 12th century a major *Phrygian centre, where MIDAS is thought to have been buried.

Gutians A people who lived in the Zagros mountains, east of southern Mesopotamia. From a small power-base in the Diyala region they invaded the kingdom of *Akkad in the early 22nd century and established their own dynasty, which was defeated by UTUHEGAL.

Hamath Syrian town in the Orontes valley, modern Hama. It occupied an advantageous position on an interchange of important routes from the Phoenician coast to Mesopotamia and beyond. In the 1st millennium it was the capital of a small *Aramean kingdom with the same name.

Harran City in northern Upper Mesopotamia, already known from the *Hittite archives (mid-2nd millennium). It was conquered by the *Assyrians in the 8th century In the *Neo-Babylonian period it became under Babylonian control. It was an important cult centre of the moon god Sin. His temple was richly endowed and rebuilt by NABONIDUS, whose mother was a priestess there.

Hattusa City in central Anatolia (modern Boghazköy). In the early 2nd millennium it was the location of an Assyrian trading colony and in the mid-2nd millennium it was capital of the *Hittite empire. It was destroyed in the 13th century, though later inhabited again by the *Phrygians.

Hittites Indo-European people who settled in Anatolia in the 18th century, taking the name of the indigenous population, the Hatti, whose territory around the bend of the river Halys (Kizilirmak) they conquered. By the mid-2nd millennium they became a major military power, on a par with Egypt, *Assyria and *Mitanni. At that time they wrote their language in *cuneiform, later they developed a hieroglyphic system of writing. The empire disintegrated in the 13th century, and although the previous heartland around *Hattusa was devastated, the Hittites continued to prosper in southern Anatolia, where a number of small kingdoms retained a precarious independence in the first half of the 1st millennium, in the face of Assyrian pressure. They left a number of inscribed monuments from that period (usually referred to as Neo-Hittite) which used the hieroglyphic system of writing.

Hurrians A group of peoples speaking a Caucasian language, who inhabited the north-eastern borders of Mesopotamia from the last quarter of the 3rd millennium. Judging from patronyms, Hurrian people were present in all parts of the Near East for most of the 2nd millennium, but especially in south-east Anatolia, northern *Mesopotamia and eastern Iran. They achieved the greatest political importance between 1500 and 1200, within the framework of a kingdom called *Mitanni. The Hurrians wrote their language in *cuneiform (for instance a letter in the *Amarna correspondence written by TUSHRATTA).

Isin City in central Lower Mesopotamia. After the collapse of the *Ur III, ISHBI-ERRA founded the First Dynasty of Isin (*c.* 2017–1794), making Isin the capital; it was conquered by RIM-SIN of Larsa.

Israel Semitic-speaking people who take their name from a legendary ancestor Jacob, also known as Israel, the forefather of the ten tribes of Israel, which settled in *Canaan in the late 2nd millennium. After the division of the kingdom founded by DAVID, Israel became an independent political unit, often in conflict with its southern neighbour *Judah. The kingdom of Israel ceased to exist in 721, when its capital Samaria was destroyed by the Assyrians and the population deported.

Jerusalem City in middle Palestine. After the conquest by DAVID (*c.* 1000), it became the capital of the united kingdom of *Israel and *Judah, and main cult centre of Yahweh. After the division it remained as capital of Judah. It was conquered by the Babylonians in 587 and rebuilt during the *Achaemenid period in the 6th century.

Judah Region in Palestine, south of Jerusalem, named after one of the sons of the tribal ancestor Jacob. After the division of the monarchy under REHOBOAM it was the name for the southern kingdom which lasted from 931 to 587.

Kalhu (modern **Nimrud**) Assyrian city on the Tigris, founded by SHALMANESER I (13th century), much enlarged in the 9th century by ASHURNASIRPAL II, who made it his capital. The *Medes and Babylonians destroyed the city in 612.

Kanesh City in Cappadocia (modern Kültepe). In the beginning of the 2nd millennium it was inhabited by the local, Hattian, population and benefited from the Assyrian trade colony (*karum* Kanesh) next to it, which dealt in the import/export of metal and textiles. Extensive *cuneiform archives have been recovered.

Kassites A people speaking a little-known language, who appear in Mesopotamian sources in the first third of the 2nd millennium. After the *Old Babylonian dynasty, kings with predominantly Kassite names ruled Babylonia (from the 16th to the 12th century), an epoch known as the Kassite period.

Khorsabad Assyrian city, originally called Dur-Sharrukin ('Sargon's Fort') after its founder SARGON II, who built it between 713 and 707. It was dedicated in 706 and soon afterwards abandoned by SENNACHERIB, who moved the court back to *Nineveh.

Kish Mesopotamian city near Babylon (modern Tell el-Ohemir). It was an important town, seat of several dynasties, during the 3rd millennium. For some still obscure reason the title 'king of Kish' implied the hegemony over Sumer and Akkad.

Kizzuwatna Area in southern Anatolia, roughly equivalent to classical Cilicia. During the 2nd millennium it had a large *Hurrian population. Initially an independent kingdom, it came under the control of the *Mitanni and the *Hittites in the 15th century.

Kudurru Babylonian word that refers to an upright boundary stone, inscribed with title deeds to land, usually bestowed by the king on deserving individuals. Kudurrus are magically protected and guaranteed by divine symbols and curse formulae. They are a characteristic feature of the Kassite period.

Kummuh Region in southern Anatolia, classical Commagene. Like neighbouring *Melid and Gurgum, it was fought over by the *Urartians and *Assyrians in the first quarter of the 1st millennium and, under the control of one or the other, with brief periods of relative independence.

Kush Other name of Upper Nubia, and sometimes all of Nubia south of Egypt along the Nile. In the 1st millennium it was a powerful kingdom which exercised control over Upper Egypt. In the 7th century the Kushite kingdom was invaded by the Assyrians.

Lagash Sumerian city-state, including Girsu (modern Telloh). It had considerable importance in the *Early Dynastic period and the second half of the 3rd millennium. Extensive tablet finds from the period of GUDEA provide details of the economic and political affairs.

Larsa City in southern Mesopotamia (modern Senkereh), in the first quarter of the 2nd millennium seat of an *Amorite dynasty, conquered by HAMMURABI OF BABYLON.

Luwian Indo-European language, closely related to Hittite. Most of the extant sources, written in a hieroglyphic system in the first half of the 1st millennium, are from the north Syrian border region.

Lydia Region in western Anatolia, seat of powerful and wealthy kingdoms in the 1st millennium. The capital was Sardis. Lydian rulers, such as GYGES, maintained relations with Greeks as well as Assyrians and exercised control over Phrygia. Their last ruler, CROESUS, was defeated by the Persians in 540 and this marked the end of Lydian independence.

Mannaeans A people inhabiting the mountainous regions of the Zagros in the 1st millennium, called Mannaea by the Assyrians. They came under the domination of *Urartu and the Assyrians, especially under TIGLATH-PILESER III, and from then on remained allies of the Assyrians until their demise.

Mari Mesopotamian city in the middle Euphrates region (modern Tell Hariri in Syria). It was an independent city-state in the *Early Dynastic period and flourished in the first quarter of the 2nd millennium, when it was capital of an *Amorite kingdom. It was destroyed by HAMMURABI OF BABYLON in *c.* 1759. The extensive archive dates mainly from this period, but within the temple precinct inscribed votive statues from the 3rd millennium have been found.

Medes Iranian people closely related to the *Persians who inhabited the area of Hamadan in the first half of the 1st millennium. They did probably not form a coherent state, but some of their rulers, such as CYAXARES, extended their power into eastern Anatolia and they also contributed to the final defeat of the *Assyrians as allies of the Babylonians. Their main city was *Ecbatana. In the 6th century they were defeated by the Persians under CYRUS II.

Melid Small kingdom in southern Anatolia, with the eponymous capital (classical Melitene; around Malatya) in the first half of the 1st millennium. It came intermittently under *Assyrian or *Urartian domination.

Mesopotamia Graeco-Roman name (literally 'between the rivers') of a Roman province; in modern usage it denotes the geographical area between the Euphrates and the Tigris from their confluence near the Persian Gulf up to the Anatolia. Lower Mesopotamia is the area south of Baghdad, Upper Mesopotamia includes the Habur valley and the *Assyrian heartland on the Tigris. The term is also used in a cultural and historical context for the various civilisations in the area from the late 4th millennium to the conquest of ALEXANDER THE GREAT (*c.* 330).

Middle Assyrian period The time when Assyria emerged again as an important political power after a long decline, *c.* 1400–1050. Some of the most important rulers of this time were ASHUR-UBALLIT I, ADAD-NIRARI I and TIGLATH-PILESER I.

Mitanni Kingdom in northern Mesopotamia and Syria. From the 16th and 14th century it was one of the most influential powers in the Near East, dominating the Assyrians. It came into conflict with the Egyptians and the *Hittites, who under SUPPILULIUMA I, reduced it to a vassal state. The *Hurrian element was strong in the Mitanni kingdom, though the ruling elite had mainly Indo-European names.

Moab   Small Aramean kingdom east of the Dead Sea in present-day Jordan. The Bible and a monument by MESHA record hostilities against Israel in the first half of the 2nd millennium.

Mushki *see* **Phrygians**

nadītum   Akkadian term for women who fulfilled some form of ritual or priestly role, mainly during the Old Babylonian period. They were mainly dedicated to the sun god, secluded, and not allowed to have children. Some *nadītum*s were from wealthy (and even royal) families and could invest their share of their fathers' estate. Because of their childlessness some reached a greater age than usual for the time.

Neo-Assyrian period   The time from *c.* 934–610 when Assyria expanded rapidly to dominate the whole of the Near East, from Iran to Egypt, until its collapse and final defeat by the Babylonians and Medes.

Neo-Babylonian period   The time from *c.* 900–539 when Babylonia, freed from the domination of the Assyrians, became a powerful state in western Asia, under kings like NABOPOLASSAR and NEBUCHADNEZZAR II. It was conquered by the *Persians.

Nimrud *see* **Kalhu**

Nineveh   City in Assyria, near modern Mossul in Iraq. It had a very long history of occupation, documented by votive gifts found in the precinct of its most important sanctuary, the temple if Ishtar. At the end of the 8th century SENNACHERIB made it the capital of the Assyrian empire. Important archives and the so-called 'library' of ASHURBANIPAL with thousands of *cuneiform tablets, were discovered in the mound of Kuyunjik. Nineveh fell in 612 to the *Medes and was destroyed.

Nippur   City in central Mesopotamia. It had mainly cultural importance, especially during the *Early Dynastic period but also in the *Old Babbylonian time, until the middle of the 2nd millenium. Nippur was a major cult centre, the seat of the god Enlil, and a place of learning. Tablets discovered in the temple area and the scribal quarter contain examples of Sumerian literature.

Old Assyrian period   Like 'Old Babylonian' this term has philological connotations, as the language used in the written sources of the period. In historical terms it refers to the time from *c.* 2000–1800, when Assyria had a flourishing economy based on international trade, especially with Anatolia.

Old Babylonian period   Time from the end of the *Ur III to the end of the First Dynasty of Babylon (*c.* 2000–1600), also used as a linguistic term, referring to the Akkadian dialect that was used in the documents of the time.

omens   There was a great variety of divinatory techniques in the ancient Near East, and the collection of omens and their interpretation was the responsibility of highly trained scribes in Mesopotamia. Some Babylonian omens include references to historical events.

Palestine   Part of the western Near East between the Dead Sea and the Jordan valley and the Mediterranean. The name derives from a people known as the Philistines, who settled in southern Palestine after 1300. The region has the longest history of human habitation in western Asia, dating back to the early Palaeolithic age. In the 2nd millennium it was inhabited by *Canaanites and then also by the tribes of *Israel, who settled there around 1200.

Parthians   Iranian people from the area around the Caspian Sea. They rebelled against the *Seleucids and formed an empire which lasted from 140 to AD 224, which eventually included Mesopotamia. The Parthians fought tenaciously and with considerable success against the Romans in Syria.

Pasargadae   Iranian city founded by CYRUS II (6th century), though the site had been inhabited in prehistoric times and the 3rd millennium. It contained the *Achaemenid royal residence, as well as royal tombs. It was destroyed by SELEUCUS I in the 3rd century.

pastoralists   People whose main form of subsistence is the herding and raising of sheep and goats, with a nomadic or semi-nomadic way of life. Pastoralists have existed in the Near East for millennia since it allows them to utilise land that is too marginal for the growing of crops. Pastoralists are usually tribally organised with strong kin loyalty, and are often good fighters. Due to the fact that literacy was a prerogative of the urban population, pastoralists 'who have no cities and don't know bread', were generally described as uncivilised, hostile and dangerous. In fact their relationship with settled populations could vary considerably, from a mutual beneficial interaction to destructive raiding. The archive of Mari has proved a fertile source for studies of ancient Near Eastern nomadism and pastoralism.

Pattin(a)   Small *Aramaic kingdom in the Amuq plain on the lower Orontes in Syria during the first half of the 1st century, usually dominated by the Assyrians who called it Unqi.

Persepolis Iranian city, founded by DARIUS I (late 6th century) as a royal residence and ceremonial centre, destroyed by ALEXANDER THE GREAT in 330.

Persians Iranian people who formed two empires in the ancient Near East. The first was the *Achaemenid empire, founded about 550 by CYRUS II and conquered by ALEXANDER THE GREAT between 334 and 323. The second was the *Parthian empire (140 to AD 224).

Philistines The name appears the Bible, referring to a people who had settled in the south of Palestine before DAVID (c. 1000). In Egyptian sources there are groups of people called *Prst* ('Peleset') who fought against RAMESSES III's army, as part of the 'sea-people' (13th century). Some of them settled in southern Palestine, in parts usually controlled by Egypt.

Phoenicians Graeco-Roman term for *Canaanites who inhabited the western and coastal parts of *Palestine and Syria in the late Bronze Age. It is also used to describe the inhabitants of the Mediterranean coast who managed to retain their independence from *Aramaic, *Israelite, *Assyrian and Egyptian domination in the first millennium. They founded colonies in other parts of the Mediterranean.

Phrygians A people who lived in central Anatolia and who formed a state that lasted from the mid-12th century until about the 6th century Their state suffered from attacks by the *Cimmerians, the *Urartians and *Lydians, and they were for a while paying tribute to the Assyrians, who called them the Mushki. They are also known from later Greek sources which emphasise their great wealth, derived from agriculture, trade and metal-work. One of their major cities was *Gordion.

Ptolemies A Hellenistic Dynasty, founded by PTOLEMY I SOTER, one of the generals of ALEXANDER THE GREAT, which ruled Egypt from 306 to 30. Also known as Lagides after an ancestor of Ptolemy's.

Saïte Dynasty Egyptian dynasty which ruled from Saïs in the Nile delta from 664–525. The Saïte period refers more generally to the later phase of Egyptian culture, from the 7th century to about AD 100.

Sam'al City and small kingdom in south Anatolia, in the Taurus region (modern Zinjirli). The local population spoke Luwian until the *Arameans conquered it in the 10th century. It became part of the Assyrian empire by the 8th century.

Samaria Palestine city, capital of the kingdom of *Israel from the time of OMRI (late 9th century), destroyed in 721 by the Assyrians.

———

Sardis   City in western Anatolia, capital of *Lydia until its capture by the Persians in *c.* 540. It continued to flourish under the *Achaemenids and throughout the Hellenistic period.

satrap   A term derived from the Persian word *kshatrapavan* that refers to the governor of a district. DARIUS II divided the *Achaemenid empire into 20 great satrapies. The head of each province, the satrap, was responsible for collecting taxes and functioned as supreme judge and arbiter. He was also in charge of maintaining roads and ensuring their safety.

Scythians   A group of nomadic peoples, originating from central Asia, who appeared in Anatolia in the first half of the 1st millennium. Like their contemporaries the *Cimmerians they fought on horseback. They clashed with the armies of the *Urartians, *Phrygians and Assyrians. The *Persians under DARIUS I fought them in central Asia.

Sealand   Translation of an Akkadian term for the marshes of southern Babylonia. In the mid-2nd millennium there was a Dynasty of the Sealand, mentioned in the king lists, which profited from the Gulf trade. There was a Second Dynasty of the Sealand in the 11th century. In the *Neo-Babylonian period it was mainly occupied by *Chaldean tribes who fought against the Assyrians, often allied with *Elamites.

Second Dynasty of Isin A   A Babylonian dynasty based on Isin (1158–1027). NEBUCHADNEZZAR I was its most prominent and successful ruler.

Seleucids   Hellenistic dynasty (305–64), founded by SELEUCUS I NICATOR, a general of ALEXANDER THE GREAT.

Shimashki   Region in Iran, north-east Khuzistan. From *c.* 220–*c.* 1900 it was a kingdom with its own dynasty; sometimes ally, sometimes rival, of *Elam.

Shubat-Enlil   City in the Habur valley in northern Syria (modern Tell Leilan). In the *Old and *Middle Assyrian period it was an important provincial centre.

Sidon   City on the Phoenician coast, 25 miles north of *Tyre, an important harbour in the second half of the 2nd millennium, especially for the trade with Egypt. It was destroyed in 677 by the Assyrian king ESARHADDON.

Sippar   City in central Mesopotamia. A large number of economic texts from the *Old Babylonian and *Neo-Babylonian periods have been found there.

'sister-son'   An Elamite title found in royal genealogies. There are indications that brother–sister marriage could occur in Elamite royal families, and descent could pass through the female line.

Sogdiana Region in central Asia, around Samarkhand. In the 6th century it was integrated into the *Achaemenid empire by CYRUS II and later conquered by ALEXANDER THE GREAT.

Suhu Region along the middle Euphrates, in the 1st millennium a wealthy *Aramean state, which was first made to pay tribute to Assyria (9th century) and then became a province of Assyria, until the Babylonians under NABOPOLASSAR incorporated it in their realm (7th century).

sukkalmah *Elamite title, derived from Sumerian, designating a high office and, usually, command over the armed forces. For a period of Elamite history, *sukkalmah*s held power over the country, and were independent from Mesopotamia (mid-2nd millennium).

Sumer Name for southern Mesopotamia from the 3rd to the mid-2nd millennium. It did not form a political unit in itself but was divided into several entities similar to city-states.

Sumerians Inhabitants of southern Mesopotamia in the 3rd millennium who spoke Sumerian, a language that has no connections with any of the known linguistic groups. Sumerian was written in *cuneiform and, like Latin in the Middle Ages, remained in use for some text genres long after it ceased to be a spoken language.

Sumerian King List A document compiled in the *Old Babylonian period (*c.* 19th century) which lists rulers in Mesopotamia from the 'beginning' to the end of *Ur III. It has a theoretical framework that assigns overall leadership ('kingship') to one city at a time, which clearly contradicts historical realities. It includes kings with exceedingly long reigns before and immediately after the 'Flood'.

Susa Iranian city in the plain of the Ulai river. It had a long history of occupation, spanning five millennia. It was the capital of *Elam until it was destroyed by the Assyrians in the 7th century.

Synchronistic History Assyrian chronicle written at the time of ADAD-NIRARI III (*c.* 800). Its purpose was to trace Assyria's relationship with Babylonia in the aftermath of the destruction of the city by SENNACHERIB. It has a decidedly 'nationalistic' bias but is a useful source of historical information, especially if consulted in combination with *Babylonian chronicles of the period.

Tabal Region in central Anatolia, corresponding roughly to Cappadocia. It was an independent buffer state between *Phrygia and *Assyria until it was incorporated into the Assyrian empire in the 8th century.

Terqa City on the Middle Euphrates, north of *Mari, capital of the small kingdom of Hana in the *Old Babylonian period.

Tummal texts The Tummal was an important sanctuary at Nippur. There are texts from the Old Babylonian period which list the kings who had contributed to the building over the centuries in a chronological sequence.

Tushpa City and fortress in eastern Anatolia (modern Toprakkale near Van). In the 1st millennium it was the capital of the *Urartian kingdom, supplied with fresh water by a canal built by MENUA and surrounded by orchards. It was destroyed by the Medes in *c.* 590.

Tyre City on the Phoenician coast, like its sister city *Sidon a wealthy port, profiting from the Egyptian trade with Syria-Palestine, especially in the second half of the 2nd millennium. In the 1st millennium the Assyrians imposed tribute. ALEXANDER THE GREAT conquered Tyre in 332. It continued to prosper in the Hellenistic and Roman periods.

Ugarit Wealthy city-state on the Mediterranean coast of Syria (modern Ras Shamra) during the second half of the 2nd millennium. Numerous tablets, written in *Akkadian *cuneiform, as well as in an alphabetic adaptation, were recovered in the ruins of the city.

Umma Sumerian city in southern Mesopotamia, mainly known from tablets discovered at Girsu, which describe its long-standing war with *Lagash in the *Early Dynastic period.

Unqi *see* **Pattin(a)**

Ur City in southern Mesopotamia with a long history of habitation, from the prehistoric to the *Seleucid period. It was the seat of several dynasties in the 3rd millennium and reached its political apogee with the Third Dynasty of Ur (*Ur III). It was also an important trading post, especially for maritime trade across the Persian Gulf, a famous cult centre as the city of the moon god, and a place of learning, yielding thousands of *cuneiform tablets.

Ur III (Third Dynasty of Ur) A dynasty founded by URNAMMU which ruled over most of Mesopotamia and parts of *Elam from *c.* 2112–2004. It relied on a centralised and highly differentiated bureaucracy which used Sumerian as the main means of written communication.

Urartu   Kingdom centred around the Lake Van region in eastern Anatolia, that extended east to include Lake Urmia, north to the Caucasian mountains and west as far as northern Syria, during the first half of the 1st millennium. The Urartians were skilful engineers of fortresses and artificial waterways, and excellent metal workers. They came into conflict with the Assyrians and various Anatolian states, such as *Phrygia.

Uruk   City in southern Mesopotamia (modern Warka in Iraq), with a history of continuous habitation from the 4th millennium to the *Seleucid period. It was the seat of dynasties in the 3rd millennium, but thereafter mainly a religious centre, with temples of Ishtar and the sky god Anu.

Washshukanni   Hurrian city, capital of *Mitanni, in the 2nd millennium, destroyed by the Hittites. The site has as not been located.

Yamhad   Name of the Amorite city and kingdom of Aleppo in the first half of the 2nd millennium; allied with *Mari.

ziggurat   Babylonian word which describes a type of religious building consisting of several superimposed platforms, accessible by one or more ramps. It became a characteristic of Mesopotamian religious architecture. Several examples have been excavated, and there are descriptions and architectural sketches on cuneiform tablets. At least some ziggurats, like the famous Etemanki at Babylon, had a shrine on the uppermost platform.

Outline of the main historical periods

Mesopotamia

c. 2600–2350	Early Dynastic period
c. 2350–2150	Dynasty of Akkad
c. 2150–2000	Third Dynasty of Ur (Ur III)
c. 2000–1800	Isin-Larsa Dynasties
c. 1800–1600	First Dynasty of Babylon
c. 1600–1155	Kassite Dynasty
c. 1900–1400	Old Assyrian Period
c. 1400–1050	Middle Assyrian Period
c. 1155–1027	Second Dynasty of Isin
c. 1026–1006	Second Dynasty of Sealand
979–732	Dynasty of E
934–610	Neo-Assyrian Empire
626–539	Neo-Babylonian Dynasty
550–330	Achaemenid Empire
311–126	Seleucid period

Anatolia

c. 1650–1420	Old Hittite Kingdom
c. 1420–1200	Hittite Empire
c. 750–650	Urartian Kingdom

Syria-Palestine

c. 2500–2300	Kingdom of Ebla
c. 1775–1760	Kingdom of Mari
c. 1480–1330	Mitanni
c. 1370–1185	Kingdom of Urartu
c. 1000–935	United Monarchy of Israel
931–720	Kingdom of Israel
931–587	Kingdom of Judah
311–63	Seleucid period

Iran

c. 2500–2200	Dynasty of Awan
c. 2200–1900	Dynasty of Shimashki
c. 1900–1500	period of *sukkalmahs*
c. 1450–1100	Elamite classical period
c. 720–550	Median period
640–330	Achaemenid period
250–88	Parthian period

Bibliography

Abou Assaf, A., Bordreuil, P. and Millard, A.R. (1982) *La Statue de Tell Fekheriye et son inscription bi-lingue assyro-araméenne* (Études assyriologiques 7) (Paris).

Agostino, F. (1998) 'Ein neuer Tent über Abī-simtī; und das Elūnum Fest in Puzrish-Dagan', *Zeitschrift für Assyriologie* 88: 1–5.

Albright, W.F. (1956) 'The Nebuchadnezzar and Neriglissar chronicles', *Bulletin of the American Society of Oriental Research* 143: 28–33.

Allen, L.C. (1978) *The Books of Jehu, Obadaiah, Jonah and Micah* (London).

Alster, B. (1973) 'An Aspect of "Enmerkar and the Lord of Aratta" ', *Révue d'Assyriologie* 68: 101–10.

——(1985) 'Sumerian love songs', *Révue d'Assyriologie* 79: 127–59.

——(1980) (ed.) *Death in Mesopotamia*, 26ième Rencontre Assyriologique Internationale (Mesopotamia 8) (Copenhagen).

Amiet, P. (1976) *L'Art d'Agadé au Musée du Louvre du Paris* (Paris).

Anderson, R.T. (1960) 'Was Isaiah a scribe?', *Journal of Biblical Literature* 79: 57–8.

Archi, A. (ed.) (1988) *Eblaite Personal Names and Semitic Name Giving. Papers of a Symposium held in Rome, July 15–17 1985* (Rome).

——(1990) 'Imar au IIIe millénaire d'après les archives d'Ebla', *Mari: Annales de Recherches Interdisciplinaires* 6: 21–38.

Asher-Grève, J. (1985) *Frauen in altsumerischer Zeit* (Malibu, Calif.).

Astour, M. (1986) 'The name of the ninth Kassite ruler', *Journal of the American Oriental Sociey* 106: 327–31.

Balcer, J. (1987) *Herodotus and Bisitun* (Weisbaden).

Batto, B.F. (1974) *Studies on Women in Mari* (Baltimore).

Bauer, T. (1933) *Das Inschriftenwerk Assurbanipals* I–II (Leipzig).

Beal, R.H. (1993) 'Kurunta of Tarhuntassa and the Imperial Hittite Mausoleum', *Anatolian Studies* 44: 29–40.

Beaulieu, P.-A. (1989) *The Reign of Nabonidus King of Babylon 556–539 BC* (New Haven, Conn.).

Berger, P.R. (1973) *Die neubabylonischen Königsinschriften: Königsinschriften des ausgehenden babylonischen Reiches (626–539 a.Chr.)* (Neukirchen Vluyn).

Berlin, A. (1979) *Enmerkar and Enšuḫkešdanna* (Philadelphia).

Boese, J. (1982) 'Burnaburiaš II, Melišipak und die mittelbabylonische Chronologie', *Ugarit Forschungen* 14: 15–26.

Borger, R. (1988) 'König Sennacheribs Eheglück', *Annual Review of the Royal Inscriptions of Mesopotamia Project* 6.

Bosworth, A.B. (1996) *Alexander the Great, the Tragedy of Triumph* (Oxford).

Bottéro, J., Cassin, E., and Vercoutter, J. (eds) (1965–7) *Die altorientalischen Reiche*, 3 vols (Frankfurt am Main); translated as *The Near East: The early civilizations*, 3 vols (London).

Braun-Holzinger, E.A. (1977) *Frühdynastische Beterstatuetten* (Berlin).

Briant, P. (1973) *Antigone le Borgne. Les débuts de sa carrière et les problèmes de l'assemblée macédonienne* (Paris).

——(1987) *De la Grèce à l'orient: Alexandre le Grand* (Paris).

——(1992) 'La date des revoltes babyloniennes contre Xerxès', *Studia Iranica* 21: 7–20.

——(1992b) *Darius, les perses et l'empire* (Paris).

——(1996) *L'Histoire de l'empire perse. De Cyrus à Alexandre* (Paris).

Brinkman, J.A. (1968) *A Political History of Post-Kassite Babylonia 1158–722 B.C.* (Rome).

——(1969) 'Ur: "the Kassite period and the period of the Assyrian kings" ', *Orientalia* 38: 310–48.

——(1972) 'Documents relating to the reign of Aššur-nādin-šumi', *Orientalia* 4: 245–8.

——(1976) *Materials and Studies for Kassite History, Vol. 1: A catalogue of cuneiform sources pertaining to specific monarchs of the Kassite Dynasty* (Chicago).

——(1983) 'Bēl-ibni's letters on the time of Sargon and Sennacherib', *Révue d'Assyriologie* 77: 175–6.

——(1984) *Prelude to Empire: Babylonian society and politics 747–663 BC* (Philadelphia).

Brinkman, J.A. and Dalley, S. (1988) 'A royal Kudurru from the reign of Aššur-nādin-šumi', *Zeitschrift für Assyriologie* 78: 76–98.

Brosius, M. (1996) *Women in Ancient Persia: 559–331 BC* (Oxford).

Burn, A.R. (1973) *Alexander the Great and the Middle East* (Harmondsworth).

Bryce, T.R. (1988) 'Tette and the rebellion in Nuhassi', *Anatolian Studies* 38: 21–8.

Burstein, S.M. (1978) 'Babyloniaca of Berossus', *Sources of the Ancient Near East* I, 5: 142–81.

Cameron, A. and Kuhrt, A. (eds) (1983) *Images of Women in Antiquity* (London).

Cancik-Kirschbaum, E.C. (1996) *Die Mittelassyrischen Briefe aus Tall Šeh Hamad* (Berlin).

Cardascia, G. (1951) *Les Archives des Murāšu: une famille d'hommes d'affairs babyloniennes à l' époque perse* (Paris).

Carter, E. and Stolper, M.W. (1984) *Elam: Surveys of political history and archaeology* (Berkeley).

Charpin, D. and Durand, J.M. (1983) 'A propos des "Archives de Šumu-Yamam" ', *Mari: Annales de Recherches Interdisciplinaires* 2: 117–21.

——(1985) 'La prise du pouvoir par Zimri-Lim', *Mari: Annales de Recherches Interdisciplinaires* 4: 293–343.

——(1985b) 'Les archives du divin Ašqudum dans la residence du "Chantier A" ' *Mari: Annales de Recherches Interdisciplinaires* 4: 453–66.

——(1994) *Florilegium Marianum II: Receuil d'études à la memoire de Maurice Birot* (Paris).

Charpin, D. and Joannès, F. (eds) (1991) *Marchands, diplomates et empéreurs: études sur la civilisation mésopotamienne offerts à Paul Garelli* (Paris).

Charvát, P. (1978) 'The growth of Lugalzagesi's empire', in B. Hruška and G. Komoróczy (eds) *Festschrift für L. Matouš* (Budapest): 43–9.

Civil, M. (1985) 'On some texts mentioning Ur-Namma', *Orientalia* 54: 33–6.

Cluzan, S., Delpont, E. and Mouliérac, J. (eds) (1993) *Syrie, Mémoire et Civilisation* (Paris).

Cogan, M. and Eph'al, I. (eds) (1991) *Ah, Assyria... Studies in Assyrian History and Ancient Near Eastern Historiography Presented to Hayim Tadmor* (Jerusalem).

Cogan M. and Tadmor, H. (1977) 'Gyges and Ashurbanipal: a study in literary transmission', *Orientalia* 46: 65–85.

——(1981) 'Ashurbanipal's conquest of Babylon: the first official report – Prism K', *Orientalia* 50: 229–40.

Cohen, S. (1973) 'Enmerkar and the Lord of Aratta', dissertation (University of Pennsylvania).

Cole, W.S. (1996) *Nippur IV. The Early Neo-Babylonian Governor's Archive from Nippur* (Chicago).

Colledge, M.A.R. (1967) *The Parthians* (London).

Comay, J. (1993) *Who's Who in the Old Testament* (London).

Cooper, J. (1980) 'Apodictic death and the historicity of "historical" omens', in B. Alster (ed.) *Death in Mesopotamia* (Copenhagen).

——(1983a) *The Curse of Agade* (Baltimore).

——(1983) *Reconstructing History from Ancient Inscriptions: The Lagash-Umma border conflict* (Sources from the Ancient Near East 2/1) (Malibu, Calif.).

——(1986) *Sumerian and Akkadian Royal Inscriptions. Vol. I: Pre-Sargonic Inscriptions* (AOS Translation Series I) (Winona Lake, Ind.).

Cooper, J.J. and Heimpel, W. (1983) 'The Sumerian Sargon legend', *Journal of the American Oriental Society* 103: 67–82.

Dalley, S. (1984) *Ebla and Karana: Two Old Babylonian cities* (London).

——(1989) *Myths from Mesopotamia: Creation, the Flood, Gilgamesh and others* (Oxford and New York).

——(1996) 'Herodotus and Babylon', *Orientalistische Literaturzeitung* 91, 5/6: 526–31.

Dalley, S. and Postgate, N. (1984) *The Tablets from Fort Shalmaneser* (London).

Dalley, S., Hawkins, J.D. and Walker, C. (1976) *The Old Babylonian Tablets from Tell al Rimah* (London).

Dandamaev, M.A., *et al.* (1976) *Persien unter den ersten Achämeniden 6.Jahrhundert v.Chr.*, trans. H.D. Pohl (Wiesbaden).

Deller, K. and Millard, A. (1993) 'Die Bestallungsurkunde des Nergal-Āpil-kūmūja von Kalḫu', *Baghdader Mitteilungen* 24: 217–42.

Dietrich, M. (1998) 'Bel-ibni, König von Babylon (703–700)' in M. Dietrich and O. Loretz (eds) *dubsar anta-men. Festschrift für Willem H. Ph. Römer* (Münster): 81–108.

Dietrich, M. and Loretz, O. (1981) 'Die Inschrift der Statue des Königs Idrimi von Alalakh', *Ugarit Forschungen* 13: 201–69.

——(1993) 'Besitz der Tiša-Lim, Zuwendungen des Königs von Ebla an die Königin von Emar', *Ugarit Forschungen* 25: 93–8.

——(eds) (1995) *Vom Alten Orient zum Alten Testament: Festschrift für Wolfram Freiherrn von Soden zum 85. Geburtstag am 19.Juni 1993* (Neukirchen-Vlyun).

di Vito, R.A. (1993) *Studies in Third Millennium Sumerian and Akkadian Personal Names* (Rome).

Donbaz, V. (1990) 'Two Neo-Assyrian stelae in the Ankiya and Karanmanmaras Museum', Royal Inscription of Mesopotamia Annual Review 8: 5–24.

Donner, H. and Röllig, W. (1962–8) *Aramäische und Kanaanäische Inschriften*, 3 vols (Wiesbaden).

Dossin, G. (1939) 'Les archives épistolaires du Palais de Mari', *Syria* 20: 97–113.

——(1939b) 'Iamhad et Qatanum', *Révue d'Assyriologie* 36: 46–54.

——(1948) 'Šibtu, reine de Mari', *Actes du XXIe Congrès Internationale des Orientalistes (Paris 23–31 Juillet 1948)* (Paris): 421–3.

——(1950) *Archives royales de Mari, I: Correspondance de Šamši-Addu et de ses fils, transcrite et traduite* (Paris).

——(1952) *Archives royales de Mari, V: Correspondance de Iasmah-Addu, transcrite et traduite* (Paris).

——(1952b) 'Le royaume d'Alep au XVIIIe siècle avant notre ère d'après les "archives de Mari" ', *Bulletin de l'Acadamie Royale de Belgique, Classe des Lettres* 229–39.

——(1954) 'Le royaume de Qatna au XVIIIe siècle avant notre ère d'après les "Archives de Mari" ', *Bulletin de l'Académie Royale de Belgique, Classe des Lettres* 417–25.

——(1967) *Archives royales de Mari, X: La correspondance féminine* (Paris).

——(1970) 'Archives de Sumu-Iamam', *Révue d'Assyriologie* 64: 17–44.

Dougherty, R.P. (1929) *Nabonidus and Belshazzar: A study of the closing events of the Neo-Babylonian Empire* (Yale Oriental Studies 1) (New Haven, Conn.).

Drecksen, J.G. (1996) *The Old Assyrian Copper Trade in Anatolia* (Istanbul).

Durand, J.M. (1985) 'La situation historique des Šakkanakku', *Mari: Annales de Recherches Interdisciplinaires* 4: 147–72.

——(1985b) 'Les dames du palais de Mari', *Mari: Annales de Recherches Interdisciplinaires* 4: 385–436.

Edzard, D.O. (1957) *Die 'zweite Zwischenzeit' Babyloniens* (Wiesbaden).

——(1981) *Studi Eblaiti* IV: 89–97.

——(1997) *Gudea and his Dynasty* (Royal Inscriptions of Mesopotamia: Early Periods 3/1) (Toronto).

Eilers, W. (1971) *Semiramis: Entstehung und Nachhall einer altorientalischen Legende* (Vienna).

Fadhil, A. (1990) 'Die Grabinschrift der Mulissu-mukannišat-Ninua aus Nimrud/Kalhu und andere in ihrem Grab', *Baghdader Mitteilungen* 21: 471–82.

Fales, F.M. and Postgate, N. (1992) *Imperial Administrative Records. Part 1. Palace and Temple Administration*, State Archives of Assyria VII (Helsinki).

Fales, F.M. and Jacob Rost, L. (1991) *Neo-Assyrian Texts from Assur: Private Archives in the Vorderasiatisches Museum of Berlin. Part 1*, State Archives of Assyria Bulletin V (Helsinki).

Farber, W. (1983) 'Die Vergöttlichung Naram-Sins', *Orientalia* 62: 67–72.

Finkelstein, J. (1961) 'Ammisaduqa's Edict and the Babylonian "Law Codes" ', *Journal for Cuneiform Studies* 20: 95–118.

Fitzmayer, J.A. and Kaufman, S.A. (1992) *An Aramean Bibliography. Part 1: Old Official and Biblical Aramaic* (Baltimore and London).

Foster, B. (1982) *Umma in the Sargonic Period* (Hamden).

——(1982b) *Administration and Use of Institutional Land in Sargonic Sumer* (Mesopotamia 9) (Copenhagen).

——(1985) 'The Sargonic victory stele from Telloh', *Iraq* 47: 15–30.

——(1993) *Before the Muses: An anthology of Akkadian literature*, 2 vols (Bethesda, Md.).

Frahm, E. (1997) *Einleitung in die Sanherib Inschriften. (Archiv für Orient-forschung Beiheft 26)* (Vienna).

Frame, G. (1995) *Rulers of Babylonia: From the Second Dynasty of Isin to the end of the Assyrian domination (1157–612 BC)* (The Royal Inscriptions of Mesopotamia: Babylonian Period, vol. 2) (Toronto).

Frayne, D.R. (1990) *Old Babylonian Period (2003–1595 BC)* (The Royal Inscriptions of Mesopotamia: Early Periods, vol. 4) (Toronto).

——(1993) *Sargonic and Gutian Periods (2334–2113 BC)* (The Royal Inscriptions of Mesopotamia: Early Periods, vol. 2) (Toronto).

——(1997) *Ur III Period (2112–2004 BC)* (The Royal Inscriptions of Mesopotamia: Early Periods, vol. 3/2) (Toronto).

Fuchs, A. (1994) 'Die Inschriften Sargon's II aus Khorsabad', dissertation (Göttingen).

Funck, B. (1984) *Uruk zur Seleukidenzeit* (Berlin).

Gadd, C. (1926) 'Clay Cones of Utu-Hegal, King of Erech', *Journal of the Royal Asiatic Society*: 648–88.

——(1951) 'En-an-e-du', *Iraq* 13: 27ff.

——(1958) 'The Harrran inscriptions of Nabonidus', *Anatolian Studies* 8: 35–92.

Galter, H.D. (1984) 'Die Zerstörung Babylons durch Sennacherib', *Studia Orientalia* 55: 161–73.

——(1990) 'Eine Inschrift des Gouverneurs Nergal-ērēš in Yale', *Iraq* 52: 41–9.

Galter, H.D., Levine, L.D. and Reade, J. (1986) 'The colossi of Sennacherib's palace and their inscriptions', *Annual Review of the Royal Inscriptions of Mesopotamia Project* 4: 32.

Garelli, P. (1963) *Les Assyriens en Cappadoce* (Paris).

——(ed.) (1974) *Le Palais et la royauté* (Paris).

Gates, M.H. (1984) 'The Palace of Zimrilim at Mari', *Biblical Archaeology* 47: 70–87.

Gelb, I.J. and Kienast, B. (1990) *Die altakkadischen Königsinschriften des dritten Jahrtausends v.Chr* (Freiburg im Breisgau).

Gelb, I.J., Purves, P.M. and Rae, A.A. (1943) *Nuzi Personal Names* (Chicago).

Ghirshman, R. (1966–70) *Tchoga Zanbil*, 4 vols (Paris).

Glassner, J.J. (1986) *La Chute d'Akkade: l'événement et sa mémoire* (Beiträge zum Vorderen Orient 5) (Berlin).

——(1988) 'Le récit autobiographique de Sargon', *Révue d'Assyriologie* 82: 1–11.

Goetze, A. (1947) 'Historical allusions in Old-Babylonian omen texts', *Journal of Cuneiform Studies* 1: 253ff.

——(1963) 'Šakkanakkus of the Ur III Empire', *Journal of Cuneiform Studies* 17: 1ff.

Goodnick-Westenholz, J. (1983) 'Heroes of Akkad', *Journal of the American Oriental Society* 103: 327–36.

——(1997) *Legends of the Kings of Akkade* (Winona Lake, Ind.).

Gordon, C.H. and Rendsburg, G.A. (eds) (1990) *Eblaitica: Essays on the Ebla Archives and Eblaite language 2* (Winona Lake, Ind.).

Grabbe, L.L. (1992) *Judaism from Cyrus to Hadrian. Vol. I: The Persian and Greek Periods* (Minneapolis).

Grayson, A.K. (1972) *Assyrian Royal Inscriptions*, vol. 1 (Wiesbaden).

——(1975) *Babylonian Historical-literary Texts* (Toronto Semitic Texts and Studies 3) (Toronto).

——(1976) *Assyrian Royal Inscriptions*, vol. 2 (Weisbaden).

——(1980) 'The chronology of the reign of Ashurbanipal', *Zeitschrift für Assyriologie* 70: 227–45.

——(1987) *Assyrian Rulers of the Third and Second Millennium BC (to 1115 BC)* (The Royal Inscriptions of Mesopotamia: Assyrian Periods, vol.1).

——(1991) *Assyrian Rulers of the Early Millennium BC* (1114–859 BC) (The Royal Inscriptions of Mesopotamia: Assyrian Periods, vol. 2).

——(1993) 'Assyrian Officials and Power in the 9th and 8th centuries', *State Archives of Assyria*: vii.

——(1996) *Assyrian Rulers of the Early First Millennium BC (858–745 BC)* (The Royal Inscriptions of Mesopotamia: Assyrian Periods, vol. 3).

Green, P. (1991) *Alexander of Macedon 356–328: A historical biography* (Harmondsworth).

Grillot, F. (1988) 'A propos d'un case de "Lévirat" élamitique', *Archaeological Journal* 276: 61–70.

Grimal, P. (ed.) (1965) *Histoire mondiale de la femme: Préhistoire et antiquité*, vol. I (Paris).

Grosz, K. (1988) *The Archive of the Wullu Family* (Copenhagen).

Gurney, O. (1990) *The Hittites*, rev. edn (Harmondsworth).

——(1993) 'The Treaty with Ulmi-Teshup', *Anatolian Studies* 43: 13–28.

Hallo, W.W. (1966) 'The Coronation of Urnammu', *Journal of Cuneiform Studies* 20: 133–41.

Hallo, W.W. and Simpson, W.K. (1971) *The Ancient Near East: A history* (New York).

Hallo, W.W. and Van Dijk, J.J. (1968) *The Exaltation of Inanna* (New Haven, Conn.).

Hallock, R.T. (1977) 'The use of seals on the Persepolis Fortification Tablets', in McG. Gibson and R.D. Biggs (eds) *Seals and Sealings in the Ancient Near East* (Malibu, Calif.), 127–133.

Hamilton, J.R. (1973) *Alexander the Great* (London).

Harris, R. (1962) 'Biographical notes on the *Nadītu* women of Sippar', *Journal of Cuneiform Studies* 16: 1–12.

——(1975) *Ancient Sippar: A demographic study of an Old-Babylonian City* (Nederlands Historisch-Archaeologisch Institut te Istanbul).

Hawkins, J.D. (1974) 'Assyrians and Hittites', *Iraq* 36: 67ff.

——(1979) 'Some historical problems of the Hieroglyphic Luwian corpus', *Anatolian Studies* 29: 153ff.

——(1986) 'Royal statements of ideal prices: Assyrian, Babylonian and Hittite', in J.V. Canby, E. Porada, B.S. Ridway and T. Stech (eds) *Ancient Anatolia: Aspects of change and cultural development (Essays in honor of Machteld J. Mellink)* (Madison,Wis.) 93–102.

——(1988) 'Kuzi-Tešub and the "Great Kings of Karkamiš" ', *Anatolian Studies* 38: 99–108.

Hawkins, J.D. and Morpurgo Davies, A. (1978) 'On the problems of Karatepe: the hieroglyphic text', *Anatolian Studies* 28: 103–120.

Hinz, W. (1967) 'Elams Vertrag mit Naram-Sin von Akkade', *Zeitschrift für Assyriologie* 58: 66–96.

——(1972) *The Lost World of Elam* (London).

Hirsch, H. (1963) 'Die Inschriften der Könige von Agade', *Archiv für Orientforschung* 20: 1–82.

Houwink ten Cate, P. (1967) 'Mursili's north western campaign: a commentary', *Anatolica* 1: 44–61.

——(1970) *The Records of the Early Hittite Empire (c. 1430–1370)* (Leiden).

——(1983/4) 'The history of warfare according to Hittite sources: the Annals of Hattusili I', *Anatolica* 10: 91–109; 47–83.

Hrouda, B., Kroll, S. and Spanos, P.Z. (1992) *Von Uruk nach Tuttul. Eine Festschrift für Eva Strommenger* (Munich and Vienna).

Hunger, H. (1972) 'Neues von Nabû-zuqup-kēna', *Zeitschrift für Assyriologie* 62: 99–101.

——(1992) *Astrological Reports to Assyrian Kings*, State Archives of Assyria VIII (Helsinki).

——(1996) *Astronomical Diaries and Related Texts from Babylon by the Late Abraham J. Sachs, Vol. 3: Diaries from 164–61 BC* (Helsinki).

Jacoby, F. (1958) *Die Fragmente der griechischen Historiker Dritter Teil* (Brill).

Jacobsen, Th. (1939) *The Sumerian King List* (Assyriological Studies, no.11) (Chicago).

——(1953) 'The reign of Ibbi-Suen', *Journal of Cuneiform Studies* 7: 36–47.

——(1987) *Harps that Once . . . Sumerian Poetry in Translation* (New Haven and London).

Joannès, F. (1979–80) 'Les successeurs d'Alexandre le Grand en Babylonie', *Anatolica* 7: 99–116.

——(1980) 'Kaššara, fille de Naboukodonosor II', *Révue d'Assyriologie* 74: 183–4.

Johansen, F. (1978) *Statues of Gudea, Ancient and Modern* (Mesopotamia 6) (Copenhagen).

Kärki, I. (1984) 'Die sumerischen und akkadischen Königsinschriften der altbabylonischen Zeit', II. Babylon, *Studia Orientalia* 55: 37–94.

Kataja L. and Whiting, R. (eds) (1995) *Grants, Decrees and Gifts of the Neo-Assyrian Period* State Archives of Assyria XII (Helsinki).

Katz, D. (1987) 'Gilgamesh and Akka: was Uruk ruled by two assemblies?', *Révue d'Assyriologie* 81: 105–14.

Katzenstein, H.J. (1973) *The History of Tyre* (Jerusalem).

Kitchen, K.A. (1986) *The Third Intermediate Period in Egypt*, 2nd rev. edn (Warminster).

Klein, J. (1981) *The Royal Hymns of Shulgi, King of Ur* (Ramat Gan).

——(1981b) *Three Shulgi Hymns: Sumerian royal hymns glorifying King Shulgi of Ur* (Ramat Gan).

Klengel, H. (1991) 'Tuthalija IV. Prolegomena zu einer Biographie', *Altorientalische Forschungen* 199: 224–38.

——(1992) *Syria. 3000 to 300 B.C.* (Berlin).

Koch, H. (1992) *Es kündet Dareios der König... Vom Leben im persischen Großreich* (Mainz/Rheine).

Koldewey, R. (1914) *The Excavations at Babylon* (London).

Kovacs, M.G. (1989) *The Epic of Gilgamesh* (Stanford, Calif.).

Kramer, S.N. (1952) *Enmerkar and the Lord of Aratta* (Philadelphia).

——(1967) 'The Death of Ur-Nammu', *Journal of Cuneiform Studies* 21: 104–22.

——(1983) 'The Ur-Nammu Code: who was its author?', *Orientalia* 52: 453–6.

——(1991) 'Lamentations over the destruction of Nippur', *Acta Sumerologica* 13: 1–26.

Kraus, F.R. (1958) *Ein Edikt des Königs Ammiṣaduqa von Babylon* (Leiden).

——(1984) *Königliche Verfügungen in altbabylonischer Zeit* (Leiden).

Krecher, J. (1970) *Das Geschäftshaus Egibi in Babylonien in neu-babylonischer und achämenidischer Zeit* (Münster).

Kühne, H. (1973) 'Ammištamru und die Tochter der "grossen Dame" ', *Ugarit Forschungen* 5: 175–84.

——(1995) 'The Assyrians on the Middle Euphrates and the Habur', in M. Liverani (ed.) *Neo-Assyrian Geography* (Rome).

Kuhrt, A. (1995) *The Ancient Near East c. 3000–330 BC*, 2 vols (London).

Kuhrt, A. and Sherwin-White, S. (eds) (1987) *Hellenism in the East* (London).

Kupper, J.R. (1948) *Archives royales de Mari III: Lettres* (Paris).

——(1953) *Archives royales de Mari VI: Lettres* (Paris).

——(1957) *Les Nomades en Mésopotamie au temps des rois du Mari* (Paris).

Kutscher, R. (1989) *The Brockman Tablets: Royal inscriptions* (Haifa).

Lambert, M. (1949) 'Les Dieux vivants à l'aube du temps historique', *Sumer* 5: 8–33.

Lambert, W.G. (1957) 'Ancestors, authors and canonicity', *Journal of Cuneiform Studies* 11: 1–14.

——(1960) *Babylonian Wisdom Literature* (London).

——(1962) 'A catalogue of texts and authors', *Journal of Cuneiform Studies*, 16: 59–77.

——(1965) 'Nebuchadnezzar King of Justice', *Iraq* 27: 11 ff.

Landsberger, B. and Balkan, K. (1950) 'Die Inschriften des altassyrischen Königs Irishum, gefunden in Kültepe', *Belleten* 14: 219–96.

Lane-Fox, R. (1973) *Alexander the Great* (London).

Lanfranchi, G.B. and Parpola, S. (1990) *The Correspondence of Sargon II: Letters from the northern and northwestern provinces* (Helsinki).

Laroche, E. (1966) *Les noms des Hittites* (Paris).

Larsen, M.T. (1976) *The Old Assyrian City State and its Colonies* (Mesopotamia 4) (Copenhagen).

——(1982) 'Your money or your life: a portrait of an Assyrian Businessman', in M.A. Dandamaev *et al.* (eds) *Societies and Languages of the Ancient Near East: Studies in honour of I.M. Diakonoff* (Warminster).

Leichty E., de Ellis, M. and Gerardi, P. (eds) (1988) *A Scientific Humanist: Studies in memory of Abraham Sachs* (Philadelphia).

Leick, G. (1991) *A Dictionary of Ancient Near Eastern Mythology* (London).

——(1994) *Sex and Eroticism in Mesopotamian Literature* (London).

Lemaire, G. and Durand, J.M. (1984) *Les Inscriptions araméennes de Sfiré et l'Assyrie de Shamshu-ilu* (Geneva and Paris).

Lerberghe, K. van and Voet, G. (1991) *Sippar-Ammanum, the Ur-Utu Archive* (Ghent).

Levine, L.D. (1982) 'Sennacherib's southern front: 704–689 BC', *Journal of Cuneiform Studies* 34: 28–58.

Lewis, B. (1980) *The Sargon Legend* (Cambridge, Mass.).

Lewy, H. (1952) 'Nitokris-Naqia', *Journal of Near Eastern Studies* I, 11: 264–86.

Limet, H. (1968) *L'Anthroponymie sumérienne dans les documents de la 3e dynastie d'Ur* (Paris).

Lipiński, E. (1975) *Studies in Aramaic Inscriptions and Onomastics I* (Louvain).

——(1994) *Studies in Aramaic Inscriptions and Onomastics II* (Louvain).

Liverani, M. (1979) *Three Amarna Essays*, Monograph on the Ancient Near East I: 9 (Malibu, Calif.).

—— (1993) *Akkad, The First World Empire* (Padora).

Malamat, A. (1956) 'A new record of Nebuchadrezzar's Palestinian campaigns', *Israel Exploration Journal* 6: 246–55.

——(1968) 'The last kings of Judah and the fall of Jerusalem: an historical-chronological study', *Israel Exploration Journal* 18: 137–56.

——(1983) *Das davidische und salomonische Königsreich und seine Beziehungen zu Ägypten und Syrien* (Vienna).

Malbran-Labat, F. (1975) 'Nabû-bēl-šumāte, prince du Pays-de-la-Mer', *Journal Asiatique* 263: 7–37.

Marello, P. (1997) 'Liqtum, reine de Burundum', in *Mari: Annales de Recherches Interdisciplinaires* 8: 455–9.

Margueron, J.L. (1982) *Recherches sur les palais Mésopotamiens de l'Age du Bronze* (Paris).

Matthiae, P. (1989) *Ebla. Un imperio ritrovato* (Turin).

Mayer, W.R. (1988) 'Ein neues Königsritual gegen feindliche Bedrohung', *Orientalia* 57: 145–64.

——(1995) 'Sanherib und Babylon. Der Staatsmann und Feldherr im Spiegel seiner Babylonienpolitik', in M. Dietrich and O. Loretz (eds) *Vom Alten Orient zum Alten Testament. Festschrift für Wolfram Freiherrn von Soden zum 85. Geburtstag am 19.Juni 1993* (Neukirchen-Vluyn): 305–32.

—— (1998) 'Nabonids Herkunft' in M. Dietrich and O. Loretz (eds) *dubsar anta-men. Festschrift für Willem H. Ph. Römer* (Münster): 245–62.

Mayrhofer, M. (1979) *Die Altiranischen Namen* (Vienna).

Michalowski, P. (1977) 'The death of Šulgi', *Orientalia* 46: 220–25.

——(1981) 'Tudanapšum, Naram-Sin and Nippur', *Révue d'Assyriologie* 75: 173–6.

——(1982) 'Royal women of the Ur III Period: part III', *Acta Sumerologica* 4: 129–39.

——(1989) *The Lamentation over the Destruction of Ur* (Winona Lake, Ind.).

Miroschedji, P. de (1985) 'La royaume d'Anšan et de Suse et la naissance de l'empire perse', *Zeitschrift für Assyriologie* 75: 265–306.

Moran, W.L. (1992) *The Amarna Letters* (Baltimore and London).

Myers, J.M. (1965) *Ezra, Nehemiah* (Garden City, NY).

Na'aman, N. (1974) 'Sennacherib's "Letter to God" on his campaign to Judah', *Bulletin of the American Society of Oriental Research* 214: 25–39.

——(1991) 'Chronology and history of the Late Assyrian Empire', *Zeitschrift für Assyriologie* 81: 242–67.

Neu, E. (1974) *Der Anitta Text* (Wiesbaden).

Neugebauer, O. (1955) *Astronomical Cuneiform Texts*, 3 vols (London).

Niccacci, A. (1994) 'The Stela of Mesha and the Bible: verbal system and narrativity', *Orientalia* 63/3: 226–48.

Nissen, J.J. (1965) 'Eine neue Version der Sumerischen Königsliste', *Zeitschrift für Assyriologie* 57: 1–5.

O'Brien, J.M. (1992) *Alexander the Great: The invisible enemy* (London and New York).

Oded, B. (1979) *Mass Deportations and Deportees in the Neo-Assyrian Empire* (Wiesbaden).

Orlin, L.L. (1970) *Assyrian Colonies in Cappadocia* (The Hague and Paris).

Orthmann, W. (1971) *Untersuchungen zur späthethitischen Kunst* (Saarbrücken Beiträge zur Altertumskunde 8) (Bonn).

Otten, H. (1975) *Puduhepa. Eine hethitische Königin in ihren Textzeugnissen* (Wiesbaden).

——(1981) *Die Apologie Hattusilis III; Das Bild der Überlieferung* (Wiesbaden).

——(1988) *Die Bronzetafel aus Boghazköy: Ein Staatsvertrag Tuthalijas IV* (Studien zu den Boghazköytexten, Beiheft 1) (Wiesbaden).

Paley, S.M. (1976) *King of the World: Ashur-naṣir-pal II of Assyria 883–859 B.C.* (Brooklyn).

Parpola, S. (1970) *Letters from Assyrian Scholars to the Kings Esarhaddon and Ashurbanipal, Vol. I* (Neukirchen-Vluyn).

——(1980) 'The murderer of Sennacherib', in B. Alster (ed.) *Death in Mesopotamia* (Copenhagen): 171–82.

——(1983) *Letters from Assyrian Scholars to the Kings Esarhaddon and Ashurbanipal, Vol. II* (Neukirchen-Vluyn).

——(ed.) (1993) *Letters from Assyrian and Babylonian Scholars* (Helsinki).

——(1997) *Assyrian Prophecies*, State Archives of Assyria IX (Helsinki).

Parpola, S. and Watanabe, K. (1988) *Neo-Assyrian Treaties and Loyalty Oaths*, State Archives of Assyria II (Helsinki).

Parrot, A. (1956) *Le temple d'Ishtar* (Paris).

Pettinato, G. (1980) *The Archives of Ebla. An Empire Inscribed on Clay* (Garden City, New York).

——(1986) *Ebla. A New Look at History* (Baltimore).

Pitard, W.T. (1987) *Ancient Damascus* (Winona Lake, Ind.).

Popko, M. (1984) 'Zur Deutung des Tawagalawa-Briefes', *Altorientalische Forschungen* 11: 199–203.

Porter, B.N. (1993) *Images, Power and Politics: Figurative aspects of Esarhaddon's Babylonian policy* (Philadelphia).

Postgate, N. (1973) 'Assyrian texts and fragments', *Iraq* 35: 13–36.

——(1992) *Early Mesopotamia: Society and economy at the dawn of history* (London).

Pritchard, J.B. (1969) *The Ancient Near Eastern Texts Relating to the Old Testament*, 2nd edn (Princeton).

Ranke, H. (1905) *Early Babylonian Personal Names* (Philadelphia).

Rashid, S.A. (1979) 'The Babylonian king Nabonidus in Tema', *Sumer* 35: 1172–4.

Reade, J. (1983) *Assyrian Sculpture* (London).

Reiner, E. (1985) *'Your thwarts in pieces, your mooring rope cut': Poetry from Babylonia and Assyria* (Ann Arbor, Mich.).

Reisman, D. (1973) 'Iddin-Dagan's Sacred Marriage Hymn', *Journal of Cuneiform Studies* 25: 189–202.

Röllig, W. (1964) 'Erwähnungen zu neuen Stelen König Nabonids', *Zeitschrift für Assyriologie* 56: 218–60.

Rollinger, R. (1993) *Herodots Babylonischer Logos*.

Römer, W.H.Ph. (1980) *Das Kurzepos 'Bilgameš und Akka'* (Neukirchen-Vluyn).

——(1985) 'Zur Siegesinschrift des Königs Utuhegal von Unug(+−2116–2110 v.Chr.)', *Orientalia* 54: 274–88.

Rouault, O. (1977) *Mukannishum. L'administration et l'économie palatiale à Mari* (Archives Royales de Mari XVIII) (Paris).

Roth, M.T. (1991) 'The dowries of the women of the Itti-Marduk-balatu family', *Journal of the American Oriental Society* 111/1: 19–37.

Roux, G. (1966) *Ancient Iraq* (Harmondsworth).

Russell, H.F. (1984) 'Shalmaneser's campaign to Urartu in 856 BC', *Anatolian Studies* 34: 171–201.

Rutten, M. (1958–1960) 'Un lot de tablettes de Manana', *Révue d'Assyriology* 52: 208ff.; 53: 77ff.; 54: 19ff.

Sack, R.H. (1972) *Amēl-Marduk 562–560 B.C. A study based on cuneiform, Old Testament, Greek, Latin and Rabbinical sources* (Neukirchen-Vluyn).

——(1977) 'The scribe Nabu-bani-ahi, son of Ibna, and the hierarchy of Eanna as seen in the Erech contracts', *Zeitschrift für Assyriologie* 67: 42–52.

——(1978) 'Nergal-šarra-uṣur, king of Babylon as seen in the cuneiform, Greek, Latin and Hebrew sources', *Zeitschrift für Assyriologie* 68: 129–49.

——(1982) 'Nebuchadnezzar and Nabonidus in folklore and history', *Mesopotamia* 17: 67–131.

——(1983) 'The Nabonidus legend', *Révue d'Assyriologie* 77: 59–67.

Saggs, H.W.F. (1962) *The Greatness that was Babylon* (London).

——(1995) *Babylonians* (London).

Sasson, J. (1973) 'Bibiographical notes on some royal ladies from Mari', *Journal of Cuneiform Studies* 25: 59–78.

Schippmann, K. (1980) *Grundzüge der Parthischen Geschichte* (Darmstadt).

Schmökel, H. (1971) *Hammurabi von Babylon* (Darmstadt).

Schneider, T. (1996) 'Rethinking Jehu' , *Biblica* 77: 100–7.

Schniedewind (1996) 'Tel Dan Stela: new light on Aramaic and Jehu's "revolt" ', *Bulletin of the American Society for Oriental Research* 302: 75–90.

Schramm, P. (1972) 'War Semiramis assyrische Regentin?', *Historia* 21: 513–21.

——(1973) *Einleitung in die assyrischen Königsinschriften. Zweiter Band 934–722* (Handbuch der Orientalistik. Ergänzungsband V) (Leiden).

Selz, G.J. (1992) 'Eine Kultstatue der Herrschergemahlin Šaša', *Acta Sumerologica* 14: 245–68.

Shea, W.H. (1978) 'Menahem and Tiglath-Pileser III', *Journal of Near Eastern Studies* 37: 43–9.

Sherwin-White, S. and Kuhrt, A. (1993) *From Samarkand to Sardis: A new approach to the Seleucid Empire* (London).

Sigrist, M. (1985) 'Mu Malgium basig', *Révue d'Assyriologie* 79: 161–8.

Smelik, K.A.D. (1985) *Historische Dokumente aus dem alten Israel* (Göttingen: English translation 1991).

Smith, S. (1957) 'Yarim-Lim of Yamhad', *Revisti degli studi orientali* 32: 155–84.

Sollberger, E. (1954–6) 'Sur la chronologie des rois d'Ur et quelques problèmes connexes', *Archiv für Orientforschung* 17: 10–48.

——(1959) 'Byblos sous les rois d'Ur', *Archiv für Orientforschung* 19: 120–2.

Sollberger, E. and Kupper, J.R. (1971) *Inscriptions Royales Sumeriens et Akkadiens* (Paris).

Spalinger, A. (1974) 'Aššurbanipal and Egypt: a source study', *Journal of the American Oriental Society* 94: 316–28.

Spycket, A. (1981) *La Statuaire du Proche Orient* (Paris).

Stamm, J.J. (1968: original edn 1939) *Die akkadische Namensgebung* (Leipzig).

Starr, I. (ed.) (1990) *Queries to the Sungod. Divination and Politics in Sargonid Assyria*, State Archives of Assyria IV (Helsinki).

Starr, R.F.S. (1937–39) *Nuzi. Report on the Excavations at Yorghan Tepe near Kirkuk* (Cambridge, Mass.).

Steele, F.R. (1948) *The Code of Lipit-Ishtar* (Pennsylvania).

Steible, H. (1991) *Die neusumerischen Bau-und Weihinschriften* (Stuttgart).

Steible, H. and Behrens, H. (1982) *Die altsumerischen Bau- und Weihinschriften*, 2 vols (Wiesbaden).

Steinkeller, P. (1981) 'More on the UrIII Royal Wives', *Acta Sumerologica* 3: 77–92.

Stol, M. (1976) *Studies in Old Babylonian History* (Leiden).

Stolper, M.W. (1982) 'On the Dynasty of Simaški and the Early Dynasty of Simaški', *Zeitschrift für Assyriologie* 82: 42–67.

——(1984) *Texts from Tall-i Malyan, vol. 1: Elamite administrative texts* (1972–4) (Philadelphia).

——(1985) *Entrepreneurs and Empire. The Murašu Archive, the Murašu firm and the Persian rule in Babylonia* (Leiden).

Storck, H.A. (1989) 'The Lydian campaign of Cyrus the Great in classical and cuneiform sources', *Ancient World* 19: 69–76.

Stronach, D. (1990) 'On the genesis of the Old Persian cuneiform script', in F. Vallat (ed.) *Contributions à l'histoire de l'Iran: Mélanges offerts à Jean Perrot* (Paris): 495–502.

Tadmor, H. (1958) 'The campaigns of Sargon II of Assyria', *Journal of Cuneiform Studies* 12: 22–40; 77–100.

Tallqvist, K.L. (1966) *Assyrian Personal Names* (Hildesheim).

Thomas, F. (1993) 'Sargon II, der Sohn Tiglat-Pilesers III', in M. Dietrich and O. Loretz (eds) *Mesopotamica – Ugaritica- Biblica: Eine Festschrift für Kurt Bergerhof zur Vollendung seines 70.Lebensjahres am 7.Mai 1992* (Neukirchen-Vluyn).

Thureau-Dangin, F. (1913) 'Notes assyriologiques: XXII. Un double de l'inscription d'Utuhegal', *Révue d'Assyriologie* 10: 98ff.

Tinney, S. (1995) 'A new look at Naram-Sin and the "Great Rebellion"', *Journal of Cuneiform Studies* 47: 1–14.

Ungnad, I. (1941–44) 'Das Haus Egibi', *Archiv für Orientforschung* 14: 57–64.

Vallat, F. (1985) 'Huteluš-Inšušinak et la famille royale élamite', *Révue d'Assyriologie* 49: 43–50.

van de Mieroop, M. (1986) 'Turam-ili, An UrIII merchant', *Journal of Cuneiform Studies* 38: 1–79.

——(1993) 'The reign of Rim-Sin', *Révue d'Assyriologie* 87: 47–69.

van Dijk, J. (1965) 'Une insurrection générale au pays de Larsa avant l'avènement de Nuradad', *Journal of Cuneiform Studies* 19: 1–25.

——(1978) 'Išbi'erra, Kindattu, l'homme d'Elam et la chute de la ville d'Ur', *Journal of Cuneiform Studies* 30: 189–208.

van Driel, G. (1985–86) 'The rise of the house of Egibi: Nabū-ahhe-iddina', *Jaarsbericht van het Vooraziatisch-Egyptisch Genootschap 'ex Oriente Lux'* 29: 50–67.

von Soden, W. (1967) 'Aššureṭelilani, Sinšariškun, Sinšum(u)lišer und die

Ereignisse im Assyrerreich nach 635 v.Chr.', *Zeitschrift für Assyriologie* 24: 24–255.

Waetzold, H. and Hauptmann, H. (eds) (1997) *Assyrien im Wandel der Zeiten* (XXXIX Rencontre Assyriologique Internationale Heidelberg 6.–10.Juli) (Heidelberg).

Watanabe, K. (1987) *Die Adê-Vereidigungen anlässlich dei Thronfolgeregelung Asarhadons* (Berlin).

Waterhouse, S.D. (1965) 'Syria in the Amarna Age: A borderland between conflicting empires', Ph.D. dissertation (Ann Arbor, Mich.).

Weinstein, J. (1981) 'The Egyptian empire in Palestine: a reconsideration', *Bulletin of the American Society for Oriental Studies* 241: 1–28.

Weippert, M. (1981) 'Assyrische Prophetien der Zeit Asarhaddons und Assurbanipals', in F.M. Fales (ed.) *Assyrian Royal Inscriptions: New horizons in literary, ideological and historical analysis* (Rome): 71–116.

Weisberg, D.B. (1989) 'Zabaya, an early king of the Larsa Dynasty', *Journal of Cuneiform Studies* 41: 194–5.

Westbrook, R. (1989) 'Cuneiform law-codes and the origin of legislation', *Zeitschrift für Assyriologie* 79: 201–22.

Whiting, R.M. (1976) 'Tiš-atal of Nineveh and Babati, Uncle of Šu-Sin', *Journal of Cuneiform Studies* 28: 173–82.

Wiesehöfer, J. (1996) *Ancient Persia from 550 BC to 650 AD*, trans. (London and New York).

Wilhelm, G. (1989) *The Hurrians* (Warminster).

Wilson, E.J. (1996) *The Cylinders of Gudea: Transliteration, translation, and index* (Neukirchen-Vluyn).

Winter, I.J. (1987) 'Women in public: the disc of Enheduanna, the beginning of the office of EN-priestess and the weight of visual evidence', in J.M. Durand (ed.) *La Femme dans le Proche-Orient antique* (Paris): 189–201.

Wiseman, D.J. (1956) *Chronicles of Chaldean Kings (626–556 B.C.) in the British Museum* (London).

——(1958) *The Vassal Treaties of Esarhaddon* (London).

——(1985) *Nebuchadrezzar and Babylon* (Schweich Lectures of the British Academy 1983) (London).

Wunsch, C. (1993) *Die Urkunden des babylonischen Geschäftsmannes Iddin-Marduk. Zum Handel mit Naturalien* (Groningen).

——(1995/6) 'Die Frauen der Familie Egibi', *Archiv für Orientforschung* 42/43: 33–63.

Yoffee, N. (1977) *The Economic Role of the Crown in the Old Babylonian Period* (Bibliotheca Mesopotamica 5) (Malibu, Calif.).

Youngblood, R.F. (1980) *The Amarna correspondence of Rib-Haddi, Prince of Byblos (EA 68–96)*, (Ann Arbor, Mich.).

Yuhong, W. (1994) *A Political History of Eshnunna, Mari and Assyria during the*

Early Old Babylonian Period (Changchun: Institute of History of Ancient Civilizations).

Zawadzki, S. (1988) *The Fall of Assyria and Median-Babylonian relations in the Light of the Nabopolassar Chronicle* (Pozman, Poland).

Zgoll, A. (1997) *Der Rechtsfall der En-hedu-'Ana im Lied nin-me-sara* (Münster).

Zgusta, L. (1964) *Kleinasiatische Personennamen* (Prague).5.

Index of personal names

Index of toponyms and rulers

Index of dynasties, peoples and tribes

Subject index

administrators 5
Amarna correspondence 1, 13, 14, 22, 89, 91, 94, 155, 168, 169
archives 5, 19, 33, 40, 46, 51, 75, 76, 77, 81, 82, 94, 108, 128, 135, 148, 153, 155, 162, 166, 174, 176
archivists 35
āšipu 171 *see* exorcists
astrologers 8, 18, 58, 116
astronomers 24, 121
authors 1, 5, 52, 56, 59, 89, 156

businessmen 5, 46, 51, 53, 77, 83, 94, 108, 113, 122, 132, 152, 155, 176; women 124, 168

chariot drivers 47, 135
chiliarch 129, 142
commanders 81, 101, 110, 130, 132, 147, 149
concubines 152, 156
correspondence 81, 90, 91, 93, 155, 179; *see also* letters
crown-princes 29, 58, 104, 112, 144, 147

deified kings 152, 153, 159
diadochi 16, 130, 142
diviners 33

divorces 15, 17, 51, 151, 162
dynastic marriages 4, 10, 11, 14, 17, 21, 26, 30, 33, 34, 39, 40, 41, 42, 44, 51, 60, 62, 68, 76, 80, 81, 85, 104, 107, 115, 134, 150, 159, 167

en 49, 75, 77, 81, 103
ensi 55, 58, 62, 79, 171
entum 52, 54, 55, 62, 97, 111, 141, 166, 175
eponyms 29, 40, 46, 64
eunuchs 23, 38, 110, 115, 121, 157
exorcists 5, 51, 102

galamahu 170
generals 4, 22, 49, 129, 130, 141
governors 29, 36, 39, 41, 52, 61, 62, 64, 76, 80, 83, 94, 107, 115, 121, 133, 138, 150, 154, 156, 159, 180

letters 5, 8, 13, 28, 31, 32, 33, 38, 41, 56, 57, 58, 66, 74, 77, 78, 79, 82, 94, 102, 113, 123, 143, 148, 151, 170

merchants 5, 9, 41, 79, 132, 168
see also businessmen
mothers 5, 7, 11, 14, 18, 34, 58, 67, 71, 91, 100, 116, 157, 163